*To Sue, my guiding light, whose encouragement and support has enabled me to pursue my dreams and whose tolerance and understanding has provided me the space to do so; to my three daughters Leanne, Jennifer and Rachel and stepdaughter Nikki all of whom I have watched grow into women any father would be immensely proud of;*
*And to Michael for sharing the dream.*

# The Boy and Me

*The*

**Boy**

*and*

**Me**

*A Pyrenean Adventure*

STEVE TAYLOR

Matador
5 Weir Road
Kibworth Beauchamp
Leicester LE8 0LQ, UK
Tel: (+44) 116 279 2299
Fax: (+44) 116 279 2277
Email: books@troubador.co.uk
Web: www.troubador.co.uk/matador


ISBN 978 1848766 631

British Library Cataloguing in Publication Data.
A catalogue record for this book is available from the British Library.

Typeset in 10.5pt Bembo by Troubador Publishing Ltd, Leicester, UK


Matador is an imprint of Troubador Publishing Ltd

Printed and bound in the UK by TJ International, Padstow, Cornwall

# *Acknowledgements*

Michael and I enjoyed the company of numerous individuals along the route of the H.R.P all of whom contributed to making the journey the enjoyable adventure that it was. People such as Gerry, the eye surgeon, who I still suspect may actually be a spy, Richard and his death defying, one handed acrobatics above a gaping chasm on our wettest day and characters such as the extremely smelly French guy in the launderette at Amelie-les-Baines and the amorous couple in the dormitory at Baysellance all combined to make our trip such a colourful and fascinating adventure.

I would like to single out both Charlie and Sue, and my old boss Keith whose support was vital and very much appreciated at the time. Their involvement and help at some of the most demanding sections of the trek were timely and provided a fresh impetus and energy (and tent) when it was most needed.

Thanks to you all, you helped make the H.R.P a most memorable, once in a lifetime adventure. My thanks must also go to my stepmum Pauline and my work colleague Lewis, whose assistance in proof reading my manuscript removed a number of errors, helped me in identifying and removing some of the less appropriate profanities and generally made the content more presentable.

## Friday 30<sup>th</sup> June 2006, Liverpool to somewhere off the coast of Brittany in the English Channel

It seemed a somewhat low key start to our big adventure. Descending from our 2<sup>nd</sup> floor council flat at 9.30am we stepped out into a deserted neighbourhood. The morning rush over; workers at work, kids at school and all the dossers and dealers still in bed. There was just a solitary pensioner eyeing us over with a look of puzzlement and suspicion as she returned home from the local shop with the morning paper. We weren't part of the everyday scenery in this Liverpool suburb.

No fond farewells for us. No tearful goodbyes. No big send off. We tottered down the quiet suburban street crushed beneath enormous backpacks. My son Michael's pack towered above him. From behind he resembled a sort of huge walking wardrobe. His backpack was gargantuan, although I put much of this down to his poor packing skills and a series of "luxury" items he had insisted in bringing along. His sponge bedroll was strapped to the top of the pack and was leaning to one side, which gave him the appearance of some sort of leaning mobile tower that was in impending danger of tipping beyond its point of balance and crashing to the ground.

It was a bright, warm and sunny morning and the estate was devoid of life except for a solitary battle scarred black tom cat lazing in the morning sun on a garden wall. Our presence did not disturb his slumber and we passed by seemingly unnoticed. In contrast, when we turned the corner into Forthlin Road we were confronted by the regular melee of tourists crowding outside Paul McCartneys former home. They had just alighted from the psychedelically coloured Magical Mystery Tour coach taking them on a tour of the Beatles former homes and hang-outs. From the looks on the mostly Japanese and American faces outside of what to us was no more than just another council house, (the only give-away being the small metal plaque next to the garden gate); we were a source of some curiosity. They eyed us up like we were part of the show, another mystery on their magical mystery tour! To an outsider both parties probably appeared equally alien in this environment. A peculiar sight in the midst of a Liverpool council estate without doubt. A father and son kitted out for a Pyrenean adventure and a group of tourists, armed with digital cameras and mobile phones, taking photographs of a post war terraced council house. We passed on by, somewhat bemused by the hush that descended upon the group, and left them to resume their Beatles Tour with our appearance and purpose remaining unexplained. We turned the corner onto the main road to wait for our bus.

After a short wait we struggled onto the number 86, attracting the attentions of yet more pensioners who were taking advantage of their free off peak bus travel. The 'twirlies,' as they are referred to in Liverpool. The name derived from their plaintiff call to the driver upon flagging down the bus on which they were not supposed to use their free pass until after 9.30am, "Am I too early? Which when said quickly translates as "am I twirly?"

We alighted some 20 minutes later outside the Lewis's department store and made our way to Liverpool's Lime Street station for our 11.09am train to London Euston. Possibly because of our attire we felt rather conspicuous but I doubt whether our teetering forms received more than a passing glance. The distance from the bus stop to Lime Street station was probably little more than about 400 metres but it was enough to make both of us even more aware of the significant weight of our packs, each of which we'd weighed on the bathroom scales at home before leaving.

It hadn't dawned on me at the time that the simplest method of weighing the packs would be to weigh ourselves with and without the packs and then deduct one figure from the other. However, thinking about it later, the combined weight of me and my pack would have exceeded the maximum 20stone on the scales and probably bust the thing. (I could have used Michael!) Instead we faffed around trying to balance the packs on the scales, struggling to ensure we didn't let any bits overhang onto the floor, trying to minimise the degree to which we supported them and hence some of the weight, whilst struggling to prevent them obscuring the scale's measuring display window. They each weighed in at just on 20 kilos, (44 pounds), without water. The water we would need to carry on a daily basis on our trek could add a further 4kg to each pack. We each carried a 3-litre hydration pack and 1 litre bottle, which were both currently empty.

The seeds of doubt, which had plagued my private thoughts

throughout the planning of our trip, were being nurtured and cultivated once again. The short walk from the bus to the train station made me doubt we could carry these monstrous sacks as far as the train let alone up and down one of Europe's major mountain chains for six weeks. I could barely carry the bloody thing down the street without my legs buckling. Michael seemed unperturbed. I kept my thoughts to myself.

We sat in one of the station cafes eating baguettes and drinking coffee. Our first sample of foreign food! Ha you don't have to go to the continent for continental food these days! It felt rather strange that there was no one around to see us off, but all family and friends were either at school or work. In contrast to the quiet of our council estate we were now surrounded by the hustle and bustle of Liverpool's main railway station, Lime Street, but here we just blended in with the other travelling public. Everyone was going about their own business unaware of two more travellers amongst the crowd. Why would they be? I wanted to walk up to people and say, "excuse me, do you realise that me and my lad are about to embark upon probably the toughest long distance walk in Europe?" I resisted the temptation of such a ridiculously embarrassing encounter and sat and drank my coffee.

Getting on the train was a challenge. They're not designed to accommodate backpacks the size of a small family car. We both careered down the centre aisle of the train in pinball fashion bouncing from side to side off alternate passengers as we encountered each row of seats until, a dozen sorries later, we reached our pre-booked designated places either side of a table. We were in a quandary over where to stow the backpacks. The luggage rack at the end of the carriage was full and the spaces beneath the seats were not tall enough, or wide enough. The alternative, the overhead storage areas, were available but, considering it was all I could do to get my pack off the ground and onto my back, the prospect of getting it above head height seemed remote to say the least. I envisaged myself straining under the weight, bulging veins and eyeballs, toppling backwards, pack still held high, the combined load of my 17 stone frame and accompanying pack crushing the old biddy in the opposite seat. I didn't relish the ensuing paperwork so we opted to double our seating allocation, I daresay much to the annoyance of the other passengers, and dumped our packs on the seats adjacent the window.

The journey to London Euston was uneventful. I spent the time going back over the all the items we'd packed and trying to establish whether we'd missed anything important. 'Bit late now,' I thought, but at least whilst still in the UK it would be possible to replace any omissions without too much hassle. We talked about our journey; trains to Portsmouth, via London, then ferry from Portsmouth to Bilbao in northern Spain. All pre-booked and pre-arranged. Then… Then, for us our journey entered the unknown. We hadn't booked any transport from Bilbao on to Hendaye, the small French coastal resort on the Spanish border, which was some 40-50 miles east of Bilbao, and the starting point of our walk.

I suppose this would be a good time to inform you just what it we were setting out to do. My son Michael and I were planning to walk the length of the Pyrenees, the mountain chain that forms a natural boundary between France and Spain. Michael, who was 18 years old, had only just completed his A levels and, in contrast to the stress of his academic studies, or more accurately, lack of studies and the stress accompanied by the prospect of academic failure, he had been quite excited about the prospect of our adventure for sometime. However, at this stage I must point out that Michael is not really the type of person for allowing his emotions to surface. I've never quite been able to work out whether he has inherited some of my "laid back" characteristics or whether his relaxed attitude is down to a more common male teenage lethargy, which seems so prevalent amongst his age group. Probably a bit of both! After much deliberation, we, or more accurately I, had decided to opt for the HRP, (Haute Randonee Pyrenees) or Pyrenean Haute Route as our preferred coast-to-coast passage. Michael was just looking forward to the adventure and had been quite content to leave all of the pre-planning to his dad. The alternative long distance paths, the GR10 (France) and the GR11 (Spain) had also been given serious consideration but there was something about the challenge of the HRP which appealed to my sense of adventure. The Haute Route had been devised in the 1970's by a Frenchman by the name of George Véron but from my study of the various Pyrenean maps it was a route that appeared to have many variations. Furthermore, the route described in our guidebook (Pyrenean Haute Route by Ton Joosten) was not always the same as that marked on the map, nor was it the same as described in other HRP guidebooks. In addition it was not a GR route and hence did not have the benefit of the red and white paint flash markers, which guided the walker on these trails, except of course where the trails coincided which was repeated many times along the way. All in all it was more of a concept than a long distance path. It straddled the French Spanish border from the Atlantic to the Mediterranean generally seeking out the higher ground, but not always. From what I could gather, whilst not adhering to the highest ground at all times, it was a true mountain trail, largely avoiding the small centres of population of the Pyrenees and seeking out the wilder more remote regions.

The idea for this walk had evolved from a trip to Corsica in 2003 when the two of us had walked for 9 days along the northern half of the GR20 long distance route through the wild and barren mountain terrain that had long been the hideout of the Corsican resistance movement. That trip had been particularly arduous with temperatures soaring to over 100 degrees Fahrenheit at times during one of the hottest Mediterranean summers on record. We learned some lessons the hard way. Don't start your walk at 11.30am, which will mean you walking during the hottest part of the day for instance. A mistake we only made once. That trip had opened my eyes to the attractions of walking in a Mediterranean climate. Having cut my teeth on the mountains of Snowdonia, Lake District and Scotland and the vagaries of the weather that accompanies these hills, the prospect of walking in shorts and t-shirt had obvious appeal. However walking in hot climates doesn't just improve your suntan. It's hard. The heat can really take its toll. You sweat much more and as a result need to take on more water. Because we would be carrying such heavy loads this would cause us to sweat even more still, requiring even more water. And so on. You get my drift. I estimated that we would need a maximum of around 4 litres of water each per day. This turned out to be sufficient for most situations, but not all!

We pulled into Euston Station and let everyone else get off first to allow us the maximum available space to alight, and to prevent injury to fellow passengers. We could save that for the underground. The London Underground is not a place for the faint hearted. The journey through to Waterloo for our connection through to Portsmouth was not nice. It was hot and the subterranean platform at Euston Underground was chocker with commuters. I thanked god I didn't have to face this commuter nightmare on a daily basis. When the train pulled in it was already full to bursting and there were several hundred people trying to get on. For the most part everybody seemed to manage to get on the train, which was nothing short of miraculous. It was uncomfortable to be so close to so many people in such heat. Such intimacy should be confined exclusively within marital relationships. I was crushed into the area between the sliding doors, which I would guess measures around 6 feet by 10 feet, with approximately 10,000 other individuals I had never met before. I was intrigued by the anonymous expressions that everybody seemed to adopt. They were de-humanised by their surroundings; programmed not to engage with the other automatons around them. Nobody returned my glances. They were all focussed on some netherworld far away. I found myself thinking 'what shall I do with my hands.' To leave them dangling by my side would have brought them into close proximity to innumerable sets of genitalia which made me feel somewhat uneasy. From some of the pretty (female) faces on view I suspected there were some lovely bottoms around though and I daresay I could probably have squeezed quite a few of them without fear of discovery or retribution. Nah, bad idea! I extracted my trapped arms upwards and tucked my thumbs under the shoulder straps of my backpack banishing such lurid thoughts. Such was the crush I'm sure my feet left the floor a few times at which stage the substantial combined weight of me and my pack was entirely supported by the crowd.

I was thankful to emerge into the relative fresh air and daylight of Waterloo station. Only moles, worms and pot-holers are adapted to spend any length of time underground in such claustrophobic conditions. We caught our connection through to Portsmouth, which, although it was travelling to our destination, entailed a further change at an intermediate station. We all alighted at some remote rural outpost and the train pulled out of the station, continuing on its journey to Portsmouth, whilst all the decanted passengers waited patiently on the platform for the next train, to Portsmouth. Somewhat confused, we eventually arrived at Portsmouth at 4.30pm and walked the mile or so past Portsmouth Naval Docks to the ferry terminal. I was very self conscious of our appearance as we walked through the streets of Portsmouth. For practical reasons we had both had our heads shaved prior to leaving home and looked like a couple of Cistercian monks, or skinheads in search of a National Front convention.

When we arrived at the ferry terminal the Germany v Argentina world cup match was attracting some interest at a bar at one end of the passenger waiting area. I showed a passing interest in the match but like much of the rest of the nation was more interested in the England v Portugal game, which was due to be played the following day. Michael wasn't and still isn't into football. Germany won 4–2 on penalties after a 1–1 draw.

Whilst passing the time in the waiting room and conscious of our imminent departure I started to feel a little concerned about the amount of cash we had between us and an irrational fear that we wouldn't be able to get any more, ever again upon leaving the UK. I withdrew a further £600, which gave us a total of £1,600 between us. Enough for the first few days at least! The boat set sail at 9.30pm.

# Saturday 1ˢᵗ July, English Channel to Bay of Biscay

I awoke at 7.30am to the mildly nauseating sensation of a gentle rocking boat in a mid Channel swell. We were somewhere off the north coast of Brittany. Because we were in an internal cabin it wasn't possible to orientate yourself with the outside world. The boat was rocking but we were confined to a small, enclosed box with no daylight and with no perspective of the external environment, just a constant swaying from side to side. I could understand why people became seasick. We showered and headed up to one of the various on-board cafes for breakfast. The day passed by painfully slowly. We weren't due to arrive at Bilbao until 7.00am on Sunday. I felt like a child on Christmas Eve. Every minute lasted an hour. The football helped pass the time but that was painful as well. There was a big crowd to watch the England game in the afternoon but the almost predictable outcome, lost on penalties after a 0-0 draw, put a bit of damper on proceedings and we spent the remainder of the time wandering about the boat. There was an impromptu game of football taking place on one of the upper decks. The players were actually quite skilful in keeping the ball on board the boat, which made me think they probably weren't English. From time to time we spotted some dolphins in the Bay of Biscay but no whales, which were apparently quite common in these waters. We ate quite well whilst on board the boat, "The Pride of Bilbao", in the belief that we may get few opportunities to do so once we started the walk.

The HRP presented it's own logistical problems in that it avoided most of the towns and villages throughout the Pyrenees preferring to remain true to its name as the High Route. This resulted in difficulties when trying to ensure you always had enough food and provisions to sustain you from one source to the next. This wouldn't be too much of an issue for the first week or so as we were starting in the foothills where the path didn't rise above 4000 feet and passed through a number of small Basque hamlets and villages.

As we looked back from the stern top deck at the boat's wake disappearing over the horizon behind us, I pondered the fortunate position I had been in which allowed me the opportunity to make this trip. My job was that of a highway engineer working in the maintenance team of Knowsley Borough Council. I had been there for over 20 years and was very much part of the furniture. Although none of the furniture had been there as long as me, so far as I was aware. Generally speaking I enjoyed my job although I likened it to spending the day in a spin dryer on occasions, so frenetic was the pace at times. I had submitted a written request to my manager a year previous seeking permission to be allowed to accumulate sufficient leave to be able to take a total of 2 months off work so I could do this walk with my son. After some deliberations, and the suggestion that to nominate a charity and organise sponsorship would be a useful tool to get management to look upon the application more favourably, permission was granted. I took up the charity sponsorship suggestion and opted to do the walk for a local children's care home, Rainbow House, after becoming aware of them through a work colleague, Steve Hardman, whose son had benefited from their good work. Steve's son was around 3 years of age and had been diagnosed with cerebral palsy. Since attending Rainbow House his development and progress had been remarkable by all accounts and this was solely down to the dedication and expertise of the staff working there. The driving force behind Rainbow House was a lady by the name of Joanne Mawdsley, whom I had come to realise, was quite an inspirational figure in promoting the place and whose tireless work had been largely responsible for getting Rainbow House up and running in the first place. Anyway I was pleased that we were able to be doing our bit for such a place and after a slow start we had been successful in obtaining pledges for several thousand pounds in sponsorship before our departure.

I had also been fortunate in having the support of my wife, Sue, who had encouraged me to pursue this dream of walking the Pyrenees. I think the prospect of having 2 months free of perpetual flatulence and smelly socks was quite an attractive proposition for her to be honest. Suffice to say I was here with her blessing and that was rather crucial. Michael had been living with Sue and I for a couple of months, although we hadn't seen much of him to be honest as he'd spent most of the time with his girlfriend Hayley at her parents home.

So here we were, sailing south with a big adventure awaiting our arrival. We were both itching to start and the time was dragging. After tea we went and watched a performance of Grease on stage, which was quite good and provided a lively evening's entertainment. That took us to around midnight and I was glad such a long day had finally come to a close. I don't know how the hell people go on "pleasure" cruises for weeks on end. I'm sure I'd be bored rigid. We returned to our cabin and went to sleep. My thoughts of trekking over mysterious mountains were eventually consumed by sleep.

# Day 1, Sunday 2nd July, Bay of Biscay to Col d'Inzola

We were up at 5.20am in order to guarantee a breakfast before disembarking at 7am. The condemned man's last meal! This was the final sustenance we would enjoy within the womb of the Pride of Bilbao, our home over the last 36 hours. We were about to be cast adrift in a foreign land of which we knew so little. Alright it was only Spain, but this wasn't one of the anglicised Costas we were about to drop into with their Union Jack bars and fish and chip cafes, thank god, it was Bilbao, a large sprawling Basque city, a hotbed of the Basque separatist movement for decades. It was the major port of Northern Spain, it's third largest city and not quite so accustomed to tourists, especially at 7am on a Sunday morning.

Access to the ship's bow and upper decks had been closed off before we approached port, which was disappointing, as this would otherwise have afforded us the opportunity to recce the lie of the land. It was our intention to walk from the ferry terminal to the bus station as some prior research had established that there were buses that ran on a Sunday from Bilbao to San Sebastian. I was reassured from my enquiries at the ship's helpdesk to hear that the bus station was only a 15-minute walk away. I dismissed the minor detail of them not being able to provide any street plan or clear directions. We eventually got off the boat and were shepherded through customs with the rest of the herd. We found ourselves alone amongst a milling crowd once again. After 10 minutes in the queue to show our passports we were deposited on the pavement outside the P&O ticket office, disorientated and trying to establish our escape route from the dock complex to the city. It was a very warm, dry and hazy morning. Everybody seemed to know where they were going except for us. People were boarding waiting coaches and taxis whilst others had friends and relatives collecting them in cars. Everyone was organised. We stood there looking around for the way out. We were in the middle of the docks, surrounded by warehouses, tall mesh and barbed wire fences and empty abandoned yards that I suspect had seen little activity for many a year. This wasn't a place designed for pedestrians. You were definitely not supposed to walk to and from the ferry terminal. We followed the route the taxis and buses were taking, sticking to the edge of the weed overgrown road way as pavements were few and far between, passing various deserted dock buildings and so out onto what, had we been in Liverpool, I would have termed "The Dock Road." It was around 7.30am on a Sunday morning. There was no traffic and not a soul in sight. We turned left and crossed the road to walk on a pavement alongside a low wire fence, the other side of which was a dirty and seemingly disused rusty rail track. On the opposite side of the railway track was a high, graffiti scrawled concrete wall beyond which rose row after row of run down looking apartment blocks stretching up the hill into the morning haze. This was where the poor people lived. I felt at home. The whole place reminded me of a 1970's Liverpool. It had an appearance of poverty and neglect. The buildings looked mostly post war but decrepit and left to rot like the tenement blocks of my home city in the 70's. Battery farm living for humans!

It was warm in Bilbao as we plodded down the dusty and deserted dock road, not really sure where we were headed. After a few minutes we became aware that some way ahead on the opposite side of the road were a group of noisy young men, who we heard before we saw. They were laughing loud and shouting to each other. I couldn't figure out what all the commotion was about until one of them walked out into the middle of the road stooping down for a moment. After a few seconds he leapt back, to roars of approval from his cohorts as a wall of flame erupted across the road. For some reason, best known to themselves they were setting the road surface alight with what I presume was petrol. As we neared the scene a solitary car approached and drove through the flames and on down the road, with barely a hesitation as though it was an every day occurrence. I felt uneasy. I didn't want us to become part of the show. We lengthened our stride and hurried past as inconspicuously as we could with our dirty great backpacks and our dirty great wallets. Our passage seemed to go unnoticed fortunately as they busied themselves preparing the next wall of flame.

A few hundred metres further up the road there was a crossing point over the railway which we used to take us to the edge of the city office blocks adjacent a large square. We looked around for signposts but there was no indication as to where the bus station might be so we conceded defeat and piled into a taxi that had been parked up nearby. I asked for us to be taken to the bus station that had buses to San Sebastian in my best

Spanish. The journey took us 15 minutes and he seemed to head out of the part of the city containing the docks area through a semi rural landscape and into another built up city centre area. I guess we covered about 6-8 miles, which made me particularly pleased we opted against walking, eventually. We were deposited outside of the main bus station and the taxi driver kindly indicated the bus we needed. It was just after 8 am and the city was just beginning to wake up, after quite a heavy night by the looks of some of the sorry looking characters around the bus station. We got on the bus with about a dozen other assorted passengers and departed for San Sebastian at 9am. The journey, with no stops en route, must have been some 40-50 miles and took us an hour and a quarter, arriving at 10.15am. Entering San Sebastian it was immediately apparent that it shared a liking for high-rise living and graffiti with its near neighbour Bilbao.

After a scan of the timetables around the bus station it turned out there were no buses on the Sabbath to our destination, Hendaye. However, before contemplating how we would progress further on our journey I became preoccupied with the more pressing priority of emptying my bowels. Apparently our body clocks had become synchronised at that stage as Michael expressed a similar urge. The public loos at San Sebastian bus station were of the mechanical, automated variety with shiny stainless steel sliding doors. So far in life I had been successful in avoiding such contraptions, regarding them with a deep suspicion. I was convinced that they were controlled by some malevolent force, which would open the doors unexpectedly whilst I was seated in deep contemplation with my pants around my ankles. Another of my fears was being trapped inside as the whole thing went into self-clean mode, which I likened to entering a car wash without the car. Fortunately, my fears were unfounded and none of these terrible things occurred and I finished well within the allotted time limit thankfully. That's another thing, knowing you have to finish within a set time. It's un-nerving which has the effect of tightening the bowel muscles, which in turn leads to you taking longer, which…

We perused the city street plan at the bus station and pinpointed the nearby railway station, no more than a ten-minute walk away and so set off to find out if any trains ran on a Sunday. It was mid morning and a number of street cafes and bars were tempting their customers off the streets with the aromas of coffee and freshly baked croissants. Not for us. We hopefully had a train to catch. Arriving at the railway station, Michael wandered off towards the platform as I scanned the timetable. Before I could digest any of the information in front of me Michael was shouting that there was a train about to leave for Hendaye, at 10.45am. I looked at my watch, 10.45 exactly. I garbled out my order for 2 tickets for Hendaye, ensuring I didn't forget my "por favor" and with tickets in hand I ran, well as much as it is possible to run with the equivalent of a washing machine on your back, onto the platform where the train was about to depart. The train doors were closed and it took us a few seconds to fathom out that a small lever to the right of the doors was used for opening them. We dived on the train and as the doors closed behind us the train jolted off on its journey. This initial lurch caught me, and my pack, somewhat by surprise to the extent that we both ended up landing in the adjacent seat, which unfortunately was occupied by an elderly gentleman. He was unimpressed at my efforts to crush him to death and similarly it seemed at my efforts of an apology, which splurted out in a rapid succession of first English, then French and then Spanish as I realised where I was. Other than expelling a huge gasp of air, which was almost his last, he said nothing. He didn't need to. His expression shouted out "get off me you big fat stupid English pillock." Having managed to alert the attentions of the whole carriage we headed off down the aisle with our back packs, bouncing from one side to the other as the train lurched out of the station, looking for the nearest seats that would accommodate all four of us.

Some thirty-six minutes later the train trundled across the bridge over the Bidassoa River, which marked the border between France and Spain, and into Hendaye, France at 11.21am. Exiting the Hendaye station we made a beeline for a small street café across the busy main road and sat down at a table and ordered our second breakfast. Hendaye is a busy little coastal border town, population 12,500, which, whilst of seemingly little international significance now, had been the focal point for some historical meetings over the centuries. On a small island, Ile de Faisans, located in the Bidassoa River, the Treaty of the Pyrenees was signed by Luis de Haro, the main Spanish negotiator and Cardinal Mazarin the French Prime Minister in 1659. This brought to an end the 30-year war between France and Spain. The Ile de Faisans or Pheasant Island is referred to as Ile de la Conference on the French 1;50,000 Pays Basque Ouest map, no doubt following the series of 24 conferences which took place prior to the signing of the treaty. The island is actually governed as a condominium under the joint sovereignty of France and Spain, who are "in charge" of the island for alternating periods of 6 months. An interesting and novel arrangement in an age of worldwide conflicts!

A more recent and probably even more significant meeting took place at Hendaye between General Franco and Adolf Hitler in 1940 when the two leaders met to discuss Spain's participation in World War 2 as part of the Axis. Despite his foreign minister, Serrano Suner, advocating such an alliance Franco opted to remain non-belligerent in the conflict, much to Hitler's disappointment. Apparently this was Franco's only excursion out of his home country during his long dictatorship. Perhaps he should have travelled more; it is reputed to broaden the mind!

Away from such decisions of state I was perusing the map to establish our precise whereabouts. We were about 2 miles from our starting point at Hendaye Plage on the Atlantic coast, which was apparently becoming a popular resort for the well healed. I wondered whether we could reasonably be associated with such a group, with me in my virtually unused pristine Scarpa mountain boots, and Michael in his slightly less pristine Brashers. More 'down at heal' maybe?

I had planned out the whole walk broadly coinciding with the recommendations of the Cicerone guidebook, "Pyrenean Haute Route," a publication that was to prove invaluable over the course of the next 2 months. I had poured over the contents of this book for months before the start of our trip and felt I knew the route already. The first day however was particularly arduous if the guidebook was to be followed to the letter, with the intended finishing point at Col de Lizuniaga, with 1300m of ascent and 1070m of descent, taking 8hrs 15mins according to the guide. One of the peculiarities of the guide for me was the practice of giving estimated times to complete each stage, as opposed to actual distances. I would personally have preferred to be given the distance with the estimated time as an optional extra but we did get accustomed to these times and, along with the details of ascent and descent, they provided a reasonably accurate means of gauging the level of arduousness we would face each day. Anyway, because of this expected late start I had long since decided to spread the first days walk over two days with an overnight stop somewhere near to Col d'Ibardin, probably in the tent. This was a lesson learnt from our first day of the GR20 walk in Corsica a few years previous when we set off from Calenzana at around noon on a blisteringly hot day and suffered significantly as a result. This lesson had been a hard one, where we had ran out of water and were both seriously dehydrated by the time we reached the Piobbu Refuge that evening at some 1580m above sea level. I remember my elation that day upon discovering that the refuge sold chilled beer. I purchased just 2 cans, not wanting to dehydrate myself any further, and then downed about a gallon of water. Anyway, this particular experience had made me very wary of taking on too much for the first day on our Pyrenean trip, hence the decision to split Day 1 into two halves. This would make the start of our adventure less of a route march and also leave the climb over our first Pyrenean mountain, La Rhune, until the second day.

After refreshments we set off down the main road towards Hendaye Plage to find the start of the walk which was apparently next to the towns Casino located on the promenade. It was a warm and muggy day and despite being attired in just shorts and t-shirt, I soon began to sweat profusely under the load of my pack. We headed off around the estuary of the Bidassoa, known as The Baie de Chingoudy, along a broad promenade, past salt marshes on one side and well manicured public gardens on the other. After about a mile and a half we left the prom and headed away from the estuary through the busy streets of Hendaye Plage and down onto the sea front. There we encountered a sweeping sandy bay with a rocky headland marking its northern extremity and the mouth of the Bidassoa the southerly limit.

We wandered down the beach to the waters edge and dipped our booted toes into the Atlantic. This was of course an essential and symbolic gesture in that we could not truly claim to have travelled coast to coast without coming into some contact with the sea at either end. We were keen to start the walk so didn't venture any further into the sea although it was tempting to strip off and dive into the Atlantic's welcoming surf. Despite the desire to get started there was also a strong inclination to linger. Now we were here at the starting point of our trek there was a reluctance to leave our comfortable surroundings. We were in a busy bustling resort and about to leave behind all the comforts of life, hotels, real beds, readily available food and drink, to spend up to six weeks in a harsh unpredictable and unforgiving mountain wilderness. We were about to begin to subject our bodies to an unfamiliar and punishing daily routine. Little did we know then the hardships we would face over the coming weeks. Ah well! It had to be done, so, after taking the obligatory photos, which made me realise later just how fat I was at the time, we headed off through the bustling town. It felt strange. This was it. All the planning, all the preparation, all the money! (Michael had sold his first ever car to fund the trip). The start of such a significant trek and here we were just walking off into the town's busy streets like any other pedestrian. I don't really know what I expected but it all felt rather odd. It was 1 o'clock. I was surprised that it appeared to be some sort of market day, with roadside stalls taking over the pavements. It seemed more like a weekday than a Sunday. We stopped and purchased some fruit and some snacks as well as buying bottled water to fill our water bottles and hydration packs. The additional 4 –5 kilos of weight was demoralising. This was the first time we had carried the packs with their full compliment of water. It was all we could do to get them off the ground. They now weighed around 25 kilos or 55lb each. My thoughts turned to the amazing strength of the Nepalese Sherpas who would think nothing of carrying double this weight at altitudes of over 5000 metres. Incredible! Here was I whingeing about some piffling little backpack.

Over the coming weeks I developed a technique of getting my pack up onto my shoulders in instalments. This required me to bend at the knee and hip, as though I was sitting on an invisible chair, which thinking about it now probably gave me the appearance of a Sumo wrestler, and involved an initial lift of the pack onto my thigh. I would then twist the top half of my body round and slip my right arm under the right shoulder strap. Then, before transferring all of the weight onto the one shoulder strap, I would then manoeuvre my right hand beneath the pack holding it in place as I bent forward transferring all the weight onto my back, before slipping my left arm under the left shoulder strap. I could then stand upright, thus transferring the weight of the pack onto my shoulders before fastening the waist strap. This seemed to me the most economic and least strenuous method of putting my pack on but did require a little room to manoeuvre.

Once we were satisfied that we had enough food and provisions to support the Chinese Army for six months we headed off through the streets of Hendaye Plage, retracing our steps around the Baie de Chingoudy. For this first day, as far as the Col d'Ibardin, our route coincided with the French GR10. This convergence of the HRP with both the GR10 and the Spanish GR11 became a regular occurrence over the coming weeks as our path crossed from France to Spain and back again many times on it's journey to the Mediterranean. The route finding as we plotted our way out through the suburbs of Hendaye required close concentration, with numerous subtle turns and changes of direction as we slowly gained height, passing under the railway in a narrow pedestrian tunnel and threading our way through the streets. After half an hour or so, we stepped out of the suburbs of the town and leaving the last of the houses behind, and entered a surrounding landscape farmland, hedgerows and dusty dirt tracks. We took a final glance back towards Hendaye before it disappeared from site as we headed over the brow of a hill on our own dusty farm track. It was very warm and muggy with a hazy sky shading the full glare of the sun. My t-shirt was soaked in sweat and I was ever conscious of the crippling weight of my pack as the shoulder straps bit deep into my flesh. The waistband that was distributing much of the load onto my hips seemed to make little difference to the discomfort and aching in my shoulders. Michael didn't complain. He trundled along with his gargantuan load and a supplementary carrier bag of shopping in one hand. There was no room in his pack for the extra bits of food we'd bought in Hendaye!

Some ten minutes after passing out of site of Hendaye our route brought us out onto a main road, the N10, onto which we turned left, followed for some 50m or so before picking up a path on the opposite side of the road which entered an area of woodland. The path was carpeted in many years leaf-fall and gave the appearance that it was seldom used. It's seemingly abandoned state made me doubtful we were still en-route and that this wasn't some disused former way through the woods that would peter out into a tangle of briars, resulting in a lengthy retracing of our footsteps. My fears were unfounded. After some ten minutes or so we emerged from the trees onto a broadening track which became a narrow tarmac road and led us through the small Basque hamlet of Garlatz, comprising a handful of scattered red roofed houses.

It was here we met our first fellow long distance walkers. Two young women were on the road ahead, map spread out between them discussing their route with some uncertainty and looking rather puzzled. It turned out they were Belgian and were walking the GR10. They had apparently set out from Hendaye much earlier than us and were having difficulty with the route finding. We confirmed that unless we were both lost they were on the right route and passed on our way leaving them to contemplate their clearly uncertain progress. That was the one and only time we ever saw them. I sometimes wonder if they ever made it. Further along the road we passed the bemusing sight of a woman mowing the most enormous lawn using a modest sized hover mower. The lawn was probably the size of about 3 tennis courts but more importantly was on a very steep slope. She was cutting from top to bottom and then back again in endless repetition. I would gauge it was between a 1 in 2 and 1 in 3 gradient and she would have been better served with a flock of sheep to keep the grass short. We marvelled at her energy and sheer fitness to be able to take on such a daunting task. I couldn't resist taking a photo as she marched up hill pushing the mower with her back to us. I don't know if she was simply ignoring our mild curiosity but she seemed to remain oblivious to our presence as she stuck to her task. I drew a parallel between her labours and the challenge that we were facing although I suspect she probably finished slightly before us.

Shortly after this spectacle, continuing along narrow country lanes and tracks we passed under the A63 Autoroute by way of a new pedestrian tunnel. The GR10 seemed very disjointed at this stage, flitting from short sections of track and path onto quiet country lanes and back again. It was tricky to follow with some obscure and easily missed turn-offs. Soon after the tunnel we passed through the outskirts of another small hamlet, Biriatu, which, it was hard to believe, had been the scene of an assassination on 18th November 1984. A dancer named Christian Olaskoaga had become the latest victim of the GAL (Grupos Antiterroristas de Liberación) who were responsible for 27 killings between 1984 –1987. GAL were death squads illegally set up by officials within the Spanish government to fight the Basque Seperatist movement ETA (Euskadi Ta Askatasuna, Basque for *"Basque Homeland and Freedom"*). It was difficult to contemplate such a violent act in a peaceful little back-water such as Biriatu. By the time of our walk ETA had declared a "permanent" ceasefire (22nd March 2006) although this situation changed again on 30th December 2006 following detonation a van bomb in a parking building at the Madrid Barajas international airport. The peace and tranquility of the Basque countryside did not suggest a region in political turmoil.

Upon leaving the village we began a steady ascent on paths and tracks, heading into the foothills of the Pyrenees and leaving civilisation behind. The landscape was in many ways similar to some parts of the Welsh hills on which I had cut my teeth in my early walking and climbing days, with fern, gorse and broom adorning the hillside. As we slowly ascended the terrain became rockier and the track we were on quite rough. We were making a traversing ascent beneath a row of crags which guarded the summit of what on the map was a somewhat modest hill with the rather tongue twisting name of Xoldocana. The Basques are very generous in their use of Xs and Zs in their language. The crags of Xoldocana towering above us disappearing into the misty haze were an early indication of what was to come. They were rocky and precipitous and belied the modest elevation of 486 metres of the mountain. The walking was tiring as we climbed higher and we stopped for our first 'sit down' break some thousand feet above the Bidassoa River, which meandered through the wooded valley below. I was glad we were only doing a so-called half days walk according to the guidebook. The ten minutes or so seated at the edge of the path was a welcome reprieve from the exertions of the ascent and gave some respite for my aching shoulders. We resumed our trek and after another half hour or so, following a steepening ascent on a forest track, found ourselves taking a further break at the Col de Poiriers where we sprawled on the grass eating the bananas we had purchased earlier. We were both tired although I doubt we had covered seven miles since leaving Hendaye. The entry in my logbook says simply, "both knackered." The Col de Poiriers was at a height of some 350 metres and would probably have made a good viewpoint but for the haze having reduced the visibility down to no more than about a mile. We were enjoying the rest and were loath to press on. We discussed the excellent qualities of our resting point as a potential campsite, with numerous patches of flat grassy ground and plenty of firewood nearby. We eyed the next section of path with some dismay as it ascended the hillside off to our right. It was tempting to stay put. We were still some 200m below the highest point of the day, a large hill called Mandale. The French/Spanish border, which had up until now followed the middle of the Bidassoa River in a south easterly direction, turned away from the river at 90 degrees in a north easterly direction towards us and passed over the summit of Mandale. The GR10 and HRP remained north of the summit ridge on the French side.

Resisting the temptation to set up camp we forced ourselves to our feet once more and set off up the steep hillside towards our next landmark, the Col de Joncs (419m). The landscape reminded me of The Clwydian Hills in North Wales with pine plantations, short-cropped grass and heather. Just beyond the col we ascended into a thick damp mist, which reduced visibility to about 30-40 metres. Fortunately the path was quite well defined at this point and we didn't experience any problems with the route. The path skirted around the north side of Mandale and levelled off following a narrow balcony across the steep hillside. We soon came alongside a pine forest and slowly descended out of the mist and into the curious surroundings of Col d'Ibardin. The path we were on joined the end of a tarmac road, which descended past restaurants, hotels and gift shops lined up on the southern side of the road. It was 5pm and it seemed the majority of the tourists had gone home. Col d'Ibardin was a remnant of the days before the relaxed trading of the European Union in Western Europe when national borders were littered with such trading posts and opportunities to avoid excise duties. This strange collection of tourist tat, various cafes, bars and hotels now seemed alien and out of place in an otherwise rustic environment. However, I was happy to take advantage of its presence by extending our contact with the civilisation and the prospect of our evening meal in one of the numerous restaurants. According to our map there was a campsite located just east of the Col d'Ibardin where the D404 road crossed the border from France to Spain. We passed the last of the buildings and reached the col. There was no sign of any campsite so we continued on the HRP, now leaving the GR10 for the first time and descending the D404 down into Spain. After a short descent we turned off on a secondary road, still seeking the elusive campsite but to no avail. We wandered off the road to the left believing the campsite may be close by but it was nowhere to be found. Returning to the road we were both now very tired and just needed to stop walking. We reached the end of the tarmac road at a large isolated building, the Restaurant Okalarre from where the route joined a path, which descended gently down a wooded hillside. There were no suitable camping areas anywhere. The few patches of grass in the woods were either too small to accommodate a tent or at an awkward angle. I was beginning to despair of ever finding a suitable site. We were now over a mile from Col d'Ibardin and the prospect of returning there for a meal at a restaurant was one of diminishing attraction. We emerged from the woods at the Col d'Inzola and lo and behold, the perfect campsite! A purpose built picnic site sat in a small field surrounded by a fence. It had picnic tables and benches, flat, though rather long grass, and more importantly a fresh water supply in the form a tap in the middle of the site. There was even a small hut which was unlocked and had benches, tables and gas stoves, but no gas. The site had panoramic views down over the Bidassoa Valley and was simply perfect. I don't suppose it was particularly intended for bivouacking but I was too tired to care. We dumped the packs, a wonderful feeling in itself, and pitched the tent. Michael volunteered to return to Col d'Ibardin to obtain some food for tea and tomorrows lunch. He returned 45 minutes later empty handed. The shops were shut. We resorted to what we referred to as camp food, the dehydrated meals, of which we carried about five or six each, including desserts. Although they didn't quite have the same impact as a rump steak and chips they were surprisingly appetising and being eaten direct from the foil bags even saved on the washing up. We sat at the wooden benches looking down into Spain and enjoying the peace and quiet of our surroundings. We hadn't seen anybody since Col d'Ibardin and had the picnic site very much to ourselves. Our bellies were full and spirits high as we discussed our day, which had started on a boat in the Bay of Biscay and ended 1000 feet up a Spanish hillside. Considering the potential for things to have gone wrong with transport from Bilbao to Hendaye, for us to have reached a point a mile beyond our original destination was very satisfying.

We were forced to retire to the tent at 9.10pm due to a fine, light drizzle. After two cups of Earl Grey tea and some snack bars we settled down into our sleeping bags listening to the fine rain pattering down on the tent as the light faded.

# Day 2, Monday 3rd July, Col d'Inzola to Col de Lizuniaga

Monday mornings are such a drag. Not today though. Peace, tranquillity, birds singing, wisps of light mist in the valley below and a blue sky and bright sun. Bliss! It was 8am as I clambered out of the tent. Michael showed no sign of life. I made myself a cup of tea and sat at one of the picnic benches savouring the surroundings. It was a fine morning, the first of many. Rolling green hills stretched into the distant Spanish haze. White buildings with their red tiled rooves marked the numerous Basque settlements nestling in the valleys below. Although the overnight rain had soaked the long grass around our picnic site it was drying out quickly in the warm morning sun. A herd of goats emerged from the adjacent woodland heralding their arrival with the clanging and tinkling of their bells as they grazed their way along perimeter fence of our campsite. I looked in the tent. Michael was playing dead. I told him all the jingling was because Santa had arrived but that didn't seem to illicit any response.

We were expecting a relatively short day so far as the walking was concerned with the intended destination being the Col de Lizuniaga. Michael had obviously picked up on this fact the day before and decided that in the circumstances a lie-in was an appropriate start to the day. We had five to six miles of walking which was to take us over our first real Pyrenean mountain, La Rhune, which at 905 metres, just short of 3000 feet, was to make a relatively short walk into a tough day. Michael eventually stirred at 9.30am and after a cup of tea headed off back to Col d'Ibardin to buy some food for lunch. I wrote up my log whilst waiting for Michael to return. It occurred to me that I had now worn the same clothes since leaving home and I probably didn't smell too good but I can't say I'd noticed… yet! We each had one full change of clothes for our trip but I was reluctant to wear a second set of clothes without the opportunity to wash the first set. Actually the situation was a little more complicated than that. There was the facility available to wash the clothes here at this picnic site with running water available. We had soap we could use for such occasions but I suppose I didn't really want the inconvenience. I was about to face a seemingly hot day ascending a

3000ft mountain with a large pack. Whatever clothes I was wearing would be saturated in sweat by the end of the day and it would be nice to be able to put on fresh clothes then. However, we were camping again that night and not guaranteed the prospect of being able to wash either ourselves or our clothes so if I wore clean gear today, by the end of the day I would then have 2 sets of dirty clothes and nothing to change into. I did have the luxury of 3 pairs of undies and 3 pairs of socks but wanted to conserve these for the moment. We were expecting to book into an inn at the small Basque town of Arizkun tomorrow night and this would give us a chance to clean ourselves and our clothes and change into clean ones.

Michael returned at 10.40am with baguettes, cheese, tomatoes, chorizo, apples, nectarines, a litre carton of pineapple juice and mayonnaise. A particularly large bottle of mayonnaise in fact! I suggested to him that since it needed to be carried a bottle of mayonnaise was somewhat of a luxury. He said he loved the stuff and that he'd carry it! We made our lunch, packed away the tent and gear and promptly ate the food we'd prepared before setting off. It was 12.10pm by the time we finally left camp, at which stage a party of French walkers arrived to use the picnic site for its intended purpose. We picked up a wide forest track that soon began to ascend towards La Rhune.

La Rhune is an iconic mountain in Basque culture. It is held to be a sacred place in their mythology with numerous tales abounding. It was alleged to have been the venue for gatherings of witches, or akelarre, and up until the 18th century the local villages paid for a monk to live on the mountain to keep the witches away. A sort of ecclesiastic bouncer! Probably the most unique feature of La Rhune was its cog railway to the summit, which reminded me of Snowdon in North Wales. It was first opened in 1924 and has operated as a popular tourist attraction ever since, with up to 350,000 visitors per year in modern times. The mountain had also played a significant part in European history. It was used by French troops as a defensive position towards the end of the Peninsular War, but Wellington's forces drove those of Marshal Soult off the mountain during the Battle of Nivelle on November 10 1813, this action leaving France open for Wellington's successful march north to Paris.

More recently the mountain had been used as a smuggling route for refugees during both the Spanish Civil War and Second World War, presumably travelling in opposite directions dependant upon the war in question. We were ascending on the Spanish side of the mountain, no doubt in the footsteps of previous refugees and wouldn't encounter the railway until reaching the summit. No easy way up for us. The route was straightforward enough to follow being on a broad, forestry type track for the majority of the way but it was 2000 feet of grinding ascent. It was very, very hard. The weight of the packs was crippling and we needed many short breaks. At our last sit down rest before the summit at the Col Zizkouitz we were joined by a herd of native pottock ponies. They were of nervous disposition and trotted off when I tossed my apple core in their direction. Shame really, they might have carried our packs to the summit for us! They had apparently been used in the past to assist smugglers in their cross border trade.

The last few hundred feet were particularly steep and we really struggled with constant stops to catch our breath and recover. I described it in one word in my log, "knackering." Only the second day and I'm running out of suitable adjectives to describe our level of tiredness. The summit was engulfed in mist although it was still comparatively warm. We went into the summit café and enjoyed an afternoon treat of lemonade and ice cream. There were lots of people around, including one or two school parties. Because of the thick mist we didn't get to see the extensive views available from the summit, which apparently extend along the Basque coast from Biarritz to San Sebastian and inland to some of the higher Pyrenean mountains that awaited us. Even in the mist we were conscious that the summit was a cluttered place with various buildings, TV masts and all manner of cairns and viewpoint features as well as all the paraphernalia associated with the railway. One impressive feature was a granite obelisk erected in 1859 to commemorate the ascent of La Rhune by Empress Eugenie de Montijo. No such accolades for us. A mint cornetto and a can of tango each was our reward!

After our refreshment break, we left the summit café and set off on our descent towards the Col de Lizuniaga. For the first time we were heading away from distinctive tracks and paths into an area of poorly defined and in some places non-existent trails. To add to the difficulty we were in a thick Atlantic mist, which obscured any landmarks and made route finding that little bit trickier. The conditions called for use of compass as well as map and we struck out across the summit plateau on a bearing, compass in hand, leaving the clutter of buildings behind us. Every now and then a numbered border stone would loom up out of the mist confirming we were still on route. Twenty-five, twenty-six. Upon reaching the edge of the plateau we picked up a path which descended steeply down a broad stony gully until we emerged from the mist on to slopes of short, well grazed grass and tall green ferns where the path splintered into a myriad of animal tracks fanning out before us. In places the ferns were 4-5 feet high completely masking the path. We stumbled on down until border stone twenty seven confirmed we were still en-route and we pressed on to a small grassy plateau and border stone twenty nine where our guide book advised, "pay attention, because the junction can easily be missed." It was easily missed and sure enough we missed it. We picked up and followed a faint but well marked path, which continued to descend, but as it dropped began to turn more westerly. After descending a few hundred feet I realised the error but decided to continue on the path we'd chosen, as opposed to re-tracing our route, partly because we were still going down and in generally the right direction but more due to not relishing the re-ascent. The path we were on joined a well defined but rough vehicle track and we stuck with it until it took a complete change of direction and started contouring round the mountain turning first to the west then north; the complete opposite way to where we needed to be headed. We needed to get back on the path which I believed was probably located on a ridge over to the east of where we were stood but which was now separated from us by a steep sided ravine. We headed off the track in an easterly direction contouring around the rough steep hillside through some dense patches of gorse towards this ravine. There were numerous narrow animal tracks that helped us on our way but not having the same tough hides as the sheep and cattle that had preceded us, our bare legs soon became scratched and bloodied by the dense scrub of mountain gorse. The descent into the ravine was steep and awkward and strewn with loose rock and scree. We scrambled down to the stream at the bottom of the gully, taking a welcome drink of cool, clear mountain water before making our way out onto the open hillside once more. The east side of the ravine was less steep and we were able to escape its clutches quite easily. Sure enough we soon picked up our intended path that was indeed descending the crest of the ridge as I had suspected. Relieved to be back on track and still retaining at least the minimum requirement of blood to preserve human life, we descended quickly on the dusty path over rough, dry scrubland to the Col Golmendia, which was marked by border stone number thirty-two and a large wooden barn. We rested for a while on one of the various logs that were layed out around the col before pressing on to our day's objective of Col de Lizuniaga.

After a short ascent from Col Golmendia on a well-defined dirt track we descended past meadows to emerge at a large bungalow and adjacent farm buildings at Lizuniaga. The guidebook referred to a Hostal-Restaurant at the col, which allowed walkers to use the lawned area fronting the property in which to pitch a tent. The bungalow was indeed a restaurant. There was a suggestion in the guidebook that in return for their hospitality of free camping they expected your patronage in the restaurant. In this respect we were only too happy to oblige and booked a table for 2 at 8pm, at the same time as asking whether we could pitch our tent. After the disappointment of missing out on a restaurant meal at Col d'Ibardin the temptation of a restaurant meal here was totally irresistible. Camp food, whilst practical and providing basic nourishment, had to be regarded as a last resort when more appetizing and substantial alternatives were available.

After pitching the tent in a prominent position at the edge of the lawn, or more accurately, small field, which overlooked the Valle de Baztan, we boiled up some water and sat and drank tea, eagerly anticipating our feast to come. It occurred to me that we were right on the French – Spanish border and I wasn't certain whether the restaurant was on French or Spanish time, although we were just inside Spain. There was an hour difference between the two. Michael came to the rescue. He had noticed that the restaurant had a sign displaying CERRIDO (closed) 17.00 – 20.00. He then pointed out that since my watch was displaying Spanish time and we had arrived at Lizuniaga at 17.10, when the restaurant was indeed closed, then they must be on Spanish time. It was good to see his A level education wasn't being wasted. And of course 'Cerrido' was Spanish!

Before we dined we removed the sweaty clothes that had by now begun to take on a life of their own. Unfortunately there was little we could do with our sweaty bodies with no toilet facilities available until the restaurant opened, so we had to make do with a rub down with a towel. Not ideal, but something which was to become more commonplace as our trek progressed. I used the spare time we had to book our accommodation for tomorrow evening at the Fonda Etxberria in the small Basque village of Baztan. My brief excursions into the Spanish language were heavily supported by a little phrase book that we had brought along. It gave us the ability to communicate our accommodation and meal requests but was severely exposed if I was subsequently asked any questions. I finished the "conversation" with a lady at the Fonda Etxberria not entirely certain whether my attempt to book a room for two with an evening meal and breakfast for tomorrow evening had been entirely successful. We would just have to turn up tomorrow and see!

At 8pm we went and sat at the terrace fronting the restaurant and ordered a couple of beers whilst perusing the menu. We each chose a 3-course meal that incorporated lots of red meat, washed down with a bottle of house red wine, 2 more beers and a large jug of water. It was a most enjoyable meal and at 48 euros I thought it represented quite good value. Whilst we were dining another walker arrived and camped on the lawn. He was Spanish and also took up the option to dine at the restaurant. Sleep on the hard ground came a little easier that night with the benefit of the anaesthetic qualities of the alcohol we'd consumed.

## Day 3, Tuesday 4th July, Col de Lizuniaga to Arizkun

Today was to be our first full day of walking according to the guidebook and with over 2500ft of ascent and an estimated duration of 7hrs 15mins would be a tough test. We arose at 6.45am to a misty grey sky but dry conditions. After a breakfast that comprised of tea, muesli bars and the remains of the pink grapefruit juice, we topped up of our water containers and started out at 8.10am, a few minutes after the Spanish bloke who had been camped alongside us. We never did see him again. It remained misty and rather cool as we crossed the D406 road at the col and slowly ascended on dirt roads and forest tracks. After about a mile our path was joined by the GR11, ascending up to meet us from the Basque town of Vera de Bidassoa to the west. We continued our gentle ascent, skirting around the 698m bulk of Ibanteli, to arrive at a deserted Col de Lizarietta. The Col was the meeting point of a number of tracks and was crossed by a minor road on which a single car drove past in the short time we rested there. There were a couple of buildings at the Col, a house and what appeared to be a bar/souvenir shop which looked like it had been closed for years. The Col marked the point where we had rejoined the border and were accompanied by periodical border stones once again. Except for the single passing vehicle and the sound of a distant chain saw in the forest below us there were no signs of life around the Col. We continued on dirt tracks through heavily forested hillsides and were curiously passed by a couple of Gendarmes in a police land-rover as we approached the Col de Narbalatz. The area didn't strike me as a hotbed of crime. There was nobody around to commit it! Upon attaining the Col de Narbalatz the path left the border ridge and headed down through deciduous woods into Spain. It was also at this stage that the mist started to break up and what had started off as a cool day, ideal for walking, transformed into an uncomfortably hot late morning and afternoon. We descended into a wooded valley to cross a small stream where we stopped for a cuppa in the shade of the tall trees.

This was our last respite from the searing heat of the sun for some hours. We emerged from the woods passing a small farm and into more open land, remaining on dusty dirt tracks, surrounded by low scrub bushes. We took advantage of a water fountain at the side of the track in an obscure little corner of a field before ascending a steep stony track in a southerly direction onto open hillsides. The fountain would most likely have gone un-noticed had it not been referred to in the guidebook. We had entered an area of open heath and grassland interspersed with thickets of birch and oak trees, quite different from the morning's landscape of thickly forested hillsides. So far as we could see there were rolling hills stretching into the distance in all directions but unfortunately the hazy conditions limited the view to probably no more than a couple of miles. It seemed strange that although we were now some 2000 feet above sea level there wasn't really any indication that we were so high. Being accustomed to the type of bleak moorland landscape that would prevail at this sort of altitude in the UK it was odd that our surroundings were more akin to the rolling downs of Southern counties of England. The heat was punishing and the hats we wore, whilst protecting us from the sun, acted as a layer of insulation. Any brief areas of shade were heralded with a removal of headwear to try to assist the cooling process. I felt like my body was liquefying. The sweat was running down my face and dripping from my nose and chin. After half an hour or so walking on open hillside we entered an area of woodland and were so glad of the shade it provided. It seemed like a good place for lunch. We were actually at a pass, the Col de Irazako, but it was imperceptible from the lay of the land, further disguised by the covering of trees. We found a fallen tree that made an excellent bench and we were soon joined for lunch by a noisy herd of small wild ponies. They lazily grazed all around us as we consumed the remaining bent and battered baguette, purchased the previous morning at Col d' Ibardin, with a mixed filling of cheese, tomato and the everlasting chorizo, supplemented of course by lashings of mayonnaise. We realised at this stage that baguettes don't exactly keep too well when confined to a hot backpack for a day and a half. This one would have been more suited to knocking nails into concrete than actually being eaten. Thank god (and Michael) for the mayonnaise. It did at least offer a modicum of lubrication when trying to digest the culinary equivalent of a brick.

The sad thing about lunch breaks is that they come to an end and you eventually have to get going again. We tarried under the shade of the trees for probably best part of an hour, not wanting to be exposed to the full heat of the afternoon sun again. Just as we were setting off a smartly dressed man and woman rode past on two majestic looking black horses. They both looked most elegant on their sleek and well-groomed steeds as they disappeared off down the track. In contrast, we were both looking rather dishevelled and certainly not smelling too good in our sweat soaked attire. In the league of smelliness I was undoubtedly well ahead of my son. The clothes I had removed the previous evening at Lizuniaga were now quietly fermenting in a plastic bag somewhere in the depths of my pack, whilst my sweat glands were actively employed contaminating their replacements. There was no doubt about it, I stunk! Absolutely and completely stunk! It was a phenomenon of which I had become ever more distinctly aware over the last 5 or 10 years of my life, more or less since turning 40. Once I was engaged in any strenuous physical activity the resultant perspiration held such a strong odour it was truly offensive. It was essential that whatever clothes I had on must be instantly washed to prevent a slow but certain process of disintegration. In addition and in order to stave off bodily decomposition and general rot I must immediately be immersed beneath a hot soapy shower, followed instantaneously by all over coverage in deodorant. Failure to adhere to this strict regime could result in the onset of a meltdown process of atomic proportions! Over the years some insidious physiological metamorphosis had taken place that had resulted in my perspiration taking on the aromatic qualities of a skunk. I recall one incident when walking into a bar following a particularly arduous day in the Scottish Highlands when within a couple of minutes I had established my own 5 metre exclusion zone, so powerful was the whiff of stale sweat and body odour. Still, it had its advantages. I would always be guaranteed a seat on a bus!

We soon left the forest, still following the GR11 with its periodical red and white markers, although some were so badly faded as to be almost invisible at times. About a mile after our lunch stop we dropped down to another col that was crossed by a minor road, Col d'Ursua. Once again there was little sign of any traffic and we passed on quietly un-noticed, continuing up the next ridge on another dirt track, still both baking under the afternoon sun. We found the next section through a forest a little confusing in places and took the wrong track at one stage. We corrected the mistake after about a hundred metres or so, after I checked our direction with the compass. After half an hour we emerged from the forest onto open hillside once more and had a long break, sheltering from the sun under a solitary oak tree, and drinking large amounts of water. I was concerned that our water was not going to last the day and there didn't appear to be many opportunities to top it up. It was around this point where our route moved onto the second of our series of maps, the Spanish 1:40,000 Alduides/Baztan map. Despite the improved scale there was little to recommend the new map over the previous one, which being French, and focusing on detail in France, at the expense of the minor detail in Spain, such as forests, paths etc, etc, had deteriorated into a vagueness which made it impossible to trace the route. Nevertheless we regarded it as a minor milestone to have completed the entire first map. We spent some time sat under that tree, 45 minutes according to my log, babbling away, about what, I cannot truly recall. In my log I make a vague reference to the conversation somehow being manoeuvred onto rabbits eating their own poo! How on earth we got onto that particular subject I have no idea. But I also went on to remark, "us too soon." Whether that was meant to refer to us eating rabbit poo or …no…perhaps I should leave that particular train of thought just there.

After our rest we continued on to our next col, Col de Esquisaroy, 556m, from which we began a quite steep 900 feet ascent to take us over a ridge of high hills which barred our way to Arizkun. At the start of the ascent we encountered a burst black PVC water pipe that was spraying a jet of water across the path. I was down to my last half litre of water and didn't give a thought to guzzling probably a pint or more of this surprise water supply. It was only afterwards I realised that this water may not have been suitable for drinking. It played on my mind for the rest of the day that what I'd drank might have been contaminated in some way. This may simply have been a pipe that was supplying a cattle trough or the likes. I had to hope my sturdy constitution would stand up to any bugs I may have ingested. I had once been told that I could probably eat dog shit without an adverse reaction although I had never deigned to put this theory to the test.

The weather took a further twist and as we neared the top of the ridge and we were soon enveloped in a thick, damp mist that reduced visibility to no more than 50m. Whilst this was a welcome relief from the oppressive heat of the afternoon sun it came at a price. We were approaching a section of the walk where the route finding was to prove particularly difficult. The GR11 was a relatively distinct path but we needed to part company with it, high on the ridge at a place called the Col Bagacheta. Now that wouldn't have been too difficult, so long as we could locate the col in the first place. According to the guidebook the route was quite straightforward. However, the reality didn't quite match the simplicity of the route described. The guidebook was at best rather vague and occasionally somewhat misleading, and at worst downright wrong.

After we'd ascended on an eroded dirt road to a point some 730m up the ridge we needed to leave the road behind and join a path at a small metal cross according to the guidebook. This wasn't too easy to spot but we did locate it successfully and set off along the path. So far so good! It was after this that our problems began. Here the guidebook simply states, "climb south to the Col Bagacheta." It doesn't happen to mention a whole raft of intervening detail which was rather critical to continuing on the correct route. The first of this missing critical detail was apparent after approximately half a mile or so when the path we were on joined a dirt track at right angles. Then to compound the confusion, and coincidentally a few metres to the left of this junction, was another col, to all intents and purposes having identical characteristics to Col Bagacheta. The map didn't really assist much because not only was this mystery track not shown, nor the col named, the presence of a col was not identified on the less than satisfactory map. This is probably due to the fact that there was little height difference between this new col and the sections of ridge either side of it to the north and south, and certainly not enough to merit a contour ring. So on the map the appearance was that of a slight change in the gradient of the overall ridge. Anyway, in the mist we reasonably believed this point to be the Col Bagacheta and left the GR11 heading generally NNE along the track in search of a path that headed in a NE direction as per the guidebook instructions. It didn't of course exist. We struck off the dirt track following a bearing, stumbled through deep heather and bilberry for a couple of hundred metres, slowly descending on a NE compass bearing until a plantation of conifer trees, some 40-50 feet in height, loomed up ahead of us out of the mist, directly across our line of travel. Unfortunately our Spanish 1:40,000 map didn't include such minor detail as forests, further affirmation of my strongly held belief that Spanish maps were and are completely bloody useless. Our encounter with the forest confirmed my growing suspicions that we were looking for the path in the wrong place or that it simply didn't exist. There was little sense in pursuing this lost cause any further so we retraced our steps to the un-named col and returned to the junction of the GR11 path with the track.

The only remaining option was to continue to follow the track/GR11 south, which would lead us off the ridge and bring us down to the valley a few miles south of our intended path. Michael agreed and we set off again heading south on what we believed was the GR11. After about 10 minutes we came to a fork in the path not shown on the map, nor mentioned in the guidebook. We opted for the right fork as this maintained a more southerly direction. The mist persisted and added to our disorientation. The path was more or less level but descended slightly at times, until we arrived at yet another junction with a dirt track. It was like ground-hog day but as it turned out, *this time we were* at the Col Bagacheta! We turned left and, similar to before, in a few paces arrived at the col. The track we were on continued in a NNE direction, but, heading off to the right at a bearing of 60 degrees was a faint path. It was where it was supposed to be, according to the guidebook, but far from distinct. We followed the path into the mist and initially it stayed level but then swung around to a southeast direction and began to descend, gently at first but then at a steeper angle. We were on the right path after a deal of confusion. In deference to the guide book author, Ton Joosten, he does say at the end of the chapter for Day 2 that, "If visibility is poor it makes sense to follow the GR11 all the way to the village of Elizondo, 4.5km south of Arizkun. Follow the N121b from there to Arizkun to join the Haute Route." I have strong suspicions that Mr Joosten probably did exactly that and was unable to provide a full description of the precise HRP route, because he hadn't actually been there. His guide book was generally very good but this was an aberration which caused us quite some confusion at the time.

As we descended this unfrequented and faint path the mist developed into a fine mizzle. It was a different day to the sauna we had been walking through earlier. It was cool and dank and for the first time on our trek we needed our waterproof jackets, more to stay warm rather than dry. My clothes had long since reached saturation point with perspiration for me to be bothered about trying to keep dry. The path we were on had an air of neglect. It appeared to have fallen into disuse and in no way resembled what you would expect of such an auspicious long distance mountain route. As we descended out of the mist, in places the path became very difficult to follow and occasionally disappeared completely. The abandoned nature of this forgotten way was nowhere more obvious than a point where we passed through a gap in the ridge where it was buried under a tangle of massive fallen beech trees. We had to improvise and scrambled under, over, around and through a battlefield of enormous trunks and branches. It was as though some catastrophic Armageddon like tempest had cut a swathe through this copse of otherwise towering beech trees. An abandoned, semi-derelict hill farm, for which the trees had no doubt been planted to provide shelter, maybe a couple of hundred years ago, perpetuated the deserted image of the landscape. We picked up an overgrown access track to the farm which descended down past a small, well maintained chapel into the quaint but deserted hamlet of Azpilkueta. From there we followed empty tarmac roads past fields of arable crops and occasional Basque houses down into the Baztan Valley towards Arizkun.

My water had long since run dry and as we approached Arizkun I dragged Michael into a small bar on the edge of a small industrial estate. The two beers I had did not "touch the sides" and could have quite easily been followed by many more. Michael stuck to diet coke. There were half a dozen locals drinking and chatting in what had the appearance of a café more than a bar, with small square tables scattered randomly around the floor, each with four flimsy wooden chairs. It reminded me of some of the greasy spoon cafes that had formerly adorned Liverpool during the sixties and seventies. It gave the impression it was stuck in a time bubble.

It was quite a wrench leaving the bar. We were both very tired and rather footsore after a long arduous day. We needed to find our accommodation and were still half a mile or so outside of the village. We peeled ourselves away from the seduction of more alcohol and continued relaxation (or I did anyway) and made our way across fields on an old cobbled path over an ancient stone bridge and up a narrow passage between buildings to emerge on the main street of Arizkun. We turned right along the main road, passing a newly built pelotta court as we approached the centre of the village. My previous evening's attempt at booking had been successful and we were expected at the Fonda Etxberria. The woman who greeted us led us out of the building across the road towards the village square where we were shown our accommodation in a terraced property with various rooms. Communication between us was rather sketchy but we established that we would be dining at 7.30pm, which would thankfully provide us with a couple of hours in which to clean up.

The accommodation was basic and simple with two old creaky sprung beds, an equally old and creaky wardrobe and a couple of small chairs furnishing the bedroom. A single small window looked out across the fields we had crossed earlier when entering the village. The bathroom was at the end of the hall and contained a cast iron bath, toilet and basin. I pulled rank and got in the bath first and after a valiant attempt at bathing in two inches of tepid water, which I had to empty and refill half way through the operation due to the sheer volume of filth and scum that threatened to simply relocate itself around my body, I eventually emerged cleaner than when I started. Feeling at least partially refreshed I changed into my one remaining set of clean clothes, and after Michael had finished in the bath, (after I had cleaned it) I proceeded to wash my dirty clothes, hanging them out of the bedroom window to dry.

We made our way back across to the hotel and sat at the only table that had been set for dinner in the bar area. The room we were in served many purposes from dining area to shop, bar, restaurant, café, impromptu social gathering place and general community meeting room. It was generally quiet with its only other customer being an elderly gentleman sat at the bar smoking his pipe. Our hostess brought our food from an adjacent room in between tending a young child and serving drinks to the elderly bloke at the bar. From time to time villagers wandered in and out of the shop/bar area, viewing our presence with a sort of mild inquisitiveness, exchanging brief discourse with the gentleman at the bar before disappearing back out onto the street again. Our meal was simple but appetizing and comprised a vegetable soup, which was delicious, followed by fish and lettuce soaked in olive oil. Fortunately there was plenty of bread to provide the necessary carbohydrates. The dessert of homemade apple sponge was wonderful but I could have eaten another six helpings. We settled for orange juice to wash it all down and retired to our room by 9pm after a long and hard day.

# Day 4, Wednesday 5ᵗʰ July, Arizkun to Aldudes

Despite my acute tiredness, sleep had been in short supply. I had spent the night in fitful short bouts of slumber interrupted by the continual chimes of the village church clock at fifteen minute intervals interspersed with the frequent barking of village dogs. There had been light rain falling for most of the night, and despite us having brought our laundry inside before going to bed it was still on the wet side of damp, with our socks being dampest of all.

Breakfast was of the continental variety but appreciably more sustaining than the muesli bars of the previous two mornings. It comprised a large plateful of toasted/crunchy mini baguettes with apricot jam and butter washed down with lashings of tea and coffee. I could have done serious damage to a large English breakfast in truth, but, when in Rome! After breakfast we purchased a fresh baguette, tub of Philladelphia cheese spread, two tomatoes, four apples and four oranges.

We eventually set off at 9.30am on what was described as an "easy day" according to our friend Mr Joosten, with 800m of ascent and a predicted duration of 5 hours. In spite of its diminutive size Arizkun was adorned with some fine and rather grand looking buildings. We wandered slowly up out of the village admiring the solid and substantial Basque architecture of what appeared to be an impressive village hall. The local church with its infernal bell was an edifice otherwise worthy of admiration. There was nobody about. The impression left by Arizkun was that it was a self-contained village, quietly getting on with life, little touched by the modern world. The whole place had a quiet, confident self-assuredness. Its robust and sturdy buildings were a statement of boldness and self-belief. It had an old reliable air about the place cast in centuries of tradition.

We left the village and joined a narrow concrete road, soon turning off onto a path through a section of forest. Once again our impression was that few people had ever had cause to use the path. It was partially overgrown and frequently blocked by numerous fallen branches resulting in regular mini diversions. After five or ten minutes we emerged from the trees back onto the concrete road we had left earlier, but further on, where we continued a steady gentle ascent towards the northern end of a ridge of hills that were to occupy our efforts for the rest of the day. After a turn off to a farm on our right hand side the concrete road became a dirt track with open fields to our right behind a largely hawthorn hedgerow and a deciduous forest on our left. A short way further up the track I noticed that the waist strap on my pack was particularly wet and realised that the tube from my hydration bag must have got trapped underneath it when I put my pack on in the village. The water bag was completely empty and I was left with just a litre bottle to sustain me for the day. I knew this would never be anywhere near enough to last and was doubtful of our prospects of encountering any potable water source based on the previous three days findings. Most streams had been dry and any water sources we had encountered were of dubious quality at best, made more questionable through the constant presence of both farm and wild animals. Now rather concerned we continued up the track in the shade of the woodland canopy and within a couple of minutes, as if placed there to solely discredit my misgivings, we came across a small woodland stream. It was no more than a trickle but just sufficient to be able to refill my water bag. It took a few minutes to fill the container with great care taken not to stir up the sediment on the stream-bed. However thirsty I may become I did not relish drinking muddy water. For the first time on the trip we used the water purification tablets we had brought along, the disinfectant like taste of which we were able to eradicate by the use of neutralising tablets. Reassured we pressed on up the hill and into the forest.

As we neared the apex of the ridge we emerged from the forest some six hundred feet or more above the valley of the Baztan Ugaldea River. The weather was similar to yesterday morning with a mist and haze limiting the views. We crossed to the eastern side of the ridge where we found a small abandoned quarry alongside the track with numerous loose boulders providing a variety of seating that offered the opportunity, not to be missed, for elevenses. We boiled up some water and enjoyed a cup of soup each. Curiously, we were joined by a basset hound type dog, which appeared from nowhere. He was a friendly little chap and obviously enjoyed our company as he howled in a most mournful manner when we packed up and left. He followed us up the track for a few hundred metres before deciding to turn back. We continued ascending on dirt tracks for a couple of miles, slowly gaining height until an altitude of approximately 750m where the track we were on came to an abrupt end. The path continued very faintly, on the other side of a fence, traversing across a field of cattle towards a corner at the crest of the ridge on the edge of an old dense forest. The guide book made me chuckle with it's instructions, "cross a fence and try (no path, no marks) to follow the crest." It was somewhat disconcerting to be blindly stumbling through the forest with such limited directions, however after a few minutes heading generally south we actually encountered what appeared to be the remnants of a old way through the woods. It was dubious at times and intermittent in nature but just when we thought we had lost it completely it would reappear continuing to take us in the general direction required. We eventually emerged at the summit of a hill called Burga, (874m) on the edge of a steep drop.

It was an indication of the difference in climate from the UK that we should be on the edge of a dense broad-leaved forest at nearly 3000feet above sea level. Initially we considered this a good point to stop for lunch but a mist started to sweep in through the trees behind us and after our experiences getting lost in the mist the previous day we decided to descend from Burga to the col below and take lunch there. There was some semblance of a path for most of the descent though once again, the way was faint and blocked by fallen branches in many places and seemingly very little used. I felt the urge to sing as we descended and rattled off various country and western and Beatles ballads, much to the amusement of Michael who chose not to join in and probably thought his father slightly mad. We arrived at the Col de Basabar, an intersection of several dirt roads and sat down on a low dry stone wall to eat lunch. A fine drizzle started to fall, sufficient to merit the wearing of a hat. The peace and solitude were rudely interrupted when a scrambler motorbike came roaring up through the forest ripping up the dirt and stones on the road in front of us. For the next fifteen minutes we were subjected to an almighty racket and inundated with fumes as this Neanderthal meatball on wheels decided he would entertain us with his prowess on a motorbike. After four days of serene tranquillity this was an assault to the senses. I sat there seething as this moron did wheelies up and down in front of where we were seated, disappearing over the brow of the hill before tear-arsing back into view again seconds later. I got the impression he thought we were an appreciative audience. God knows why. Some people are so bloody obtuse. Did he not realise that his presence on this noise machine that was shredding the earth beneath it was no less than a grossly unwelcome and obscene intrusion. Throughout the whole 'show' my only thought was, "why don't you just f★★★ off?" Eventually he did, thankfully and the natural balance resumed as the quietness of the forest returned once again.

The drizzle ceased after lunch and we continued on into the afternoon on vague paths and long lost trails through oak and beech forests with frequent stops to check our whereabouts. We crossed the Col de Berdaritz back into France once again at boundary stone No. 117 and descended to the village of Les Aldudes. Spirits lifted by virtue of descending to our day's destination I began to sing again. It was something that only ever occurred on downhill sections. Hey Jude was amongst the handful of tunes that came to mind and as we marched down the dirt track I belted out the chorus of "nah nah nah nanana nah, nanana nah, hey Jude". Michael looked on in a sort of bemused and silent embarrassment. This wasn't cool. 'Dad's being an arse again,' is what I swear he was thinking.

It did turn out to be the easy day that our friend Ton Joosten had suggested. As was often the case during the walk we arrived at our destination in mid afternoon, 3pm, and had time on our hands before the hotel/bar opened. We were booked into another night of comfort, this time at the Hotel Baillea, which was located on the opposite side of the village square to the village church. Les Aldudes was very quiet, except for the regular peel of church bells. There wasn't a sole around. We sat at some benches outside of the hotel until the drizzle returned again when we sought shelter beneath the porch entrance to the church. It was quite cool and we needed to resort to wearing fleeces. We got the camp stove out and boiled some water having our second cup of soup of the day.

With the time we had available we took a look around the church and its grounds. The adjoining cemetery was particularly elaborate with the most ornate and grandiose headstones. The graves were immaculately tended with not a blade of grass out of place. It was a very relaxing place to spend the afternoon but we were both eager to book into the hotel and get cleaned up, fed and watered. There was still no sign of life at the hotel so I knocked on an entrance door next to the bar which appeared to be access to a private residence. The lady of the house descended from some upper floor and let us in. It was a basic hotel with many rooms. We were led up to the second floor and down a dark corridor to a small room with twin beds and a washbasin. There was a small en-suite shower cubicle, which answered our first priority. The toilets were located at the far end of the rather spooky corridor outside our room. The toilets were reminiscent of a school toilet block with rows of white china washbasins and toilet cubicles.

It was a building full of character with creaky floorboards and solid stone walls. The window to our room looked out on to the River Nive at the bottom of a garden full of ducks. The eaves above our window where festooned with the nests of house martins that were swooping around in the evening sky collecting insects to feed their young. After a refreshing shower we headed off to the nearby filling station to obtain provisions for the next days walk. We decided to leave the bread for the next day when we were told we could collect a fresh baguette after 8.30am. Our shopping list comprised cheese, an onion, bananas, apples a Bounty Bar (me) and a Lion Bar (Michael), both of which we ate there and then. We returned to the hotel and had a couple of beers at the bar before returning to our room where I rang Roncevalles to book our next night's accommodation. I rehearsed my lines carefully for ages, in Spanish once again, before making the call to the Casa Sabina hotel. I completely lost the plot when I started the conversation by greeting the bloke who answered the phone with "buenos dias senora", to which he responded by asking whether I would like to continue the conversation in English! I was bloody annoyed with myself for falling at the first hurdle but willingly conceded to his sensible suggestion, booking a room for 2 with evening meal for very reasonable sum of 50 euros.

Dinner at Les Aldudes was most welcome when it arrived at 8pm. There were only two other guests sharing the dining room where we were all treated to a large vat of vegetable soup that filled and refilled our bowls on at least 3 occasions. This was followed by a homemade bacon quiche, which was absolutely delicious. Now Michael normally could not stomach eggs in any of their various guises and was dismayed that the main course comprised a bacon quiche. However, his hunger got the better of him and he devoured it with little thought after the initial mouthful. Another first for Michael was the red house wine that accompanied the meal. He had confined his wine drinking to the relative safety of whites and fashionable rosés and the full-bodied flavours of red wine were a new experience for his uneducated palate. Our meal that night came with a most pleasant and unexpected surprise. The quiche, which we had believed to be the main course was simply an appetiser for the actual main course which turned out to be a monster bowl of pasta along with a silver platter of 8 pork steaks (between the 2 of us) and a bowl of lettuce drizzled in olive oil, supplemented by copious amounts of French bread. I thought it was my birthday. The food was superb and to finish it all off we enjoyed a large bowl of chocolate ice cream. I couldn't move. It was the first time my belly had been full in nearly a week. What bliss!

I decided to have a stroll after dinner to try and walk off some of the calories of our monster meal. Outside of the small square that housed our hotel, the church and the local school, Les Aldudes comprised a string of houses arranged along half a mile of the main road. The river ran through the village behind the houses on the west side of the road. The place seemed deserted. It looked like we were staying at the only hotel in the village. Where the houses finished there was a curious garage that had numerous US Army vehicles in various stages of dismantlement parked on the forecourt. I ambled back along the riverbank on a quiet path squeezed between the ends of gardens and the waters edge. Upon return to the hotel I found the door to be locked and had to shout up to Michael to come and let me in again. Before going to bed I spent the next hour or so planning our route over the next few days. We were already looking forward to our first rest day at Lescun where my brother-in-law, Charlie and his wife Sue were coming out to meet us and walk with us for a few days. Lescun was still five days walk away so we weren't even halfway yet. My heavy eyelids eventually got the better of me and I dozed off to the accompaniment of those church bells hoping it wasn't all night again!

## Day 5, Thursday 6th July, Les Aldudes to Roncevalles

The bells did ring all bloody night; every half hour to be precise. Only half as bad as Arizkun! We should always be thankful for small mercies! The only one I can't remember hearing was the six o'clock chime. Whether that was because it didn't actually sound or I had finally succumbed to the exhaustion brought on by enforced sleep deprivation I don't know, but I wouldn't want to live there and listen to them every night. After collecting our baguette from the garage we set off on our walk to Roncevalles Abbey. We had established that the best means of transporting the baguettes we had for lunch most days was to roll them up inside Michael's bed mat. This was fine so long as it didn't rain and the mat was rolled sufficiently tight to retain the baguette, which didn't always happen!

Our route struck off up a set of concrete steps almost opposite the garage. The steps were most inconspicuous and would have easily gone unnoticed had we not been looking for them. We then immediately lost the very faint path and had to resort to ascending vertical heather and gorse. After several minutes of painful scrambling we relocated the path and resumed our walk. We followed various paths, tracks and roads for several miles ascending into patches of mist that were slowly dissolving in the morning sun. The route took us across open hillsides of heather, ferns and gorse until reaching the apex of the ridge at the Col de Mizpira (832m). From this point we headed over the next summit on the ridge, Errola (907m). The views were once again rather disappointing with a mist and haze limiting how far we could see. The path then descended steeply some 170m to the next pass, Col de Meharrozteguy (733m). We found these descents most frustrating. Hard gained altitude was always conceded grudgingly and seemed such a waste of earlier efforts. We resorted to our ritual elevenses of soup at the col, sheltering from a cool breeze behind a dry stone wall that formed one side of a series of sheep pens. As usual our soup was supplemented by muesli bars and a handful of the contents of the large sealed plastic bags of mixed fruit and nuts that we both carried.

The remainder of the day's route to Roncevalles was somewhat nondescript taking us through large tracts of first broad leaved then pine forests. We continued south gradually ascending the ridge of hills which led onto the summit of Lindus, which at 1220m was the highest point of our trip so far. Although we spent much of the day on a tarmac road after the Col de Meharrozteguy it was virtually deserted. We saw a group of four cyclists when we stopped for lunch and a small pickup wagon some time later. These were our only encounters with humans on some 7 miles of road. Our lunch stop was at a junction of roads and tracks high up on the wooded ridge at yet another col, the Col d'Hauzey, where there was surprisingly a tap, supplying fresh water at the side of the road. There was actually more to this tap than met the eye and its incredibly powerful jet took Michael and me completely by surprise when he went to take a drink, as it exploded onto the stones below totally drenching him from the waist down. I roared with laughter as he stood there dripping.

We pressed on after lunch, rejoining the border once again at border stone 152, Col de Burdincurutch, at a point where the route leaves the road and ascends over the summit of Lindus. We were tired and it was an easy decision to opt to bypass Lindus, which we skirted to the north on our now familiar tarmac road. This narrow strip of tarmacadam had become our companion over the past few hours and we were reluctant to part company with it. Its presence had allowed us to just plod along taking just the occasional glimpse at the map to affirm our position and made for easy, if not a little monotonous walking. We continued up the road reaching the Col de Lindux, where we were rejoined by the HRP path. There, the French / Spanish border took a sharp turn to the north to follow the ridge that ends above St Etienne de Baigorry. Crossing once again into Spain, we slowly descended on our thread of lonely tarmac through a densely wooded ridge towards the Puerto de Ibaneta or Col de Roncevaux. Once again I found myself singing under a warm afternoon sun. I was interrupted when we heard the heavy lorries below us toiling up to the col on the busy N135 long before we emerged from the trees.

Our arrival at the col heralded us rejoining the GR11 once again which came up to meet us from the south side of the ridge. It was also our first acquaintance with the GR65, or pilgrims' path, "Camino de Santiago" which ascended from the French town of St Jean Pied de Port on its journey over the Pyrenees before heading off west to finish at Santiago de Compostella in northwest Spain. The GR65 did seem to have many alternative starting points as this was not the only time we encountered this pilgrim's route on our journey. We passed a small chapel at the col, Ermita de San Salvador, and descended on the GR65 down through beech forests in Spain to emerge at the monastery of Roncesvalles.

The village of Roncesvalles had, around the year 778AD, been the scene of a bloody battle between a rearguard band of King Charlemagnes soldiers, led by Count Hruodland, or Roland, as he became more popularly known, and an army of 400,000 Saracens. From my perusals of maps and guide books I had become aware of various references to Roland who seemed to have given his name to a number of landmarks around the Pyrenees, most famously the Breche du Roland above Gavarnie which we were to see later on our journey. Anyway, Roland had apparently fought at the front of the battle with his sword, Durandal, a reference which brings a certain mysticism and Lord of the Rings type aura to the tale. Despite his heroism the enemy hordes could not be defeated and his small band of soldiers were being overwhelmed. Roland was urged by his comrade Oliver to summon aid from Charlemagne by sounding his horn that had been given to him by the King. The horn could only be sounded by Roland apparently and was so powerful that upon hearing it birds fell from the trees, the ground shook, chimneys fell from houses and people cried out with the pain from their ears. (Sounds a bit like my singing.) He could only sound the horn when in the deadliest peril but for whatever reason Roland refused to sound the horn now. It was only when a few of his Frankish knights remained alive that he raised the horn, but it was too late. By the time Charlemagne arrived the band of soldiers were slain and Roland lay dying. It is said that on stormy nights the ghostly echoes of a horn can be heard through the mountains.

Returning to 2006AD we were booked into one of only two hotels in the village and sat outside on the terrace of the Casa Sabina for an hour, drinking beer, resting our weary feet and watching the world go by. When we came to confirm our accommodation, for some reason our original booking of a room for 50 euros was no longer available and the only room left was at the somewhat unrealistic cost (for us) of 100 euros. My Spanish was of no standard to begin to challenge why and from the blank looks that greeted my English protests it was clear I was not going to persuade the proprietors to change their mind. It was all a little frustrating but I was already feeling guilty about the amount we had spent in pampered comfort in hotels and my conscience couldn't live with a 100% hike in the cost of B&B so we headed off in disgust looking for alternative accommodation. The prospect of camping in the beech woods above the village was probably the most likely outcome. Our guidebook mentioned the possibility of staying at the monastery although this was supposedly only available to pilgrims on the Camino de Santiago de Compostella. Quite how these pilgrims could be distinguished from us less holy walkers I wasn't quite sure. We decided to pass on this idea and headed off to look for a place to camp. On our way out of the village we passed La Posada Hotel and made an impromptu enquiry as to available accommodation there. We were in luck and got a twin room with half board. We chose the "pilgrims dinner" for our evening meal and I immediately became apprehensive as to just what a pilgrims dinner consisted of, contemplating that it may be a rather modest offering at the very least! In the couple of hours up to our mealtime my imagination conjured up an ever-diminishing plate of meagre food until I had convinced myself that we would be faced with no more than a glass of water and the crusty end of a week old baguette.

At dinnertime we descended to the reception area outside of the dining room to join a host of other eager and hungry pilgrims. When the doors to the dining room opened and all the "pilgrims" who were gathered outside the dining room door were finally let in, my worst fears were confirmed. We were served with a plate of plain pasta, a large jug of water and a small basket of dry bread, which equated to 1 baguette between 8! My heart sank. Eight euros for that! I could quite easily have eaten all 8 servings myself. In my enquiries at the bar earlier I had asked about breakfast and were told it was 6 euros. I joked with Michael about what we'd get for 6 euros. The humour was not lost around the table where the fellow diners were equipped with sufficient understanding of English to appreciate the point. The co-pilgrims amongst the variety of European nationalities that were present were obviously equally disappointed. We all emptied our dishes and sat in eager anticipation of more food. As time passed and the dishes were whisked away our spirits ebbed and I contemplated the contents of our packs and what we had to eat to supplement this meagre ration. An eternity had passed by when the waitresses emerged from the kitchen with more food. Our misgivings had been misplaced as they served each guest with a large grilled trout and plate of chips, with 2 bottles of red wine per table to help it down. And more bread. The mood lifted and an almost party atmosphere overtook the room. Our table was blessed with an Italian bloke who seemed most adept at procuring more wine and we somehow ended up with six bottles on our table. Every time we were getting low he disappeared off and re-appeared moments later with yet another bottle from somewhere or other. A most resourceful chap whom I was most pleased happened to sit at our table. He was like an Italian version of the Artful Dodger. Our table was by far the liveliest, boisterous even, due partly to a broad understanding of English and no doubt an excess of alcohol compared with everyone else. We were eventually herded out of the dining room into the bar where the wine and conversation flowed freely. I lasted until 9pm but was feeling knackered and went off to bed, leaving Michael with a full glass of wine and a full wallet still in the bar. He assures me he came to bed himself at 10pm although I didn't hear a thing.

## Day 6. Friday 7*th* July. Roncesvalles to Egurgui

I awoke feeling rather groggy and worse for wear. Michael, who is definitely not a morning person, was obviously intent in spending the whole day in bed. After much moaning and groaning, mostly from Michael, we eventually descended to the bar area and partook of a modest continental breakfast with gallons of coffee. How I would have loved to see a plate of sausage, eggs, bacon, mushrooms and fried bread laid out in front of me. Still the baguette and butter was the standard fare and more than we had when camping. We set off and retraced our route up through the beech woods back to the Col de Roncevaux. There was thick damp cloud covering the forest and upon arrival at the col we emerged to a grey and dismal scene. The visibility was down to no more than 50 metres with a fine mist in the air that bordered upon rain. The ground was cloaked in a covering of fine water droplets and a carpet of spider's webs sagged under the weight of their watery load.

Fortunately, our route initially set off up a narrow tarmac road to the east of the col, which made our route finding straightforward. The single-track road made its way up into the grey murk giving us the assurance of a definite and unmistakeable path. It was not cold and we walked in shorts and t-shirts as we had done each day so far. We were passed by the occasional car as we ascended the narrow strip of rather perished and potholed tarmac which zig-zagged in a general north easterly direction up the open hillside towards our first checkpoint of the Port de Cize or Col de Lepoeder, which, at 1430m was another altitude record on our trip so far. At times the mist deteriorated further to a fine rain that forced us to don our waterproof jackets. We shortcut a number of the zigzags and each time welcomed being re-united with the road again which was like an umbilical chord sustaining our existence. On some of the longer short cuts we became quite concerned that we may have wandered off route altogether and were most relieved each time as the road once again re-appeared out of the mist. We arrived at the col without realising at first and because we were on a section of the path which was not covered by our maps we were entirely reliant upon the guidebook for directions. We were due to turn off to our left on a track and whilst there was a track at this point it was not way-marked and I wasn't at all certain of where we were. Instead of turning off we continued along the tarmac road for a further 50 metres or so until we encountered the red and white paint flash of the GR11 with a large cross painted through it. Interpreting the meaning of this paintwork to mean, "NOT THIS WAY STUPID," we turned around and headed off down the track into the mist with the higher ground of Mendi Chippi to our left and steep conifer clad slopes down to our right. The track or dirt road we were on was not only the HRP but served as both the GR11 and GR65, Camino de Santiago as well.

It soon became clear that this camino was far more frequented than our chosen Grand Randonnee and this section where all three paths, GR11, GR65 and HRP combined was clearly the busiest section of our route so far. We soon started meeting pilgrims heading up towards Roncesvalles from St Jean Pied de Port. At first we witnessed just a steady trickle of fellow travellers, then as we crossed over the Col d'Intzondorre and dropped down, and out of the mist, which slowly burnt away behind us, we passed dozens of pilgrims heading in the opposite direction. Since leaving La Rhune we had seen only one group of walkers on day 3 shortly after our afternoon siesta under the solitary oak tree. Not since the first day and our brief encounter with the two Belgian girls had we met any other long distance walkers. Until now we had felt like the only people in the mountains most of the time and it was quite a contrast to find so many people walking in the hills.

We stopped at a sort of makeshift bench at the side of the track to make a cup of tea and were immediately joined by a young Italian lad with whom we shared a cuppa. He was one of the many pilgrims and was heading up to Roncesvalles on his long journey to Santiago de Compostella. He was quite impressed with our Earl Grey tea and thanked us profusely before heading off to resume his pilgrimage.

Our route continued through forest along the dirt track, levelling out with views below us to our left down the valley towards St Jean Pied de Port. The trees slowly thinned out and where the track swept round to the north near a spring, the Fontaine de Roland, we left the Camino de Santiago and followed the GR11 over a broad grassy ridge to a fence that marked once again the French/Spanish border. This path was noticeably quieter than the GR65 and once again we had the hills to ourselves. We followed the border for about a mile passing a number of border stones, numbers 200-204, heading gently downhill towards our next pass, the Col d'Arnosteguy where a tarmac road came up to meet us from St Jean Pied de Port. Ahead of us rose the steep limestone ridge of Urculu, the summit of which disappeared into the lingering banks of mist. We passed nervously through a large herd of white cattle that were lazing around at the col and spotted a couple of fellow walkers, heading in the same direction a few hundred metres ahead of us. This was to be our first encounter with fellow HRP walkers but we didn't realise this at the time since they had stopped for lunch just away from the path and we passed them by some 50 metres away, stepping back into Spain, where our French map deteriorated to a level of vagueness that was actually so confusing in places it was worse than useless. We reverted to the guidebook once again which took us over our next col, Col d'Orgambidé and down into the valley below where we took lunch.

We'd purchased a baguette from the hotel at Roncesvalles and filled it with chorizo or saucisson, a sort of French salami, which Michael had purchased on day two when we were camped at the Col d'Inzola. Our first encounter with this particular delicacy had been on our trip to Corsica some years previous when three days into our trek along the GR20, and suffering a severe meat deprivation, we had been provided with a length of saucisson as part of a packed lunch we had purchased from a mountain refuge. It was devoured with great gusto and we thought it was absolutely fantastic. Now I wasn't so sure. To say it required a significant amount of chewing was being kind. It had a saltiness that the body craved and that no doubt gave it its longevity but my god it was tough. It had the texture and consistency of leather and was impossible to break down by chewing alone. In this respect it was akin to chewing gum. Once you had reached a certain point there was no benefit in chewing any further since it was never going to alter the digestibility of the bloody stuff. It was to the digestion system what a Tesco carrier bag is to the environment. It biodegradability would be measured in tens of thousands of years and here I was subjecting my digestion system to a Herculanean task of turning this stuff into energy to sustain my efforts. It was helped along its way with lashings of mayonnaise, which acted as an initial lubricant but was soon swallowed long before the meat followed. I chewed and chewed to the point of submission and then, admitting defeat, spat out the remains most of the time, finding it completely indigestible. Michael loved it and couldn't understand what all the fuss was about.

We pressed on after lunch and soon joined a narrow tarmac road, which had been just a dirt track when the guidebook was written, so was initially a little confusing. We were now very much in limestone country with outcrops and escarpments of white rock amongst the surrounding grassy hills. After about a mile on the road, we spotted the two blokes we had passed earlier at the Col d'Arnosteguy. They must have contoured around the hill above us when we were having lunch to save on any re-ascent and so we hadn't seen them pass. We slowly caught them up and walked along together for a while. They were both French, I would guess in their late fifties, and were walking the HRP in stages. This section was their final one and they were walking for 10 days as far as Candanchu. It seemed odd to do the walk in such a way where you finished on the start section but, 'all to their own,' I thought. Our conversation was kept to a minimum by our limited understanding of each others language and our naturally faster pace eventually took us ahead of them. We reached a T-junction, and, apparently, an imperceptible col, which surprisingly actually had a name, the Col d'Orgambidé, where we crossed into France again and turned right, still on a tarmac road. Not a single car passed us throughout the afternoon as we slowly descended to meet the valley rising from St Jean Pied de Port. After a few miles we turned off the road and dropped down to the river below to our left. This was our first taste of the HRP where there was simply no path at all. We made our way down as best we could through tall spiky grass and heather to arrive at a small dilapidated footbridge, the Pont de Chubigna. We crossed the small river and picked up a little used path which followed the stream north remaining at the same level as the river fell away below us. After 5-10 minutes we took a sharp right turn off on another faint and ancient path and leaving the river behind, we ascended a steep grassy slope for over a thousand feet. This was a cruel climb towards the end of the days walking which really hurt. We plodded slowly up to finally reach the Col d'Errozaté where we encountered yet another tarmac road. At 1076m, we were at a height only just above that we had reached at the highest point of the road only an hour or two before. This was of course a regular occurrence on our trek and only to be expected, but when it came at the end of the day like this it was particularly unkind. Fortunately we weren't far now from our night's camping spot. It was back to the tent again after

3 nights of relative luxury in hotels.

We descended a dry grassy riverbed initially before returning to the road where we passed a small farm with a persistent barking dog before arriving at our destination, Egurgui. It was difficult to understand why the place had been given a name. It wasn't a place at all, there was nothing there except for an unmanned refuge, Point d'Accueil Jeunes of Egurgui, but it was locked up and seemingly abandoned so we had to find a place to camp. There had been one or two cars around so I wanted to get out of sight of the road if possible and spent the next twenty minutes or so looking for a suitable spot, much to the annoyance of Michael who couldn't understand why I was being so fussy. I eventually picked a small patch of grass near to border stone 224 adjacent the river we had followed down from the Col d'Errozaté. This river actually marked the border so we were camped in Spain looking at France, ten feet away! There were a lot of cattle around the area and we had to remove several large humps of cow dung before we were able to pitch the tent. It was such a relief to ditch the packs for the day. One of our first tasks was to fill the water bags and sterilise the water. There were too many cattle around to take a chance of not treating the water. Whilst the sterilizing tablets were dissolving we put up the tent and immediately cooked tea. We were both famished. We were back to our dehydrated meals once again, which, whilst quite appetizing were never really enough to fully satisfy the appetite after a hard day's walking. We supplemented them with a dehydrated pudding, which helped slightly, but I resorted to a large handful of mixed nuts, seeds and dried fruit to try and fill the remaining gap. We decided to get a campfire going and after finding a few sticks and broken branches nearby we lit the fire and I sat writing my log whilst Michael went off collecting more sticks. This was an idyllic setting and I appreciated the tranquillity after the comparative commercialism and hustle and bustle of Roncesvalles. There was no signal for our mobile phones here between the surrounding hills, which added to the sense of isolation even though we were no more than a hundred metres from the road. There hadn't been any traffic on the road since 5pm and it was now 8.30pm.

I sat on a boulder and pondered the walk so far and was struck by its constant proximity to tarmac roads. I had expected a greater remoteness. We had never been more than three or four miles from the nearest strip of tarmac at any stage of our walk even on the desolate misty ridge above

Arizkun on day three where had lost our way temporarily! The trek so far would certainly lend itself to being supported by someone in a car, carrying all that heavy baggage. Contemplating such luxury was just wishful thinking. The thought of only having to carry a small day sack with butties, a drink and a waterproof as opposed to a mobile wardrobe was most inviting. I concluded that our degree of enjoyment was inversely proportionate to the amount of weight we had to carry and the corresponding pain we must suffer. The lighter the load the happier we would be. Not that we weren't enjoying ourselves but a reduction in aches and pains brought on by such heavy loads could only be a good thing, which would no doubt have allowed us to savour the beauty of our surroundings even more. Conversely, the satisfaction generated from the achievement of humping such huge loads up and down dale, and getting to the end of each day, was deeply fulfilling, or at least it was in retrospect if not at the time!

Michael returned with a bunch of sticks, which he dumped on the subsiding embers of our fire sending a shower of sparks into the evening sky, almost setting the tent alight. He boiled up a pan of water on the gas stove and made a hot chocolate drink for the two of us. More welcome calories. We sat and chatted for half an hour about our experiences so far. He said he was really enjoying the trip and had particularly enjoyed the socialising last night at Roncesvalles. I think he probably appreciated some alternative company from his boring old pop. You can feel rather isolated when the language barriers make it difficult to communicate. Having only each other for company each day does make you crave contact with others. A bit like marriage I suppose! We had got along quite well together though and I was enjoying the opportunity for the sort of father/son bonding session that probably just doesn't happen for most dads. The fire died down and as the light faded we crawled into our sleeping bags, listening to the water tumbling over rocks in the stream, little knowing this was to be the last night we would spend in this tent.

## Day 7, Saturday 8<sup>th</sup> July. Egurgui to Col Bagargui

I was up at 7.15am to be faced by a misty morning with cloud down to a couple of hundred feet above the tent. When camping the morning ritual of Earl Grey tea followed by a large helping of porridge was one that we followed many mornings but Michael would usually forego the porridge and even occasionally the tea. I sometimes wondered just what sustained him. He seemed to prefer an extra half hour in bed and was a bugger to get up on occasions. He eventually arose at 7.45am and after packing up the tent we got going at 9am. We faced the prospect of a very steep climb of nearly 500m or 1600 feet immediately upon setting off from the start. In addition there was no path and no marks and we made our way upwards as best we could, stringing together short stretches of sheep and cattle tracks where we could as we slowly ascended the steep grassy slopes of the Urculu Ridge. A different Urculu Ridge than the one we had encountered just before lunch yesterday by the way! The mist was burning away very quickly and it was becoming a very hot morning with the temperature up to 85 degrees Fahrenheit. We were struggling today and both felt physically drained. We made regular short stops and each found the effort a serious strain. Michael was particularly slow and I found myself having to stop frequently to let him catch up. We were really suffering in the heat and every step required great effort. Our progress up to the summit of the ridge was painfully slow. We would agree to stop at a particular rock or tuft of grass that we would pick out maybe 50 feet or so above us and spend a minute there catching our breath and mopping our brows with our sweat soaked hats. We derived scant satisfaction from these mini milestones, as each one seemed to bring us no closer to the top. We ascended in baby steps, melting in the heat as the final remains of morning mist dissolved under the rising sun. For the first time I felt we were entering the mountains. Our surroundings up to now had amounted to little more than large hills, with the notable exception of La Rhune. After an hour of grinding ascent we were still a few hundred feet below the summit ridge of Urculu, the non-existence of any path and our own lethargy began leading us into a tendency to avoid direct ascent and to contour around the mountain to avoid the painful effort of upward progress. The slope we were on was getting steeper as we progressed clockwise around the mountain until we rounded a ridge and started heading up towards the Col Curutche. Steep, rock-strewn slopes cascaded down to the valley below. Our route traversed up directly across them. There was a vague hint of a very narrow sheep track, which headed in the direction we wanted to go, so we pressed on with an ever-steepening gradient beneath our feet. Such terrain focuses the mind and I recalled the words of the mountaineer Edward Whymper, the first person to ascend the Matterhorn, when he advised taking the utmost care with the placement of each step knowing that a simple slip or stumble could be your last. The trekking poles were of great assistance in this sort of terrain providing additional contact with the ground and the extra stability that this afforded.

We reached the col without mishap and took a long break, taking on plenty of water. As we sat at the col taking in our surroundings we became aware that we were being watched. Up on the horizon above us there were a dozen sets of eyes observing our every move. We could just make out the silhouettes of some large dark shapes some 300 feet above us on the skyline. Griffon vultures. We were treated to an aerial display of unrivalled splendour as one by one they took to the sky. They spiralled ever upwards effortlessly on the thermals, their enormous wingspan making them look like some prehistoric pterodactyls as they surveyed their territory for easy meat. Right now I think we were looking a good prospect.

The heat was making the going very tough and I was pleased to note in our guidebook that the route dropped down slightly from the open ground of the col to gain the shade of a small forest, the Bois de Néquécharre, where we savoured the shade from the trees, and enjoyed being able to walk without our hats. We joined a distinct stony track through the forest, which contoured around the Sommet d'Occabe, providing relief from the earlier relentless ascent. After a mile or so, as the trees began to thin out, we decided it was time for our morning tea and took advantage of the last remnants of the shade of the trees to enjoy a refreshing cup of Earl Grey. We had a large supply of Earl Grey T bags that we had brought with us from England. Sufficient to last the whole trip I hoped. I had been introduced to Earl Grey tea by my wife Sue some years ago and found it to have more flavour than your normal tea and had brought it with us for this particularly refreshing taste. This isn't an advert, honest!

We lingered at the edge of the trees for half an hour or more, not relishing re-entry into the full heat of the late morning sun. Reluctantly we eventually pulled on our packs and set off onto the Sommet d'Occabe. As we reached the open plateau the macabre sight of some thirty or more Griffon vultures gorging themselves on a horse carcase, some 100m away, greeted us. We stood and watched for as while until a couple of walkers appeared over the horizon and approached the dining area. The griffons hopped away with a sort of bouncing gait and one by one took to the air. They were ungainly birds on the ground and certainly needed a substantial take off area but they were undoubted masters of the sky. The appearance of other walkers in significant numbers heralded our rejoining the GR10 once again. The first time the two paths had crossed since parting company on the first day at the Col d'Ibardin. The Sommet d'Occabe seemed to be at the centre of a popular area for walkers and hikers, and from a scene of complete solitude and isolation earlier we had been reintroduced to our fellow man once again.

The path skirted round the actual summit of Occabe and we weren't in the slightest bit tempted to divert there even though it was no more than a hundred feet higher and probably less than 200 metres away. We always felt we needed to conserve our energies for the main task and any minor diversions away from the prescribed route were simply unjustified. We didn't need to discuss such matters, it went without saying. We understood the parameters of our mission and they certainly didn't include an inch of additional ascent or further distance that was not part of the HRP and which didn't bring us closer to Banyuls sur Mer.

We headed east away from the summit, descending only slightly at first until reaching a densely forested ridge where the path became a track and dropped steeply down into the Iraty Forest and the valley of the Iratako River far below. It was lunchtime and we had set our sites on a small restaurant, The Chalet Pedro in the Iritako valley, recommended in the guidebook as 'a good place to have lunch.' We were making good progress when our descent to the valley was alarmingly interrupted as a group of maniacs on scrambler bikes came screaming around a bend in the forest track and forced us to dive for cover lest we be mown down. Their presence was as welcome as that of the last lunatic on a bike who had deigned to entertain us at the Col Basabar a few days previously. At least these loons weren't intent on hanging around. They shot past us and tore up the track like the devil was in hot pursuit. Such violent intrusions into our Pyrenean world were thankfully far and few between. One thing was certain, and that was the fact that this environment could not cope with a sustained assault by these machines. Half a dozen motorbikes delivered an equivalent amount of erosion as a hundred thousand pairs of walking boots. I don't cling to this as a scientifically proven fact you must understand, but simply a common sense theory that probably has a large degree of truth. This is the evidence I rely upon in support of an angry man who doesn't like sharing the mountains with noisy machines. Bastard motorbikes!

Our lunch beckoned loudly, if the rumblings within my digestive system were anything to go by. After our two wheeled roughing up we descended quickly towards the Chalet Pedro. We arrived and took our place on the terrace outside the restaurant overlooking a small field leading down to the river. We were by far the scruffiest and probably smelliest diners in the place. Although I wouldn't mind betting we were probably also the hungriest. Our appetites were substantial and we could not resist the prospect of steak, though it was hardly the sort of food to be consumed in the middle of the day, on a gruelling walk, under a 90° sun. But steak it was, and a bloody big one too. Well it wasn't actually bloody, we both chose medium/well done. Anyway, this steak was the size of a bin lid, a reference probably lost on the young in these days of wheelie bins. It would have kept a pride of lions in suspended lethargy for a month and here we were ripping into it like motorbikes up a mountain track, washed down with the added muscle stimulant of French beer. It was a marvellously satisfying meal at the time but Jesus did we pay for it later that afternoon. We supplemented our feast with a large bowl of French fries and finished with ice cream and then upon resumption of walking wondered why our legs were no longer working. We could have then done with a four hour siesta to aid digestion but we had a schedule to keep and Bagargui, with it's comfy beds, wasn't going to walk to us, so we set off some twenty minutes after finishing eating. The stiffness in our legs, accumulated over seven days of demanding terrain carrying heavy loads, was accentuated by the build up of lactic acid in our muscles brought on by an hours inactivity. Combined with the soporific effect of a couple of beers and a monster meal our will power to continue faced a powerful cocktail of retardants. It wasn't too bad at first, once we'd managed to get the packs off the ground. The first mile after leaving Chalet Pedro consisted of a relatively easy amble up the tarmac road through an area popular with campers. It was upon leaving the road that we really started to suffer the punishment for our lunchtime excesses.

We turned onto a steep path that headed up through the forest towards an un-named pass at 1190m, some 150m above us. Whilst the shade of the forest brought a welcome relief from the searing heat of the afternoon sun, the ascent was a heavy price to pay for our oversized lunch. "Body says no," was the response as the gradient steepened. My digestive system was obviously on full throttle and diverting all my body's energy towards breaking down that steak, because there was definitely none left for my legs. We both felt like we were pushing an elephant up that hill. This so-called easy walk was turning out to be a hard day given the added handicaps of the heat and the heavy lunch.

We took some 45 minutes to reach that col, with more time spent resting and catching our breath than actually walking. We felt drained. The last few steps to the highest point before where the ground levelled off beneath the trees were so satisfying. It meant a reprieve from the muscle-sapping ascent, at least temporarily. As we descended from the col into the next valley we were greeted by a bunch of cheeky French schoolboys who seemed amused at the presence of Les Anglais in this obscure corner of their nation. Much to our shame their English was far better than our French and after a brief conversation they passed on by up the path we had just descended mocking our efforts at schoolboy French and laughing out loudly. We pressed on and arrived once again at the same road we had left an hour earlier, but further up the valley, I hasten to add. Crossing a short dam we rested a while alongside a small artificial lake, laying spread-eagled for at least half an hour, neither of us wanting to make the first move on up and over the Crete de Heguichouria to Bagargui. We had another 226m of climbing ahead for which neither of us had the energy to face. The prospect of re-engaging with our backpacks was daunting in itself. We just lay there on our backs like two upturned turtles, neither of us showing the least inclination to move or even try for fear of the pain it would bring.

Inevitably the time came for us to move on and like two children who are told it's time for bed, we grudgingly rose to our feet, assumed the sumo stance, helping each other on with our monster packs and set off once again, upwards through the Iraty Forest towards our days goal of

Col Bagargui. Our destination was little more than 2 miles distant but took an eternity to cover. Unlike the morning when Michael was struggling in my wake it was my turn to lag behind, as he seemed to find a second wind. I laboured under the heavy pack and equally heavy belly with leaden legs to match and spent most of the climb through the thinning forest, heading back into broken mist once more, with my eyes fixed on the ground ahead. I would stop from time to time to catch a breath and see Michael's still leaning load as it rocked from side to side up the hillside ahead of me. I was so pleased to eventually join him at the summit of Crete de Heguichouria knowing that the final mile was all either level or downhill. This had been our hardest, if not longest day so far.

We rolled into the small complex of Col Bagargui at 4pm, two weary travellers, pleased to have completed their day's exertions. We booked two beds in the refuge (€12.50 each) at the small office located in a wood cabin next to the tarmac road. There were a number of cars parked around the area with holidaymakers coming and going. An elderly gentleman showed us to our cabin, which was split into several dormitories each with varying numbers of bunk beds. We had a room to ourselves with four bunk beds and duly sought to occupy every square inch of it as we emptied our packs, hoping no one else would turn up to share, and even if they did, would be put off by the state of the room and the smell of its occupants. It turned out that our immediate neighbours in the next dormitory were the two French guys, who we hadn't seen since yesterday afternoon. They had set off at 7am from their campsite adjacent the Refuge Point d'Accueil Jeunes at Egurgui but didn't arrive until ten minutes after us. They said they had experienced problems with navigation in the mist first thing in the morning on their ascent to Sommet d'Occabe. I suddenly didn't feel quite so bad about the seven hours we had taken to complete what the guidebook had suggested should take 5 hours 15 minutes. This helped put into perspective the next day to Refuge de Belagua which the guidebook had allotted 9 hours 50 minutes.

We set about various domestic and personal hygiene functions, which had become more pressing following two days out in the mountains. For me the first priority was a shower as I was beginning to emit some quite noxious odours again. Taking a shower after two days being encased in seriously perspiration soaked clothing doesn't just make you feel clean it completely revives you as well. The weariness of the days efforts were washed away down the plug hole along with all the muck. Refreshed and re-vitalised the next priority was washing of clothes. Some of the clothing in our bags was festering badly and in serious danger of disintegration without the introduction of soap and water, especially the socks. After multiple sink loads of washing were taken out to be draped over the fence, opposite the cabin, we also unpacked the tent that we had put away wet in the heavy mist and dew at Egurgui and left that to air in the early evening sun. Our next task was to stock up on provisions including obtaining something for our evening meal so we headed off to the small shop on the complex. We were able to purchase some canned food for our tea including some fish soup and a couple of cans of sausage and lentils. We had to stock up with two days worth of lunches and were unfortunately forced to resort to long life bread, which isn't really bread at all, but more of an open textured reconstituted cardboard, as we were to discover over the coming days.

We headed down to the communal dining room/kitchen cabin, eager to tuck into our newly purchased grub. The fish soup was first into the pan. It smelled absolutely disgusting and I did not much relish eating the stuff. It was a watery gruel and better deserved the name fish *pond* soup, the aroma of which reminded me of days spent out sea fishing with my father in a small boat off Rhyl in North Wales. On the trip back we would gut and behead the catch and by the time we reached shore our hands would be covered in fish scales and stink to high heaven for days. That was the smell of our fish soup. The aroma both filled, and emptied the kitchen simultaneously, so to speak with our fellow diners baling out onto the veranda in their droves to escape the smell. We were left alone to savour our hors d'oeuvres. We stoically served up our starter course and sat at one of the several dining tables, spoons akimbo, to tuck in. Urgh! The first spoonful confirmed my suspicions that this stuff was inedible. It actually tasted even worse than it smelled, which was saying something. It was probably more suited to the treatment of warts or de-scaling of ceramic bath tiling, but to eat, definitely not! After a spoonful each, that was swiftly spurted back into the bowls, the remainder was disposed of down the sink and no doubt cleared every drain of 99.9% of all known germs on its way back to the Atlantic from whence it came. Thankfully the lentils and sausage were somewhat more appetizing

After dinner we sat and chatted with some of our fellow diners none of whom were doing either the GR10 or HRP, both of which passed through Bagargui. Where were all the long distance walkers? Was this a fad that had now died out? That would explain the disused paths. It seemed the only long distance walkers were all heading to Santiago de Compostella. There was only Michael and I heading east for Banyuls sur Mer and the Med! After a while we toddled off to bed, collecting our now dry clothes and tent on the way. After setting the alarm on my mobile phone for 5.30am, we drifted off to sleep both conscious of a long and very demanding day ahead tomorrow. A day that was to turn into a true epic.

# Day 8, Sunday 9th July. Col Bagargui to Refuge de Belagua

We hadn't booked ahead to Refuge de Belagua. It didn't seem necessary. Places had been readily available everywhere we had stayed with only Roncesvalles having any suggestion of a shortage of beds. We were up at 5.30am, in the dark, and after a contrived breakfast of custard, jammy dodger type biscuits, dry bread and plenty of water we set off on our marathon day at 6.30am. It was still quite dark as we crossed the road opposite the little timber booking office and headed off up a winding tarmac lane of countless hairpins passing numerous holiday chalets as it climbed up through a pine forest towards Crete d'Orgambidesca. It was a cool morning but we stuck with our attire of shorts and t-shirts, relying on body heat from the exertions of a steep ascent to keep us warm. After about ten minutes on the road our route struck off on a path through the trees, still ascending, even steeper now. We soon emerged at the edge of the forest to find ourselves walking on the crest of the ridge. A blood-red sun, behind us over our left shoulders, was just beginning to rise above the mist filled French valleys. We stopped to admire the awakening landscape. A strange misty red-purple hue was cast across distant summits that stuck their heads out of the cotton wool mist that filled every depression. The mountains were like islands in a sea of grey-white stained by the filtered rays of a blood red dawn. Amongst these islands, the one that dominated, the one that rose above all the rest, like a Pitcairn rising from the vast Pacific, Pic d'Orhy. The first 2000m summit encountered on the HRP, towering Matterhorn like above the surrounding mountains. Pic d'Orhy, at 2017m was to be our highest point on the walk so far but was only one of a series of challenges to be overcome that day. The fact that we were facing 1200m of ascent and an estimated 25km distance was a challenge in itself and way beyond any of our previous 7 days walks so far. An added edge to the challenge was brought about due to the likelihood that because most of the day was spent high on the ridge we would probably not have any opportunities to replenish our water. Anyway, the limestone terrain we were passing through almost certainly meant that all of the river and streambeds would be dry this far into the summer even if we hadn't been confined to following the water table. And just to make it that bit more interesting, and probably most significant of all, it was shaping up to be a very hot day.

We continued up the Crete d'Orgambidesca passing a series of TV masts and looking down on the blanket of mist filling the valley below our feet. After a short descent to the Col Mehatze the path became somewhat indistinct and we became 'somewhat' lost. The immediate terrain was rather unremarkable and with no real landmarks to guide us we continued in the same general southerly direction with no true conviction and no hint of a path, going up and down over several minor summits, until eventually stumbling upon a deserted single-track tarmac road. For want of a better idea we followed this for a few hundred metres until reaching a junction with a dirt road on our left. This location fitted nicely with part of the description in the guidebook and sure enough it was our route. Once again, we had muddled through and with just a little good fortune we had stumbled back onto our prescribed route. We were now at the Col Lapatignegagne and at 1453m, marginally higher than our previous record altitude the day before on Sommet d'Occabe.

After a short descent on the dirt road a path struck off to the left to traverse precariously beneath the broken limestone crags of the Pic de Bizkarze. As the path swept around the broad open cirque it became narrower and even more precipitous until finally threading its way up in an outrageously delicate line through vertical crags onto the crest of the Millagate Ridge. Leaving the Millagate Ridge behind we dropped down into a broad grassy col and began to ascend once again. We were now on the final approach to Pic d'Orhy massif whose limestone pyramid of rock dominated the skyline ahead.

The gradient steepened as we slowly ascended the western apex of the Zazpigagn Ridge, which linked to the summit cone of d'Orhy. There were peculiar little hunting shelters at regular intervals, each one of them numbered. We unavoidably found ourselves engaged in a countdown to the summit as we passed each one. Attaining the westerly end of the Zazpigagn Ridge brought a sudden and marked increase in the wind, which until now had been little more than a gentle breeze. The southwesterly gale that sprang up from nowhere to accompany us along the crest of the ridge was most alarming. The ridge was a razor sharp arête, which plummeted 1000' down vertical limestone cliffs on the north east facing side and slightly less than vertical crags for a similar distance on the southern side. It reminded me very much of the Crib Goch ridge on Snowdon, but with bigger drops.

We edged our way along, buffeted by the fierce gusts of wind that would hit every few seconds. In places the narrowness of the apex made you feel you were walking a tightrope. Attempting such a precarious high-wire balancing act, in a gale force wind with the equivalent of a sail on your back, in the form of our backpacks, gave the whole experience that little extra added edge. The situation certainly focused the mind and there was little conversation between us as we concentrated completely on every single step. We both kept our trekking poles in hand, which was both a re-assurance, and at times an encumbrance, dependant on whether we were on the crest of the ridge or just off to one side. The ridge was generally quite level in height but comprised of broken rock and slabs, sometimes at contorted and awkward angles which twisted the placement of each foot and did not allow for easy progress. On this awkward and broken ground the walking poles were of great benefit and with their assistance we picked our way along the crest with some degree of added stability, with four points of contact with the ground. The essential element though was an absolute concentration on each step. A glance to one side into the void could lead to a sense of giddiness and vertigo that could cause a single misplaced foot, the consequences of which did not bear too careful thought. The down side of having the poles was when it became necessary to drop a few feet down off the crest to one side and we found ourselves needing to use our hands as much as our feet. The poles then became a serious handicap, dangling loosely from our wrists, clattering against the rock and getting under our feet.

After some fifteen of twenty minutes of nervous but steady progress we reached the point of descent, which was an open gully on our right. This led down from the ridge for some 60-70 feet to a narrow ledge, which then continued east to a small col at the end of the ridge. Although the gully was quite steep we were able to down climb most of it facing out from the mountain. I was ahead of Michael at this stage and I slowly picked my way down the gully seeking safe and solid handholds amongst the loose rock on quite a steep descent. Disaster struck. As my backside and backpack scraped along the steep gully walls behind me the outer tent stuff sack became dislodged from the pack and hit the ground behind my heels. At first I had no conception as to what it was, then, a split second later, I realised it was the tent. My instinct was to snatch for it as it hit the ground behind me but I didn't have any hands free. I was delicately balanced in a particularly steep section of the gully and to have let go with either hand would have resulted in a similar fate for me as befell the tent. For a moment I thought it was going to lodge behind my heels but this was only momentary. It toppled from behind my legs and bounced away from me down the gully, picking up speed as it tumbled. I felt helpless, all I could do was watch. I thought perhaps it may come to rest on the narrow shelf to which we were descending, some fifty feet below us but it had picked up too much momentum by this stage and bounced clear of this one possible safety net and into oblivion over a vertical precipice.

"NO, NO, NO, oh shit NO," I yelled in despair as our home and shelter disappeared down the mountain. I continued gazing down into the void and some five or ten seconds later maybe the tent reappeared, still bouncing, many hundreds of feet below us in the stone choked gully. We both watched, barely able to spot the rapidly descending green stuff sack, which by now was well over a thousand feet below us, until it disappeared from sight, probably coming to rest amongst the larger rocks and boulders that filled the lower sections of the gully a few hundred feet above the forest line.

"BASTARD, BASTARD, STUPID BLOODY BASTARD!" I cursed at my own stupidity for not securing the tent to my pack properly. What the hell were we going to do now?

I was stunned. We clambered down the remaining fifty feet of the gully to the narrow shelf that soon brought us to a deep notch in the ridge from which the route passed over to the northerly facing crags of the mountain. We sat down to gather our thoughts, but I could not see any solution other than retrieving the tent. After a brief discussion I left Michael and my back pack behind and set off down the mountain in the vain hope of finding the tiny green stuff sack amongst the battlefield of rocks and boulders down in the lower part of the gully probably as much as 2000' below us. There was no path or obvious route and the ground was quite steep. No one in his or her right mind would have considered trying to descend this part of the mountain, but I clearly wasn't, (in my right mind.) All I could think of was retrieving the tent. There seemed no other logical solution to our predicament and it was with an unstinting single-minded resolve of achieving this objective that I continued downwards. All other thoughts were expelled from my mind, temporarily at least. The ground was rough and steep and due to the convex curve of the slope I was soon out of sight of my son. As the gradient steepened below me I could see the lower reaches of the gully, where I believed the tent had come to rest. The ground I was on was extremely dangerous and comprised of steepening loose scree interspersed with well-vegetated and equally loose limestone crags. At first I didn't recognise the degree of danger I was facing. Like a typical man, instinct of the hunter, I was focused on one thing. Retrieval of the tent. Any barriers between me and my quarry were just hurdles to be overcome. I was spurred on by being able to see my objective down below. What I couldn't see was all of the mountain between me and where I believed the tent to be. The gradient had increased sufficiently for me to have to face into the rock in order to pick my handholds and I continued to down-climb into the unknown, unable to see the ever-steepening slope beneath my feet. The rock I was on was treacherous and in the process of seeking solid foot and handholds I was continually dislodging small rocks and stones and sending them bouncing down the face of the mountain beneath me. I eventually reached a section where a wall of vertical rock barred my continued descent and I was forced to traverse over to my left towards a small nose of rock which formed a sort of promontory above the confluence of two gullies. I was testing every hand and foothold before I committed to it when I reached for a large block of limestone with my left hand. Unnervingly it rattled slightly but still seemed reasonably firm. I re-affirmed my two footholds and a solid hold for my right hand. As comfortable as I possibly could be in the circumstances I gave a sharp tug to the block with my left hand, which, despite my preparations, completely caught me by surprise as the whole block peeled away from the side of the mountain. I froze and felt my heart pounding in my chest as a piece of mountain the size of a medium TV glanced off my left thigh as it went crashing down into the gully below. It echoed around the mountain as it ricocheted off the gully walls loosening what sounded like tonnes of further rock and stones in its path from the crescendo of noise of clattering masonry beneath me. I thought I hope to God there's nobody down there! It seemed an eternity before the noise of falling rocks ceased. Then silence. No rocks, no wind even, just the sound of my pounding heart pumping blood and adrenalin through my temples and my erratic breathing as the realisation of my foolish enterprise became crystal clear.

"For God's sake what the hell are you doing Taylor? Get out of here before you end up being reunited with your bloody tent far sooner than you'd wish!"

I scrambled back up to Michael without further mishap. I must have descended around 200' and was out of breath by the time I got back to the col. Michael had been joined by a couple of young French blokes and a woman. I must have appeared in a bit of a state, puffing and panting, sweating profusely and blurting out something about falling rocks as I sat and emptied half of my 1 litre drink bottle down my throat in between gasps for oxygen. They had asked Michael where we were headed and when he had replied Belagua they snorted in disbelief, gesturing that this was very far away and clearly beyond the capabilities of an incoherent, balding fat man with breathing difficulties and his hapless son. I confirmed our destination between breaths to which they laughed openly and dismissed any conceivable possibility of us attaining such a distant objective as being the insane ramblings of a demented fool, making some reference to "mad English" as they headed off up the Zazpigagn Ridge.

Michael was rather unnerved by these doubting French walkers and I tried to reassure him that whilst Belagua was a long way off we had started early and already had a lot of miles and ascent behind us, and most of the day ahead in which to cover the remaining distance. It was still only 9.30am. I don't think I managed to convince him. My mind was focused on the loss of our tent and Michael would have to deal with these doubts himself. I contemplated the prospects of retrieving the tent by some other route of descent. The only trouble was I didn't have any details of alternative ways off the mountain and more importantly I could probably spend weeks searching amongst the rocks in that gully and never find the tent. I concluded there was limited guarantee of success even if I did find a suitable and safe way down. Thoroughly disheartened I turned my back on the prospect and we donned our packs and moved on.

From this narrow notch in the ridge the path descended steep ground to the north of the mountain before turning east again, skirting below vertical crags to re-ascend back to the crest of the ridge at a small metal gate which seemed somewhat out of place with its surroundings. Our return to the ridge revealed a less severe slope to the south of the mountain and resurrected the prospect of descending for the tent. I didn't say anything to Michael but kept glancing down into Spain assessing the slope below us. As frustrating as it was I dismissed the possibility of retrieving the tent very quickly. Instinctively I felt compelled to get it back, but I feared it would be nothing but a fools' errand. It grieved me to walk away but that's what I did.

The conical summit of Pic D'Orhy was now directly above. This would be our first venture over 2000metres and heralded the first of many of the true Pyrenean mountains we would encounter on our trek. We soon found ourselves at the summit which we shared with another half a dozen other climbers. It was a milestone and we found it an uplifting experience that helped banish the gloom of our earlier misfortune. The wind had eased significantly since leaving the Zazpigagn Ridge and the rising sun was now high enough in the sky to provide welcome warmth at this cooler altitude. The French valleys were still filled with mist which seemed to be rising ever higher whilst in contrast, south of the border, the Spanish Sierras were overlooked by endless blue sky which blended with the rolling folds of land into a distant heat haze.

It was 10.15am and, as we sat taking in the scenery from the summit of Pic d'Orhy I devised a cunning plan. I rang my wife Sue. The conversation went something like this from recollection.

"Hi hun, it's me!"

"What are you ringing me for at this time on a Sunday morning?"

"Well, it's like this…erm."

"What have you done now?"

"We've er…lost the tent."

"WHAT?"

"He's lost the bloody tent, not me," interjected Michael.

"Yeh…it was actually me who lost the tent, or rather the outer tent to be more precise."

"Oh my God! Leave you on your own for five minutes and look what happens. Steve you're a bloody idiot. How on earth did you manage to lose the tent?"

"It came away from my pack and fell a thousand feet down a mountain."

"Bleedin' eejit! So you've rang me up to share in your misfortune then?"

"Well no, actually I was hoping you might be able to help."

"Oh yeh"

"Yes, you know your Charlie and Susan are coming out to meet us on Tuesday. Can you ask him to buy us a new tent and I'll pay him for it when he arrives. In fact do you think you can get him to see if he get hold of the same model we, ahem, I have lost; a Vango Storm 200+ model and that will give us a spare inner tent, poles and pegs?"

"I think you need to speak to him yourself."

"Yeh, that's probably a good idea, have you got his home number? No hold on. I'll tell you what, can you ring him, tell him the problem and I'll text his mobile with the details of the tent, ok?"

"Yeh, ok. What am I going to do with you eh, you bloody big dope?"

"Heh heh! Thanks hun, love you, speak later, bye for now."

I turned to Michael, "we'll have a new tent on Tuesday."

"What are we gonna do until then?" he quipped.

"Well we're in the refuge at Belagua tonight and we can book into a hotel in Lescun tomorrow night. Problem solved."

We descended the steep eastern flank of Pic d'Orhy towards the Port de Larrau, which, at 1573metres, was one of a number of the high road crossings over the Pyrenees. We had an odd encounter with a manic Spanish photographer on our descent. He was ascending towards us and for some peculiar reason seemed to take an instant liking to our photogenic potential. He obviously decided that we made the perfect subject material and for 5 mad minutes he must have shot some 50 or more photographs from various angles in a variety of poses. Standing, sitting, walking, taken from uphill, downhill, ground level, eye level, front, back, side. It was like suddenly being transported to the catwalk. He rambled on in pigeon English about some magazine or other and eventually departed uphill towards the summit, no doubt in search of his next victim, leaving us with the distinct impression that he was stark raving mad.

Though it was only 11.30am we were well and truly ready for our lunch by the time we reached the pass at Port de Larrau. It was a busy place with dozens of cars parked in a large car park. Part of its attraction was probably that it provided a big "leg up" for those wishing to ascend Pic d'Orhy. Michael, who is quite fair skinned, was starting to show signs of sunburn and I warned him to cover up. He was more interested in attaining a suntan and dismissed my concerns as unnecessary fuss. "You'll be sorry," I warned, and left it there.

Our lunch was not exactly the most appetizing of fare, with our long-life cardboard, er, sorry, bread and slices of individually wrapped plastic, processed cheese slices that tasted of nothing much at all, and least of all cheese. The saving grace was the onion we had purchased and of course not forgetting Michaels' everlasting mayonnaise. We sat on a grassy bank adjacent the car park, watching the various comings and goings and ignoring the inquisitive sheep that were angling for some of our lunch, but didn't get any. We crunched through raw onion and eyeing our next summit on the border ridge we were passed by our two French friends again who marched on by and over the next top, Pic de l'Achourterrigagna and out of site.

We set off after lunch, conscious that we still had two thirds of the days distance ahead of us. It was now 12 noon and we had already been on the go for 5½ hours and were beginning to feel the strain. The border ridge here comprised a series of relatively modest rises and falls and we were able to cover the distance quite quickly. We passed our French pals having their lunch at the next col, Port de Betzula. The path was becoming intermittent again and the mist that had been filling the French valleys all morning had risen to a point where it was starting to spill over the border ridge into Spain at the cols. After a couple of hundred feet rise to our next summit, Betzulagagna we dropped down into a swirling mist and had to resort to the use of the compass to stay on track. We managed to locate border stone No 240, which pinpointed our position at the Col de Bildacharreko from where we ascended on an easterly bearing, and thankfully out of the mist once again, to our next summit Gaztarrigagna. The gradients, unlike the pronunciations, were easy and gentle and we were progressing well. There were fewer walkers around since the hustle and bustle of Port de Larrau and the last person we saw on the hills that day was during our next ascent from the Col Elhurrosoko up onto the Crete Otchogorri. A solitary wanderer passed us heading in the opposite direction and soon disappeared into the many folds of mountains behind us towards Larrau. From there on that day the mountains were deserted and devoid of both people and water!

Our route finding since leaving the crowds behind us at Larrau had been aided by virtue of the HRP hugging the crest of the border ridge so we always knew we should be on the highest ground. If you could make out higher ground to one side or other then you were almost certainly veering off track. However that came to an end before the next summit of Otchogarrigagna. The route diverged from the border ridge and traversed around the north of the mountain to reach the Col Uthu. Once again there was no path or marks of any kind to guide us and we struck out on a compass bearing, which coincided with the direction of a sort of scree channel which headed up onto a broad ridge. From this vantage point we were gazing east across a wide and open grassy bowl towards the summit of Otchogarrigagna. Around the perimeter of this broad basin there was a distinct line which marked the position of a long lost ancient way, described in the guide book as a vague 'track.' It had clearly fallen into disuse over many decades and in places was barely perceptible. However, the passage of many animals had helped maintain its existence over the years, though clearly they had a tendency to wander and the path split into a myriad of narrow single tracks no more than about 6 inches wide, which made walking them somewhat difficult and ungainly. We persisted, placing each foot directly and awkwardly in front of the other until, after about fifteen or twenty minutes we reached the ridge on the far side of the bowl where the path left the grassy bowl threading its way between two lines of crags on an unlikely narrow shelf to descend gently to the Col Uthu.

We were surprised to find a small electric fence at the col, which was too high to step over, safely, so we were forced to remove our packs and crawl beneath it. Such bodily contortions did not come easy with the stiffness induced after 8 hours walking. It was 2.30pm and we had now completed two thirds of the days walk. We rested at the col and had a snack and a drink, at which stage I realised I had drunk all of my 3 litres of water in my hydration pack and had only ½ a litre remaining in my drinks bottle. The one drawback of the hydration packs is that you don't get to know they're empty until you're down to the last mouthful. They're tucked away out of sight in the depths of your pack and it's only when the hydration pack starts sucking back and you're in danger of losing your tongue down the drinks tube that you actually realise there's no bloody water left. I took the hydration pack out of my backpack just to confirm that it was in fact empty and sure enough the collapsed bag surrounding the inner tube showed I actually sucked all the air as well as water out of the bag. We still had a long way to go and only a small amount of water for a large amount of miles. Looking round from our lofty vantage point at the Col Uthu there was no sign of any water in the adjacent valleys. The impressive limestone crags of Otchogorrigagna and Chardekagagna towered above us hemming in both sides of the col. Nowhere was there any hint of any water. This was a dry and barren landscape with an uncompromising attitude towards any ill prepared travellers. We set off once again, feeling weary by now and concerned at our diminishing water supply. As we descended from the col we passed a herd of cattle who could probably knew where to find the nearest water supply. They said nothing, gazing at us nonchalantly as we passed by. The path skirted below the cliffs of Chardekagagna, finding an increasingly unlikely route between crags on ever more precipitous terrain. After a short ascent we came out at yet another col, the Port de Belhay, marked by border stone No 250.

We rested again briefly at the col with our thoughts turning towards the beckoning comforts of a proper bed and substantial evening meal at Belagua. Simple comforts that took on an enhanced significance the harder they were to come by. We rose to our feet once more, teetering under the load and pressed on along vague tracks and pathless grassy slopes. The mist came up from the French limestone gorges of Olhadubi and Kakoveta to the north and enveloped us once more; only this time with no path or marks to guide us we were entirely reliant upon our map and compass. After half an hour of faltering progress through the thick mist on pathless ground we found our way through to our next landmark, the Col de Bimbalette, and once across the border from France into Spain we were clear of the mist once again. It was peculiar the consistency with which the mist was contained entirely in France. The dividing line between brilliant blue sky and thick impenetrable mist was always on the border. It was as though there was an invisible force field, which coincided with the border and prevented the mist spilling over into Spain. From the col the HRP then avoided taking what was probably the more obvious route over the summit of the Pic de Bimbalette by taking a most improbable traverse on a narrow path across the very steep south face of the mountain, where any misplaced step could easily be your last. According to the guidebook we were now consigned to follow cattle tracks once again, although I could not envisage how any cow could possibly negotiate such a precarious route. Then, as if to demonstrate the point and allay my doubts we turned a corner to find half a dozen cows ambling along the path in the same direction as ourselves. We joined the back of the convoy. They were painfully slow and presented an impenetrable barrier of Pyrenean beef curbing our previously steady progress. We trouped along at the rear of the mini herd looking for opportunities to pass, but these did not arise, the ground above and below being too steep. Every now and then the front cow would stop and bring the whole posse, including us, to a standstill. We didn't want to rush them in case they became agitated which could cause all sorts of problems on such a narrow and precipitous path. They looked formidable beasts with large intimidating pointed horns although we were facing the opposite, less intimidating but smellier end. I couldn't see how they could ever turn around in such a confined space to bring their horns to bear on us even if they wanted to. All eight of us meandered along the narrow winding balcony for what seemed an eternity, stopping occasionally to munch upon some particularly attractive piece of vegetation, while the rest of us had to stand around taking in the views, waiting patiently for the train to start rolling again. Eventually the path came out onto the broad east ridge of the Pic de Bimbalette and we were released from our enforced convoy as the cattle dispersed and we resumed a more normal pace.

We descended the ridge to the Port d'Ordaylé, our umpteenth col of the day, to enter the swirling mist spilling over from France once again. We were both exhausted. I drained the final meagre mouthful of water from my drinks bottle. I had managed somehow to eke out the last ½ litre since the Col Uthu. Michael still had about half a litre left, some of which he kindly shared with me. We prolonged our rest at this, our final col of the day, reluctant to move and re-activate the pain. All that remained of our marathon day was a steady descent of some 2 miles on mostly grassy slopes to the Refuge Belagua. Spurred on by our proximity to what had seemed an unattainable objective earlier in the day we struggled to our feet for the final time and wearily began our descent to Belagua. A hot shower, drink of water, (maybe even beer), a cup of tea and a substantial three-course meal, which we were reliably informed, was served up at all Pyrenean Mountain refuges, was a powerful inducement to keep us moving. These dreams of basic comforts, indeed luxuries to us, sustained the pair of us over these final two miles. We fantasised over the food we would be served until it reached ridiculous proportions and we had conjured up a Henry VIII style banquet served up by nubile topless wenches. Well maybe not quite, but the imagination ran wild. We had finished the last of the water and were incredibly thirsty. I thought perhaps we might encounter some streams as we descended across the face of the mountain. The map showed numerous broken blue lines, which depicted the presence of seasonal streams. Summer was the wrong season. What little water there was came in the form muddy, baking, stagnant pools full of oxygen starved tadpoles, frog spawn and cow shit where you wouldn't contemplate washing your arse, let alone taking a drink.

We spotted a large building someway ahead and believing it to be the refuge made directly towards it. We were desperately tired. Too tired to consult the map or guidebook! It was only when we skirted the rear of the building behind a formidable security fence that it was clearly not the refuge. According to the guidebook it was an abandoned customs building. We came out on the main road next to the customs building. Finally consulting the map it became clear that the refuge was a further kilometre UP the road. I cursed, we had descended too far. Spirits dampened by our stupid error we began the long trudge uphill on tarmac. We could barely walk. My feet were sore, and my leg muscles stiff and painful. The effort of ascending even the modest gradient of the tarmac road was at the extreme limit of my capabilities. Michael seemed to be suffering even more, although to his credit he said nothing of it. He lagged behind, obviously struggling and on the brink of exhaustion. We were both feeling the effects of dehydration. I could barely produce the saliva to keep my mouth moist. That climb up the road to Belagua was a cruel and punishing final lap. I entered my own little world reciting over and over in my mind, food – drink – shower – bed; food – drink – shower – bed. I entered a trance like state watching my boots alternately striking the tarmac ahead of me. The odd car passed us on the road but I barely noticed. I kept my head down and ground out those last thousand metres from my protesting limbs. I recited some of the inspirational lines from Kipling's 'If' to myself as I entered my own little world.

*'If you can force your heart and nerve and sinew*
*to serve your turn long after they are gone,*
*and so hold on when there is nothing in you*
*except the will which says to them 'Hold on'.*

The refuge was in a bit of a dip and didn't come into view until about 200m away. It was a strange beehive like timber framed structure at the end of 100m of rough stony track which was a final punishment for the feet. We turned down the track toward the refuge. There were a couple of cars parked in the inordinately large car park adjacent the building but something about the place didn't look quite right. As we got closer Michael blurted out,

"Dad it's shut. The windows and doors are boarded up!"

"No." I didn't want to believe it. My brain refused to translate what my eyes were digesting. He was right.

"Oh no! I don't believe it. "

We scoured the perimeter of the refuge. It was closed alright. We found out later that it had been shut since the previous winter. We were completely demoralised. The implications of the situation hit us like a sledgehammer.

"What the hell are we gonna do now dad?"

"Don't know son. Let's just sit down and take these soddin' packs off our backs for a start."

We had no water and no means of obtaining any. We were both suffering from dehydration and desperately in need of a drink. All the food we had, with the exception of our processed cheese and long life bread, which was intended for tomorrow's lunch, required water to reconstitute it into edible format. And we had half a tent: the half that was great for keeping out mosquitoes, but useless in the event of the slightest hint of rain or bad weather. Things couldn't possibly get worse.

We were both crushed by the hopelessness of our situation. After so looking forward to some basic comforts, to then have them stolen from us in such a cruel fashion was soul destroying. We were at the point of total exhaustion after our most demanding day so far and faced with a series of dilemmas. Our most pressing need was water. Without it we could not continue. Without it we would both start feeling rather ill with the symptoms of dehydration quite quickly. Overcome with utter despondency we sat on a low stone wall below the refuge and pondered our fate.

While sat outside the refuge looking very forlorn and feeling totally dejected a family of four returned to one of the vehicles in the car park. Desperate, we approached them, begging for water. They kindly gave us a litre bottle, which Michael and I emptied within seconds between us. The family were local and Spanish and had been out for a walk for the day. We explained our situation as best we could and asked if they knew where we could find fresh water. The father gestured towards a stream that passed through a culvert beneath the road where he obviously believed there was water. I had looked at this stream where it passed the back of the refuge a few minutes earlier and it was no more than a muddy ditch with no suggestion of anything approaching fresh water. He clearly believed otherwise and he headed off up hill towards the culvert, obviously convinced within himself that there was water there, whilst we discussed alternative means of obtaining water with his wife. She referred to a restaurant, 10 minutes down the road. I think she meant 10 minutes in the car and about 5 miles and two thousand feet below where we were. About 2 hours walk and probably 3 hours back. Not really a viable prospect in the circumstances. The father returned a couple of minutes later to inform us there was water in the stream where it passed under the road. I was still sceptical, but went off with our two water bags, leaving Michael to erect the inner tent on a patch of flat grass just down from the refuge. I arrived at the stream some twenty yards or so from the road embankment. It was no more than a ditch of damp mud. I headed upstream towards the culvert beneath the road and sure enough here was to be found a trickle of seemingly fresh water, running down the moss covered concrete bed of the culvert. Its flow was such that it would have taken an eternity to fill each bottle. I climbed into the culvert which was probably about four feet high and walked, stooping through to the other end where I was greeted by the most wonderful, heart lifting vision. There, right in front of me in the streambed to the side of the road embankment were 2 large metal tanks, which had, I presumed, formerly supplied water to the refuge. Protruding from the lower tank was a 3-4 inch diameter pipe that had burst or had been burst. Where it connected to the tank there was a large gash in the pipe from which a geyser of water was spurting out horizontally. Hallelujah! I couldn't hide my delight and whooped out loud like a big kid. I praised our change in fortunes and, spirits lifted, filled the water bags, drinking copious amounts myself in the process. I was like the cat with the Christmas turkey and hurried back to Michael, with a new spring in my step, eager to share the good news with him. Too eager in fact! In my haste I lost my footing on the mossy floor inside the culvert and slipped and fell, skinning several knuckles on the culvert wall and puncturing one of the water bags in the process. I cursed and got back to my feet, licking away the flush of blood from my throbbing hand. I examined the water bag closely. Fortunately it had only suffered a small pinprick near to the neck of the bag, so it was possible to prevent the loss of water by keeping it upright. Anyway, it was only Michael's bag!

I returned to Michael triumphant, holding the water containers aloft. He had erected the flimsy inner tent and we quickly set about preparing our evening meal. We selected a beef hotpot from the variety of different dehydrated packets of camp food. It may not have been caviar but to us it was a meal fit for a king. It was gorgeous. We supplemented the main course with a reconstituted chocolate sponge cake and custard, washed down with a large mug of Earl Grey. Absolute heaven!

After a change of clothes and more tea we were both feeling quietly content and somewhat revitalised though still footsore and weary from our marathon day. Michael spent some time administering 'after sun' lotion to his reddened arms, neck and legs. My earlier warnings to him had gone unheeded and he was feeling rather sore now. We sat outside the tent surveying the terrain now immersed in a warm glow of evening sunshine. We watched a massive flock of several hundred sheep sweep across the mountainside above the road. They were best part of a kilometre away but the crescendo of noise from their bleating and the clanking of bells around their necks resounded across the valley. Close by, in the dry river valley below us were a herd of white cattle whose larger bells provided the base accompaniment to the higher tone and smaller sheep bells. The trials and tribulations of the day now seemed far removed as a peace and tranquillity settled over the Spanish valleys below and to the south of us. All was well in our isolated little world once again. We sat and chatted as the sun set over the mountains to the west over which we had toiled that day. A grey dusk fell over the Spanish Sierras and we crawled into our sleeping bags consumed by a deep weariness. I had even managed to find a spare water bag that I had almost forgotten I'd packed, tucked away in the deep recesses of my backpack. It had been by far the longest and hardest day. Our one remaining prayer was that it didn't rain overnight.

# Day 9, Monday 10<sup>th</sup> July. Belagua to Lescun

We awoke to a dry, still, perfect dawn, with the rising sun yet to appear over the massif of Pic d'Anie to the east. It was 6.50am. It had been the ideal night for our flimsy inner tent, four and a half thousand feet up in the Pyrenees with no wind or rain. I got up and sat outside admiring the views of misty sierras to the south. Michael was still in deep sleep, which wasn't unusual, but I could forgive him his tardiness this morning after our exertions of the previous day. I made myself a cup of tea and sat on the grass outside the tent pondering the mixture of emotions experienced the day before. Losing the tent; nearly falling off the mountain trying to retrieve it; total exhaustion of walking for 12 hours, mostly in unforgiving heat of the Spanish sun; insatiable thirst and the worry of not finding any water; the crushing blow of discovering the refuge shut and all the implications this held; and finally the elation of discovering a fresh water supply. All in all, quite a roller coaster of a day! It struck me there and then how tenuous was our hold on life in these wild and inhospitable lands. The intermittent water supplies were fragile stepping stones along our route, each susceptible to failure and capable of turning our trek into a catastrophe.

I managed to rouse Michael by 7.30am and after a cup of tea each, my second, he went to fetch more water while I made porridge. The cattle that had been down in the valley the previous evening had now ascended the hill and were all around our tent. The noise of their clanking bells was deafening. Fortunately they weren't too inquisitive and kept their distance, which was a relief. The last thing we wanted now was to be stampeded by a herd of mad cows. We packed up the tent and set off at 8.15am on what promised to be a very hot day. Our route today was to take us once again to a new altitude record over the Col d'Anaye (2040m), back into France, finishing at the Basque village of Lescun. The path soon took us away from the open pastures of Belagua into a dense beech forest. The guidebook made reference to yellow paint markers, which showed the way. They were an absolute Godsend and I would have defied anyone to follow the "path" without the guidance of those apparently ancient yellow paint flashes. There were however a few drawbacks to trying to follow these markers. Firstly, they had obviously been painted a long time ago, as many were badly faded, sometimes to the point of being completely invisible. Their faded appearance made them blend in perfectly with the profusion of yellow lichen, which adorned every rock and we mistook the lichen for path markers time after time. It wasn't until you were immediately upon top of either the markers or the lichen that you were able to differentiate between the two, and even then it wasn't always an exact science shall we say. And thirdly, there simply weren't enough of the markers to prevent frequent and confusing stops to search for the path.

The path! This faint thread of compacted earth marking the passage of ancient footfall through this densest of beech forest was in danger of becoming lost forever, with fallen trees and branches obscuring the way. There were many instances were the undergrowth of branches met from both sides across the path and our trek that day became more of a gardening expedition as we snapped our way through endless branches and twigs that blocked the way. We found we had to stop constantly to check our direction and re-affirm we had not strayed from the route. We could have done with a machete, such was the density of the trees and shrubs that blocked our way. We were slowly climbing, although it was difficult to have any true perception of altitude or position on the map, enclosed within the dense forest canopy. As we gradually gained height the trees began to thin and we eventually emerged from the forest to find ourselves delivered into a random chaos of limestone rocks, slabs, boulders and stones which formed an exquisite natural rock garden. The path, as was, became more intermittent as it played hide and seek with us across a tumble of massive rock outcrops, interspersed with an impenetrable web of scrub and vegetation. Predominantly though the landscape comprised of rock. Rough, weathered blocks and ribs of limestone shaped by millions of years of rain, ice and snow and interspersed by the skeletal stumps of long dead trees, their roots bleached white by the sun. This was a harsh and unforgiving landscape. The hardy and diminishing vegetation clung onto life. The clefts between the limestone blocks provided sufficient respite from the harsh climate to enable tough spiky grasses and pink flushes of thrift to establish themselves in this desolate terrain. Solitary Arrola pines were scattered around the wilderness, their tapering crowns like witches hats dotted around the landscape.

The route finding wasn't any easier as the paint marks became more difficult to spot amongst the increased patches of lichen. Many small cairns of loose stones supplemented the yellow dots. They were marginally easier to find than the camouflaged paint spots. It was in following the trail of a line of cairns that we became lost at one stage. The path became increasingly vague up to a point where both the paint marks and cairns just dried up. I checked my compass to confirm our direction only to find we actually headed west. Back whence we came! We retraced our steps, which was not an easy task in itself and picked up the trail again some 200 metres back. This was indeed a most wondrous, but also most confusing, gallery of razor sharp limestone architecture.

The trail meandered its way taking the line of least resistance through the confusion of rocks and boulders. Every ten yards gained was 30 yards walked. Our boots clanked through the sharp rubble and alerted lizards which scurried for cover into the nearest crevice. It was energy sapping. Every footstep was twisted left then right to fit the unnatural contortions of ground. The most energy draining aspect of the environment though was the heat, the unrelenting, baking heat of the merciless Spanish sun, now high above our heads. The temperature must easily have been 100 degrees Fahrenheit and we were slowly being cooked. The few remaining trees and bushes thinned more and more until we were left with little or no respite from the burning heat of the sun. There was no escape. The white limestone rock reflected heat straight back up from the ground and our drinks tubes were seldom away from our lips as we soaked up liquid to replenish the perspiration that was running out of us like a tap and evaporating from our clothing. Michael suffered most though. Due to his sunburn from yesterday he was compelled to cover up, wearing long trousers and a long sleeved shirt. He was like a jacket potato slowly cooking in a wrap of silver foil. My words of warning from the previous day had not penetrated the folly of his whimsical desire to improve his suntan and he was now learning the hard way. I couldn't help but feel sorry for him though. Of all the days not to have to wear long sleeves and trousers I would have ranked this one at the very top of the list.

We stopped for a long lunch under a solitary pine polishing off the remains of our indigestible long life bread and cheese. It was easy to linger under the shade of that pine tree, delaying our return into merciless heat of the midday sun. Eventually resuming our battle we emerged from the protection of our natural parasol and slowly ascended into a desert of stone as we approached the Col d'Anaye. We were lost in a moonscape of bare rock, completely devoid of all vegetation. It was of little surprise that nothing grew in this barren wilderness. We rested at the col and finished the last of our water, prematurely once again but this time with less than half of the days distance covered. I was banking on there being fresh water in the valley as we descended into France. The guidebook made reference to a fresh water supply and the map showed a 'source', or spring about a kilometre distant and some 250metres below the col. The surroundings at Col d'Anaye, whilst savage and uncompromising, were also outstandingly beautiful. Massive monolithic slabs of limestone towered above the col capped by overhanging bulges of rock which gave the appearance of a giant tsunami about to consume all before it.

We clattered down on the loose, dry stone of a steep, vague path into the Vallon d'Anaye and sure enough we soon encountered the outflow from the fresh water springs referred to as the Source de Marmitou on the map. This tumbling mountain stream was indeed a joyous site and for the second time in 24 hours I found myself reduced to an infantile state by the discovery of a fresh water supply. We drank and drank and drank. I filled my hat and tipped it onto my head, gasping as the cold clear water ran down my back. We spent some half an hour or more just frolicking in the stream like two water babies, removing our boots and immersing our steaming feet in the crystal clear mountain stream. It was such a welcome reprieve from the baking Spanish kiln in which we had spent the morning and we savoured the moment for maybe half an hour or more. Unfortunately, as with all previous and subsequent siestas they were only ever a temporary relief and after filling up our water bottles we peeled ourselves reluctantly away from our mountain oasis. Relieved to have been delivered safely from our Spanish limestone oven we set off once again.

Shortly after leaving the stream we spotted our first humans of the day, who, like us were descending but had come down from the ridge to the south to converge with our path some way ahead of us. We soon passed this party of some seven or eight French walkers. An encounter that was to prove fortuitous later! The further we descended into the valley the more the massive pillar of rock, known as Le Billaré dominated the skyline, standing like a lone sentinel at the valley entrance, its vertical walls of sheer rock thrusting some 3000 feet above the valley floor. It was an incredibly impressive scene and demanded the attention of all who came within its view. It was probably whilst paying too much attention to

Le Billaré and not enough to where I was placing my feet that I took quite a spectacular tumble that must have covered some 30 feet of hillside. Fortunately for me the final point of impact where I came to rest was mostly devoid of rocks and boulders. I must say the fall itself was adorned with technical merit and involved at least one full somersault with just a walking pole remaining in contact with the ground, my legs pointing skywards, though not necessarily both at the same time. However I must acknowledge that it would never have scored highly in any gymnastics floor routine since the landing completely lacked grace as I thudded to the ground, arse first with an almighty thump and forgot to finish with the customary curtsey. Forty minutes earlier that fall could have had far more serious consequences in far less forgiving terrain. As it was I just felt a little stupid and came away slightly winded and nursing a bruised bum. Still it amused Michael who laughed out loud.

We continued to descend passing a couple of goat herder's cabanes, located adjacent a section where the valley floor levelled off into a plateau. Just beyond these the now distinct and well-defined path entered the edge of a forest and began to descend more steeply. It was here that we decided to take a short break and it was here that I noticed the PVC map case that contained the guidebook and map was missing. It had been tucked into my waist belt and must have slipped out without me noticing. Michael was not too impressed.

"The tent yesterday, the bloody map and guidebook today! What is wrong with you?"

"Sorry son," I said feebly.

He looked at me in disgust. He didn't lose his temper but it was clear that on this particular occasion he was completely pissed off with me. To add insult to injury we tossed a coin to see who would go back and search for it and he lost. I remembered having the map when we stopped at the stream and this was some 2 kilometres and a thousand feet above where we were now. He disappeared back up the path as I contemplated the latest in a series of calamities that was turning our trek into a Carry On production.

Michael returned fifteen minutes later map case in hand. Apparently the party of French walkers we had passed earlier had picked it up on the trail and brought it down with them. Saved again! I was so relieved. I felt guilty about the whole thing and was glad he hadn't needed to travel far to get it back. Our remaining journey down into Lescun was thankfully less eventful. The valley narrowed and the path steepened. As we descended through the dense forest we could hear the River Anie thundering through the deep canyon below to our right. Occasionally we would catch sight of a spectacular waterfall or cascade. We emerged from the trees some several hundred feet above the Plateau de Sanchese, which marked the head of the tarmac road up from Lescun and was clearly a popular venue with campers and day trippers, with various caravanettes, dormobiles, and every shape, size and colour of tent imaginable dotted around the plateau.

I was intrigued as to how our path would contend with such a huge drop in height over such a short distance. We were perched seemingly on the edge of a cliff, probably some 300 feet above the plateau laid out below us. It didn't seem at all feasible that a path could possibly negotiate such terrain and it was with some trepidation that we began the descent. There were however no difficulties. The path zig-zagged down the face of the cliff with sharp hairpins and a steep gradient but it was well constructed with stone retaining walls to protect from erosion, which also shielded the user from full exposure to the drop. We soon reached the bottom and it was a relief to the legs to be on level ground again. We walked on a short way and stopped just beyond a bridge for a brief drink. Looking back over our tracks, the route up into the Vallon d'Anaye looked equally implausible from below, although the line could clearly be plotted as it twisted its way up the impressive limestone walls of the Pic de la Breque into the Vallon d'Anaye. The scenery was stunning

We turned our backs on the mountains and set off down a stony track that soon became a tarmac road, which traversed hillside pastures as it slowly descended towards Lescun. We were both tired and these last few miles down into the village seemed far longer than they looked on the map. It wasn't until we were just a few hundred metres away that Lescun finally came into view and oh what a welcome sight it was. We trudged wearily into the village centre, which seemed virtually deserted, and sat down at a table outside of the Hotel du Pic d'Anie where we had booked a room earlier. The relief of discarding the backpacks and just sitting down was immense. Le garcon appeared from the hotel bar and we ordered some drinks.

"Deux grande bierres s'il vous plait monsieur," I requested in my best GCE 'O' level French. He disappeared inside as we sat flicking away at persistent flies. It was late afternoon, probably around 4.00pm as we lazed at our table in the sun grateful for deliverance from our travails and misfortunes of the previous two days. The beer went down very easily, too easily, and was quickly followed by another. I could have sat there boozing all night but after the second we booked into the hotel and took full advantage of the opportunity of freshening up with a shower and clean clothes. I even persuaded the hotel to wash our dirty clothes, which I delivered to reception in a carrier bag. I do hope whoever handled them was wearing rubber gloves and breathing apparatus! The remainder of the afternoon and evening were spent in gentle relaxation, with more drink, a sizeable meal, (but not sizeable enough for me) and general recuperation from nine consecutive days of punishing trekking. We both relished the prospect of a full days rest the next day.

# Day 10, Tuesday 11<sup>th</sup> July. Lescun

Following a continental breakfast of copious amounts of coffee, bread and jam, which we were forced to share with a cloud of dozy flies, most of the morning was spent relaxing in the hotel. I spent half an hour or so cleaning and waxing our walking boots and our dirty washing was returned, smelling rather more pleasant than it had the previous day. Whilst lying on my bed reading the guide book I became more and more irritated by the attentions of persistent flies that would land on arms, legs, feet, nose whenever I was still for more than two seconds. Eventually I could stand no more and declared war. In a pique of temper and frustration I went on the attack and splattered dozens of these winged pests that fortunately were so slow they were just sitting ducks. To the annoyance of Michael I accompanied the successful swatting of each fly to the tune of Queens, Another One Bites the Dust. "Dum, dum, dum, dum, another one…"

He said he was going to report me to Greenpeace for cruelty to animals. I told him their remit did not include flies and that I would kill as many as I wanted!

Late morning we emerged from the confines of the hotel onto the mist cloaked steep and narrow lanes of the village. There wasn't an awful lot to see or do in Lescun. It is a tiny and quaint Basque village nestling 900 metres up in the Valée d'Aspe, comprising grey stone buildings built on a steep grassy slope and overlooking a lush green valley which is divided by dry stone walls into small pastures, interspersed with isolated farmhouses and hay barns. This morning was particularly grey, hiding the surrounding mountain grandeur in an impenetrable shroud of damp mist.

We had lunch at a small café, the Bar Berger where we both appreciated the new experience of eating fresh bread after our cardboard rations of recent days. After posting the remains of the tent back to the UK and reserving four places at Refuge d'Arlet for tomorrow night we sat outside of our hotel supping French beer. Unbeknown to us Charlie and Susan had arrived whilst we had been at the post office and heard our chatter from their hotel room above and came down to join us. It was great to see them. We had looked forward to their arrival since the start of the walk and even more so now they were bringing a replacement tent. Their company brought a refreshing addition to our conversation after the limitations of nine days of talking to hardly anyone but each other. After a short time outside we were forced indoors by the onset of a fine, drizzly rain. Charlie and Sue had flown into Pau the previous day and had travelled into the Pyrenees by a combination of train and bus and finally a taxi up to Lescun. They had brought new supplies of packet soups, nuts, dried fruit and cereal bars, which, it turned out, we would still be eating at the end of the walk.

We savoured the remainder of our rest day and re-packed our bags ready for the next days trek. Once again a hotel dinner was most welcome but it was never enough, at least not for me anyway. I had the appetite of 3 men whilst on this walk. After dinner we requested an 8am petit dejeuner, which would allow us a 9am start to our walk the next day and retired to our rooms. I had a habit of summarising the day after lights out much to Michaels annoyance. His perception of lights out was that it heralded the beginning of sleep. My continuing prattle was simply interfering with this process. After a minute or so of generally aimless one sided conversation from me he could contain himself no more.

"Go to sleep will ya!"

"Ok, sorry son."

"And another thing, when you wake up in the morning don't grunt, groan, grind teeth, snort, snore, sigh, moan, fart or emit any other such similar noises. It's bloody annoying!"

"Sorry."

. . . . . . . . . . . .

"Michael"

"WHAT!!"

"How is it you're such a grumpy old bastard at the tender age of 18?"

"Goodnight dad."

## Day 11, Wednesday 12<sup>th</sup> July. Lescun to Refuge d'Arlet

After a breakfast of baguettes, butter, marmalade and coffee we set off as planned at around 9am, and following a brief visit to the village shop, descended out of Lescun down a narrow tarmac lane into the valley to cross the small river at the Pont de Moulin. For a short section we were once again reunited with the GR10 but soon parted company with this frequent companion and its reassuring red and white way-marks to continue in a southerly direction towards the Col de Pau. The tarmac road carried on for some way up the valley until becoming a stony track just beyond a metal gate. We rested on a woodpile just inside the gate where we were surrounded by cattle. It was a misty morning and after leaving the woodpile and cattle behind our ascent began in earnest and we climbed up into the mist. At first we climbed through deciduous wood, crossing the river a couple of times before the vegetation began to thin, the gradient steepened and the terrain became more Alpine, with high pastures interspersed with bare rock and scree. Our steady upward progress was greeted by a thinning of the mist and cloud until at around 1750 metres we emerged from the grey into a blue sky world with the valleys below full of cotton wool again.

After a particularly steep section, we entered a lush green valley of flat pastures locked away in this high Pyrenean fastness. We passed a small stone cabane, The Cabane de Bonaris, where some hikers were enjoying drinks outside. As tempting as it was to join them we pressed on to the col. I was always conscious of the limitations of our sparse French vocabulary and was reminded of an embarrassing episode when in Corsica a couple of years previously when Michael and I stopped at a mountain cabane after a particularly hot and arduous day walking the GR20. There were tables and chairs set out on a sort of patio area in front of the cabane similar to the one we had just passed and I took this to mean that refreshments were available. There were a number of other hikers around and we dumped our packs and sat at one of the tables. After a couple of minutes when it became clear there was no "waiter" service I wandered over to the cabane door. A mountain weathered Corsican shepherd with an impressive beard was stood in the doorway. I approached him and asked if we could have some coca cola. Fortunately for me he had the dignity and manners to not dissolve into fits of laughter as he told me that all he had for sale was goats cheese. Very nice I'm sure but not quite what we were after at the time. I didn't wish to repeat the embarrassment of such an encounter.

As we ascended to the Col de Pau we came upon endless pastures of purple/blue iris waving in the light breeze. We stopped at the col for lunch and, surrounded by blue sky, peered out over the blanket of mist filling the Valée d'Aspe. The afternoon's walking was particularly pleasant. After a short ascent from the Col de Pau a well defined path traversed the northerly facing grassy slopes just inside France following the border ridge in a gentle descent towards the Col de Saoubathou just north of Pic Rouge, which, as it's name suggests, did indeed comprise of red coloured rock. After the initial arduous labours of the ascent this was a comparatively gentle introduction to the Pyrenees for our new companions, Charlie and Sue. That wasn't to last! We stopped at a small spring just below the path on the slopes of Pic Rouge where a young man, who we were to encounter on a number of occasions thereafter, passed us. His name was Gerry. He stopped some 50metres or so beyond the spring, which he hadn't appeared to notice. He looked exhausted and when we moved off I told him, in my best French, that there was a spring where we had stopped. He seemed grateful, thanking me before heading back to the spring.

After our refreshment stop we passed through the Col de Saoubathou and continued gently descending south easterly towards the refuge at Arlet. Shortly after Saoubathou we entered a large and confused hollow where the path fanned out amongst a tumble of random rocks and boulders. We hadn't really noticed but cloud had started to bubble up all around and as we approached the small goat herders' cabane of Lapassa we heard the first distant rumblings of thunder. It sounded some way off at first and of little concern so we pushed on to a point where the path began its final ascent of 300-400ft to the refuge. All the time we ascended the storm grew closer. The growing threat of the storm unnerved me and Michael and I pushed on at an increased pace. Charlie and Sue were struggling to keep up with us and we soon began to leave them behind. As the claps of thunder became louder and more menacing my desire to reach the refuge became more desperate. Mine and Michael's pace quickened. We did not relish the prospect of being caught out in Pyrenean thunderstorm. In the course of the next few moments the sky around us became black and the first isolated but large drops of rain splattered on the rocks around us. Out-riders of the deluge to follow. A bolt of lightning split the sky and instantaneously a deafening peal of thunder rent the air. I quickened my pace further, striding up hill in search of the refuge that could have been no more than a few hundred metres away. Such was the rush to gain shelter we hadn't stopped to put on our waterproofs. After some ten seconds or so the initial well spaced large drops of rain transformed into a maelstrom of hailstones that crashed down all around us as more thunder and lightning exploded ever closer. I could hardly breath such was our pace, my heart was pounding out of my chest as I forced myself to run up the hill. A bolt of lightning struck the top of Pic d' Aillary some quarter of a mile away and the accompanying thunder made the ground shake. I stopped to look round for Michael who was now toiling some 50m behind me and barely visible in the downpour. There was no sign of Charlie and Sue. The bombardment of hailstones, some as large as marbles, pelted down with a ferocity of artillery fire and I put my hands over my head to try and protect my battered scalp. In the space of thirty seconds the ground had been covered in a blanket of white ice, and then, as if a switch had been turned, the hail turned to a torrential rain, immediately washing away the white carpet as the ground was transformed into a cascade of water. The path was turned to a river as a deluge of water and ice consumed it, washing away the rusty red soil, stones and pebbles, which forced me off the path onto the ground alongside. Another bolt of lightning ripped through the sky. I stopped, gasping for breath and looked around. Looking up I could see the refuge some 100 metres away. I shouted down to Michael and pointed in the direction of the building. I don't know if he could hear me in the melee of noise.

For some bizarre reason I suddenly became aware that the walking poles that I was using were probably the most prominent lighting conductors within miles and in a moment of illogical wishful thinking I let go of them, leaving them to dangle from my wrists, believing that by dragging them along in this way without actually holding them I was in some way immune to their potential role as electrical conductors.

As the Lac d'Arlet came into sight and I turned towards the refuge to cover the final fifty metres to safety, a cataclysmic crack of lightning exploded immediately above. The ground shook and I was rendered instantaneously deaf by the blast. I felt like my body had detonated. The violence of this strike was such that I dropped to the ground, whether through fright or shock or the physical blast of the discharge I don't know.

"Jesus Christ," I cursed.

I trembled as I got back to my feet. Michael? I wheeled round to see him rooted to the spot some 30-40 metres away gazing at the sky in abject wonder. "Michael, for God's sake, COME ON!" I screamed.

I turned and raced for the cover of the refuge balcony and reaching it turned again to see a bolt of lightning strike the hillside some 200m away directly behind my son who was like a rabbit in the headlights and still rooted to the spot.

I screamed at him again, "MICHAEL, FOR CHRIST SAKE SON, JUST RUN WILL YA."

The occupants of the refuge were hanging out of the windows above me yelling him on like it was the last 100m of an Olympic final. Jolted from his trance by the clamouring voices he practically sprinted up the hill to join me in the comparative safety of the refuge balcony. I hugged him like I hadn't seen him for years as another lightning blast smote the earth somewhere nearby.

We stood shivering for some ten minutes under the shelter of the refuge balcony and watched the storm strafe the mountainside across the other side of the lake. There was no sign of Charlie and Sue. When the thunder and lightning had moved on we moved out from our shelter and clambered the stairs and into the refuge. We removed our packs in the entrance area and like two drowned rats left a trail of water behind us across the floor as we entered the main lounge and dining area. Our two French friends, who we hadn't seen since Pic d'Orhy had been amongst the cheering voices calling from the window some ten minutes earlier. Somebody made a cup of tea and we both sat hugging the mugs and peering out of the window at the still teaming rain, shivering and wondering where on earth Charlie and Sue had got to.

We were both soaked to the skin, still in our shorts and t-shirts. Chilled to the bone and needing to get into some dry clothes, I retrieved some dry items of clothing from the depths of my rucksack and proceeded up stairs to the dormitory to get changed, there being no bathroom or other suitable facility for this function. My intention in accessing the dormitory before the prescribed time was apparently against the rules and regulations of the refuge and the warden halted me after the first three steps, pointing out that the sleeping quarters were out of bounds before 7pm. Perplexed by the meaningless stupidity of such barmy rules and with no viable alternative to undertake my change of clothes, I certainly wasn't going back outside. I commenced stripping off in the middle of the dining room floor, which was seemingly quite acceptable, until, as I was about to remove my underpants in full view of the paying guests, I was quickly ushered to a nearby broom cupboard to complete the exercise.

Charlie and Sue turned up some half an hour or so later having sat out the storm in the lee of some boulders, which from the sound of things had provided the same degree of shelter you would get from a tea strainer. We traded notes and compared the levels of abject terror we had both experienced. Needless to say our brush with the forces of nature was not something we cared to repeat. Gerry, the guy we had seen looking worse for wear by the spring beneath Pic Rouge arrived some time later having sheltered from the storm at Cabane Lapassa as any sensible person would do in the circumstances. He turned out to be Maltese and spoke English as a first language. He was working as a trainee eye surgeon based in London and had taken a few weeks off to complete the toughest middle section of the HRP from Lescun to Pic Carlit.

We enjoyed a fine meal at Arlet that evening and even managed to dry out most of our clothes as well as the guidebook, which had been in Michaels canvas bum bag. The dormitory, when we were eventually permitted to access it after dinner, comprised 2 rows of double Alpine style bunks, but fortunately, due to the small numbers of guests there was more than enough space to spread out and have the equivalent of about 4 sleeping places each, which made for a most pleasant nights repose.

## Day 12, Thursday 13th July. Refuge d'Arlet to Candanchu

We were up at dawn, 6.45am, with the other guests at the refuge. It was a cool clear morning. The calm after the storm. Our first encounter with refuge living had been quite civilised and with the exception of the daft rule preventing access to the dormitory, had been quite a relaxed affair. Although I put this down partly to the fact that the refuge was less than half full. The scenery outside was transformed from the maelstrom of the previous evening to a tranquil blue-sky dawn with the same cloud inversion we had experienced yesterday with the valleys filled with white mist, a sharp contrast to our introduction to Arlet the previous afternoon. Breakfast comprised tea, bread and jam. What I'd give for sausage, egg and bacon! We seemed to take an eternity to get ready with Michael being the last, as usual. The call of nature, which was naturally part of everybody's morning routine, was, at Arlet, a distinctly uncomfortable and quite public affair. The toilet, unlike the rest of the living quarters, was located at ground level, and in the tradition of many French public conveniences, comprised of just a hole in the floor . For No 2's your aim had to be quite accurate, which was not so easy as it sounds since you would be concentrating more on not losing your balance as you hovered delicately above the poo hole. It's not easy maintaining your thighs at a 90 degree angle to your shins and torso with only the friction of the adjacent walls against which to brace yourself and prevent you falling on your backside in the least desirable of circumstances. To add to the feeling of discomfort in this particular loo, the door, which was more gap than door, started about 18 inches off the ground, which gave all those waiting outside a grandstand view of the inhabitant, if they felt so inclined that they wished to spectate. So the cubicle occupant, assuming the sumo stance, would stare nervously at the waiting queue of fellow bog users from their waist down, whilst they benefited from a similar view of the occupant. A toilet custom-built for the exhibitionist! Then there was the smell. Without going into too much detail it was pretty dreadful. All in all the surroundings were not exactly conducive to spending much time on the most basic of human bodily functions in this the most public of public toilets and most visits were accordingly brief.

The wash facilities were of much the same standard and comprised a cold tap on the outside wall. In defence of these rough and ready amenities I have to say I was damn pleased they existed. I would not have relished a night in the tent last night! After paying our hut fees (29euros) we eventually set off. We were obviously the least organised of all the residents since we were last to leave the hut.

This was the first day where our walk actually began with a descent. After skirting the Lac d'Arlet we ascended slightly to a broad grassy col where we took the wrong path and had to backtrack to a right hand turn off that we had all initially managed to miss. The walk was pleasant and skirted high around the Cirque de Banasse to a small pass, the Col de Lapachouaou, shortly after which the path traversed level above the next mini cirque before coming out on the skyline of the easterly ridge of the Pic d'Arri, turning sharply south west and descending in zig-zags to the Cabane Grosse where we were greeted by a friendly sheep dog. So far we had enjoyed unbroken sunshine but our descent had brought us level with the mist that was filling the valleys and shortly after passing the cabane we were enveloped in this grey gloom. Dropping down into the cloud actually coincided with our entering the rather dense Espelunguere Forest so made very little difference to our already limited views. We descended through the trees and shortly picked up a dirt road which took us down to the valley floor, the Pla d'Espelunguere where, crossing a stream we immediately began a steep 350 metre ascent of the opposite side of the valley. The last of the mist was burning off and it became hot under the midday sun. The path was particularly steep and after emerging from the trees it picked its unlikely route in a rising traverse through rocks and scree below towering cliffs to a point where its further progress seemed impossible until a 20 ft steel ladder came into view. The ladder was bolted to the rock face and led us from an ever narrowing ledge onto more open rocky ground. Michael and I had once again moved ahead of Charlie and Sue and we pushed on to the top of the climb to the Pas de l'Echelle. We entered thick woodland once again and following a half buried metal pipeline, which in places formed the surface of the path, crossed from France into Spain once more. A short distance beyond this imperceptible col we came to the beautiful Lac d'Estaens which demanded to be made a lunch stop.

The water was too inviting to turn down a swim and Michael and I stripped down to our briefs and enjoyed a refreshing dip. Charlie and Sue caught us up some 15 minutes later and we sat and devoured lunch overlooking the shimmering waters of the lake. Dark ominous looking clouds were starting to bubble up to the south and east and I was keen not to linger once lunch was finished. We pressed on and upon reaching the southeast corner of Lac d'Estaens were reunited with the GR11 for the first time since leaving Roncevalles six days ago. The reassuring red and white paint flashes guided us out of the bowl containing the Lac d'Estaens and over a low grassy pass to pass back into France again, overlooking the Valée d'Aspe.

This cleft which runs deep into the French side of the Pyrenees provides one of the few natural passes through the mountain chain and joined up with its Spanish counterpart, the Valle de Canfranc, to carry both main roads and a railway line through and partly under the mountain barrier. The railway had apparently been "temporarily" out of use since the collapse of a bridge on the French side in March 1970 brought about by the collision of a loaded freight train who's brakes had failed. Miraculously nobody was killed in the accident. The reason given for the non reopening of the line being economic, whilst since that time a new road tunnel had been installed, presumably at significant expense?

The railway, opened by Spanish King Alfonso XIII and French President Gaston Doumergue in August 1928, after 24 years under construction, was a marvel of engineering at the time. It comprised 80 bridges, 4 viaducts and 24 tunnels, the longest of which ran for 7875metres beneath the French Spanish border. One of the unique civil engineering features of the line was the spiral tunnels, which allowed the line to climb the steep gradients with the use of tunnels and loops whereby the line would cross back over itself. Unfortunately it was to experience a chequered existence as political upheaval and sheer misfortune befell the line in the form of the Great Depression of 1929, a large fire in 1931, the Spanish Civil War and the Second World War, which continually condemned the line to official disuse. The Spanish even bricked up the tunnel during the Civil War in order to prevent French invasion. The start of the 2nd World War actually heralded the re-opening of the line by the Germans although the French Resistance dynamited some of the bridges in 1944. A few years later 1948 marked the re-launch of the line as a commercial and passenger facility and although it was never profitable it continued to operate until its enforced closure in 1970.

Our continued progress was also being threatened, by the onset of further thunderstorms. We encountered a local goat herder on the path, who was gathering his herd for milking with his two dogs, (goat dogs?). He seemed unperturbed by the thunder which sounded like it was getting nearer by the minute, and after a brief chat ambled off down the hillside with his dogs darting from left to right keeping the herd in an orderly bunch as they descended towards the valley floor. We traversed the hillside above the Valée d'Aspe as the rumblings of thunder reverberated across the mountains above us. After our previous experience we were understandably nervous at the prospect of being caught on the open hillside again and niaively our entry into a dense forest, which coincided with the start of some rain, brought a perceived protection from the ominous threat of the storm which rumbled on still some miles away. I don't suppose the lightning would recognise the existence of a forest as any barrier between itself and its speedy passage to earth, via the back of my shorts, but the tree canopy did nevertheless bring a degree of comfort to our nervous onward progress.

The path wasn't easily followed through the trees with numerous false trails resulting in a stuttering progress. The presence of leaf and branch debris obscured the route in numerous places and the weaving nature of the path had obviously resulted in many earlier users continuing in the directions it had initially indicated whilst the path itself would flit off at 90 degrees, like some mischievous wood sprite, up or down hill leaving the unwary walker fighting their way through undergrowth, wondering where they had gone wrong. We eventually reached the Gave d'Aspe, a steep tumbling stream, which marked the start of some very steep ground, where there had clearly been numerous previous landslides. We parted company with Charlie and Sue at this point. They had been moving far slower than us through the forest and by the time we reached the stream where we stopped for a break, it was some 10 minutes before they joined us. Michael and I pressed on and agreed to meet up with them in Candanchu.

On the other side of the stream the trees thinned and without the binding protection of their roots great slices of mountainside had disappeared into the valley below wiping out the original path and leaving extremely steep and unstable scree slopes with precarious narrow lines of compacted stones no more than six inches wide marking the line of passage of subsequent walkers. Michael cruised across these narrow tightropes seemingly oblivious to the danger and derided my nervous and carefully considered footsteps, ably aided by the cautious placement of my two walking poles.

His easy progress reminded of my youthful days of foolhardy scrambling on the crags of Tryfan in North Wales when the immortality of youth sustained my sometimes suicidal climbing exploits. With no more than a short piece of rope that my dad used to secure the family tent to the roof rack of the car myself and my brother and various pals would pick our own route up the mountain, combining various sections of what I later realised were serious and classic climbs, oblivious to the danger in our naivety, using each other as human step ladders to get past the difficult bits. I recall one day us all sitting, drinking pop and eating our butties at a popular belay point part way up Milestone Buttress when we were joined by a rather snooty female rock climber regaled in all the correct and proper clothing and equipment. She was clearly perturbed at the prospect of sharing her belay stance with what were obviously no more than a bunch of common upstarts and asked what particular route we were climbing. Of course we had no idea and just pointed to the next intended section of rock face that we had decided to climb.

In a demonstration of petty snobbery she remarked, "Oh, you're just scrambling then!

To which I could not resist the pointing out, "Well we've reached the same point as you, by pretty much the same route, without the assistance of half a hundredweight of rope and climbing gear"

"Humph", she snorted as she moved away from our position and out of site.

"Have a nice day," retorted my brother.

After the precarious balancing act across the scree slopes Michael and I made good progress. I wondered how Sue would fare on those slopes. She had a problem with her vision, which caused her difficulty in determining the proximity of the ground at times, which gave her particular problems when descending, especially on rough ground. Charlie and Sue were familiar with mountain walking though and had walked in various mountain ranges all over the world so I trusted they knew what they were doing. We passed a party of 7 or 8 elderly French walkers who had in turn passed us earlier whilst we had been waiting by the Gave d'Aspe. As we ascended towards the Collado de Causiat which marked our second venture into Spain that day the rumbles of thunder echoed across the mountains to the south, now no more than a couple of miles away. We quickened our pace and after passing numerous ski tows soon entered the village of Candanchu. The thunderstorm moved on to the west, passing us by fortunately as we continued down an abandoned road into the deserted ski resort.

Candanchu was a curious place. It was effectively closed, the only sign of life being the various workmen that were hammering, drilling and painting the empty hotels, shops and restaurants that adorned either side of the main road. We amazingly found a bar that was open just where we joined the main road at a hairpin bend and promptly plonked ourselves at one of the tables on the front patio area overlooking the road. We were the only customers. Two pints of beer for me, and similar measures of coke for Michael were most appreciated as we sat and waited for Sue and Charlie who turned up some half hour later. They joined us and we sat relaxing and chatting remarking upon the peculiar nature of our deserted surroundings. Upon leaving the bar we went in search of accommodation, which despite our previous dubious record in this area, we had not bothered to book ahead. The village was deserted with just the occasional car passing through. We called at one refuge, the Refugio el Aguila, which was listed in the guidebook, but it appeared to be closed. Fortunately, the next one down the street, the Refugio Albergue Valle del Aragon was open and we booked in for the princely sum of 23€ per night each, including breakfast and 3 course evening meal.

After we'd booked in and all cleaned up I booked our beds ahead for the next 4 nights but was unable to secure accommodation at the Refuge de Pombie for tomorrow night. It was fully booked. Charlie and I headed off to look for a supermarket or shop of some description to purchase food for the next 5 days for Michael and I, and for the next day for him and Sue, after which they would need to return to Pau to catch their flight, which was due on Sunday. What shops there were, were all closed and we ended up walking all the way up to the top of the pass, in a thick mist, eventually arriving at the Col du Somport, where there was a shop that was open. A fact which wasn't immediately obvious. It wasn't even obvious that it was actually a shop until closer investigation. The goat herder we had spoken to earlier was selling one of his cheeses to the owner and we also bumped into Gerry, the guy we had met on the path just before Arlet. He was staying in a room above the shop, which he had no doubt been able to book due to his impressive multilingual skills.

There was certainly nothing advertising the place. From the road it wasn't recognisable as a shop let alone a gîte or guesthouse! He could speak numerous European languages fluently and could even read Arabic we found out sometime later. Fully stocked with provisions for 5 days we returned the kilometre back down the road into Candanchu to find that a supermarket had opened its doors some 50metres up the road from our refuge!

The evening meal at the refugio was excellent with a fried cheese and potato starter, pork steaks in a red wine sauce with lashings of red wine and as much baguette as you could eat as the main course, all finished off with fruit and yoghurt for afters. We got talking to a couple of Scottish blokes over dinner who were walking the GR11. Coming from Scotland and being accustomed to the cold, wet and windy conditions that prevail there they thought it would be nice to walk in the sunshine for a change. So far they hadn't been disappointed. It was an enjoyable evening in the company of the two Scottish blokes, who I would guess were in their mid fifties. We both had tales to tell of our adventures so far. It was their second attempt at walking the length of the Pyrenees. They had failed last time on an attempt at the GR10 due to the excessive weight they were carrying. (I think they were referring to their backpacks although they were 'big' lads.) We eventually went off to bed around 10.30 or so and for some reason I decided not to bother getting my sleeping bag out of my pack, and just threw my fleece over me instead. By about 2am I was frozen and had to admit defeat. I hadn't thought it would get so cold indoors! I proceeded to excavate my sleeping bag from my pack, subjecting my three comrades to the disturbing and annoying rustle of countless bin bags and carrier bags in which everything was wrapped. I'm afraid it is not possible to move plastic bags in the dark without creating the equivalent noise level of Deep Purple outdoor rock concert. Having woken the whole room I quietly lay down and slowly felt the blood returning to my legs as I dozed off until dawn.

# Day 13, Friday 14th July. Candanchu to Refuge de Pombie

'Charlie and Sue were due to part company with us today'. This is the first entry in my log for Friday July 14th. We had very much appreciated their company even though our relative walking paces were different and we had frequently left them behind, usually in a thunderstorm! It had been great to have them around and we had savoured the significant benefit of having someone else to talk to rather than just each other. After a modest breakfast and a brief photo shoot outside of the refuge we set off up the road towards Col du Somport on a hot sunny morning. Candanchu was a strange place in the summer. The refuge we had stayed in was one of the few signs of life in the whole place. It wasn't like a town or village. It didn't have any centre or focal point. It was just a mountainside of hotels, bars, winter sports shops and ski lifts strung out along a wide mountain road as it headed up to the French border. A virtual ghost town in summer, no doubt transformed as soon as the first winter snows arrived. We slipped out of town, unnoticed, plodding quietly up the road to the pass at Somport.

From the pass, which marked the French border our route turned away from the border back into Spain and continued, still on tarmac, up a deserted road to another Spanish ski resort, Astun at the head of the Valle del Astun, above the romantically named Rio Aragon, which tumbled gently seawards some hundred feet below us. The concept of a Spanish ski resort didn't fit comfortably with my pre-conceived image of Spain, and even now as we viewed the numerous ski tows and lifts scattered across the mountain slopes above the valley the prospect of skiing just didn't seem viable at all in the searing heat that accompanied our steady upward progress towards Astun.

Astun was also deserted. With the exception of a group of men hammering, sawing and painting at one of the hotels, the place was abandoned. The tarmac road came to a dead end where the hotels finished and we joined a stony track that curved downhill for fifty metres to the front terraces of the string of hotel buildings. The bar of the end hotel was open and had a freezer on the terrace outside displaying various ice creams and lolly ices. This was an irresistible draw and we all plonked ourselves down at one of the terrace tables. We were the only customers and had some difficulty in finding anyone to serve us. Eventually a lone Spanish bloke wandered out from the depths of the hotel bar and promptly moved us out from our chosen seating area to an obviously lower quality set of tables and chairs further out on the terrace? We puzzled at this manoeuvre and decided he must have been expecting more smartly attired and auspicious guests later and didn't want us perspiring on his posh chairs. We lingered in the hot morning sun, savouring our ice creams, not wanting to depart from the comforts of 21st century living into our next Pyrenean wilderness.

We discussed our plans and agreed that Charlie and Sue, who did not have a tent, would have to leave us at the Cabane de Cap du Point in order to continue down the Gave de Bious valley back to civilisation , whilst Michael and I headed off towards Refuge de Pombie for a night under canvas once again. We eventually, reluctantly peeled ourselves away from the bosom of our mid morning siesta, and donning our heavier than normal replenished packs set off up hill above Astun towards the French border at the Col de Moines.

There were a number of other walkers around that day as various groups of people headed in the same general direction as ourselves. After an hour we rested briefly alongside the shallow still waters of the Ibon de Escalas, a glacial lake which sat in a hollow below the surrounding border summits. There was always an inclination to make the rest points of a walk coincide with a lake, river or stream. This seemed especially so on our Pyrennean sojourn. The presence of water has a calming and relaxing effect in my experience. My theory is that it probably appeals to some deep primeval instinct due to its basic life sustaining properties. As so often occurred in these circumstances the urge to remove boots and sooth bruised, battered and steaming feet in the cool waters of the lake was irresistible. I sat on a rock at the waters edge in quiet contemplation, blissfully satisfied, up to my ankles in water as my feet slowly turned blue. The bliss had to end unfortunately and the downside of these beautiful interludes is the unavoidable reintroduction of feet with socks and boots.

Our path took as around the lake and on up a well-walked path to the col which was marked with the curious but apparently common presence of a finger post detailing the various destinations and not their distance but the time taken to walk there. Our arrival at the Col de Moines was dominated by the awe-inspiring view of the iconic mountain of Pic du

Midi d'Ossau. Its supremacy of the skyline was omnipotent. It appeared as some Disney like castle of towering rock that mocked the lowly summits around. It seemed out of place, almost artificial, as though it didn't deserve its home amongst more believable and credible neighbouring summits. At 2884m or 9462 feet it was certainly not the highest of the Pyrenees by far but its relative altitude to its immediate surroundings and near vertical ramparts gave it an air of impregnability. It was easy to understand how it had become an iconic symbol of the French Pyrenees.

From the col we wandered down into France until we reached yet another mountain lake, Lac Casterau, which heralded an eagerly anticipated lunch stop. Our arrival at the lake coincided with that of a large herd of sheep, which appeared from over a slight rise at the north end of the lake. They scurried along the waters edge, stopping intermittently to sip water in a leap-frog like procession that appeared to have some clear objective somewhere up the hillside beyond the lake. They made a peculiar spectacle, wary of the various walkers who had stopped to rest on the banks of the lake but resolute in pursuance of their unknown goal. The convoy of sheep eventually disappeared up the hillside and we were left to enjoy our lunch of baguette, cheese and tomato, with mayonnaise of course, basking in the warm sun on the grassy bank alongside the lake. The prospect of another swim was irresistible. Or at least it was for Michael and I. Charlie and Sue resisted the temptation.

Following lunch we descended to the valley floor and crossed the Gave de Bious by a wooden bridge. It was a relief , as always, to be back on level ground and we sauntered along the sometimes muddy path, staying close to the river until we reached the Cabane de Cap de Pount, a shepherds hut which marked the parting of the ways from our companions, Charlie and Sue. It was sad to see them leave. Their presence had provided a welcome alternative to the narrow confines of our own company. Our goodbyes were brief and they wished us luck with the remainder of our journey. Michael and I set off on a very steep and winding ascent up scree slopes and were soon labouring under the renewed effort of our second major ascent of the day. After a few moments we stopped to catch our breath and looked around for Charlie and Sue but they had disappeared from sight down the valley towards the village of Gabas. Alone again we pressed on and soon left the valley behind as we ascended below the ominous towering presence of Pic du Midi d'Ossau. Storm clouds were gathering once again as we gained height, heading for the Col de Peyreget between Ossau and Pic Peyreget. They were to be a daily unnerving presence each afternoon for the next week and we learned to tailor our walking times to avoid them where possible. Not today though. We were walking into the teeth of the storm that approached us from the east behind Pic Peyreget. We passed a number of young French walkers who were nervously contemplating their next move as the thunderstorm grew closer. The terrain became a harsh ragged landscape of massive boulders through which the path picked its way. After passing the Lac de Peyreget the rain started. As with our approach to Arlet two days previously the first drops were few and far between but splattered on the surrounding rocks like jellyfish dropped from a great height. All the time I had been eyeing up potential shelters and the onset of the rain saw us scamper across the maze of rocks and boulders to the shelter of an overhanging boulder as big as a house. Our refuge provided perfect shelter from the ravages of the storm as the rain descended in torrents and lightning strafed the cliff face of Peyreget some 400m away opposite our bolthole. Although we were sheltered from the rain it had turned cold and our clothes were wet from perspiration. We soon started to feel chill and were compelled to forego our t-shirts and shorts for the warmer alternatives of long trousers, fleeces and jackets. To enhance the comfort of our enforced rest we brewed up a cup of soup each from our not insignificant selection supplied by Charlie at Lescun.

Watching a thunderstorm from the relative safety of our shelter gave a different and somewhat more relaxed perspective to that we had experienced at Arlet. It was a spectacular show. I later learned that whilst our shelter did indeed provide a relative degree of comfort and enabled us to completely escape the rain that sort of situation is by no means safe from the uncompromising shafts of lightning that can, and often do apparently breach the overhangs in the event that they strike the tops of such boulders. A sobering thought if you're caught out in such a storm. By all accounts the safest, though definitely not the most comfortable place in an electric storm, is to sit on your pack in open ground away from cliff faces, where you'll die safely, quietly and miserably from hypothermia waiting for the rain to go off. The mountain cattle that grazed the high pastures above the boulder field seemed unperturbed by the storm and were unwittingly putting my 'safe place in a storm' theory to the test. They ambled around seemingly oblivious to the tempest that embroiled them. We spotted some izards or Pyrenean chamois as they are sometimes known, that were less at ease with the storm. They seemed quite skittish and were prancing one way then another across the mountainside as the thunder and lightning danced across the summit of Peyreget. We spent an hour hiding under that boulder. The braver, or more foolhardy French walkers we had passed earlier pressed on towards the Col de Peyreget. We watched their stooped outlines steadily progress up the path above us only to be stopped in their tracks as each bolt of lightning exploded from the sky above them. We considered ourselves wimps cowering under our rock as our French counterparts marched on regardless. They passed out of sight, and on to their destination, probably Pombie. I assume they arrived there safely since we didn't pass any corpses on our way. Perhaps they had been vaporised by 100,000 volts of earthbound electricity. Who knows?

When the storm seemed to have passed over we clambered out from our sanctuary into the open and pushed on to the col. As we approached the col there was another series of thunderclaps no more than a few miles away and we scurried under yet another overhang. As we sat looking across to Pic du Midi, the summit of which disappeared into the black misty gloom above, we spotted the single figure of a man engaged in what I can only describe as rock acrobatics on a large boulder below us. Here we were hiding under a rock like two nervous crabs whilst this exemplar of manhood did housefly impressions clinging upside down to rock faces twenty feet off the ground as the sky threatened to send down bolts from above to smite him from the rock. Bloody poser! He was an impressive poser though.

The rumbles of thunder passed away without ever getting too close and we resumed our intermittent passage to Pombie. The path picked its way through a tumble of rocks and boulders on the east side of the col until the refuge and numerous surrounding different coloured tents came into site. We pitched our brand new, unused tent some 50m or so above the refuge and the small lake that accompanied it. The evening eventually settled down as the thunderstorms dissipated and we enjoyed a pleasant but cool evening in our lofty perch some 2050metres, nearly 7000ft above sea level, with the sheer rock face of Ossau looming behind us. The sunset was probably quite spectacular that evening but we didn't get to see it as the western sky was hidden from our view by Ossau but the peaks to the east were bathed in an orange glow as we retired to our sleeping bags just after 9pm.

# Day 14, Saturday 15<sup>th</sup> July, Pombie to Larribet

Lying on the ground is definitely not conducive to a comfortable nights sleep. We had managed to pitch our tent on bumpy ground again which whilst appearing both relatively flat and level at the time, through the course of the night we discovered that it also slanted down to one side. I had spent the night frequently re-positioning myself back up hill from Michael but, each time, the pull of gravity would bring us back into close contact once again. This was not the bonding session that either of us had anticipated. Fortunately the tent and groundsheet were of course one piece of material otherwise Michael would probably have woken up looking at the stars. For me nights in the tent meant an endless routine of turning one way and then the other as various limbs ceased to function from lack of blood supply. My fitful slumbers would lurch from one position to another as the pain in an arm, leg or shoulder became too much to bear any longer. I sometimes woke in a panic believing my hand had dropped off because I no longer had any sensation there at all. Suffice to say I never really slept much when we camped. The pain kept me awake.

I was up at 6 am that morning and boiled the kettle whilst still in my sleeping bag. Michael was still asleep. When he eventually stirred and I passed him a cup of hot tea which he sat and nursed in a state of semi-coma. I finished my tea and got up to start packing. It was 6.15am. As I busied myself packing away sleeping bag, stove, pans and bedding Michael didn't budge. He sat nursing his tea meditating. After a few gentle words of coaxing I got fed up and shouted at him to move, to which he replied that he was cold. I felt rather mean but I knew these early starts were essential to try and avoid the afternoon thunderstorms and he needed to shift himself.

Today was going to be a 'big' mountain day with a height gain of 1500m (5000ft) and height loss of 1370m (4600ft). I couldn't fathom why the guidebook had graded this day as a Grade 2, which suggested it was no more difficult than the last 3 days we had encountered. It was certainly far harder than any of these three days and involved some extremely serious mountaineering. Ton Joosten alluded to the difficulties to come in his route summary, which said simply, "the first day of the Haute Route that might cause serious problems." I came to realise in time that he was a master of the understatement. The most notable feature of our journey today would be the Passage d'Orteig. This was a narrow ledge across a sheer rock face with a 200metre cliff at your feet. Whilst your progress across the Passage d'Orteig was partially assisted by a steel cable that had been bolted into the rock it was without doubt still a very intimidating section of 'path'. It was not a section of the route I particularly relished. As my years had advanced I had found that my head for heights had correspondingly diminished and immediate proximity to large vertical drops was not something I was too comfortable with. So it was with some trepidation that I faced our walk that day.

Michael eventually shifted himself and we set off, once again starting the day with a descent. The HRP took us down some 700m from Pombie towards the Vallee d'Ossau. It was a relatively easy start to the day and we enjoyed the comparatively gentle descent in the green and pleasant surroundings of these high Pyrenean pastures with the Gave de Pombie glinting in the morning sunshine below us. Now whilst I don't want to destroy this idyllic setting I feel I must mention that as we descended further it was fair to say that gravity was beginning to intervene with my digestive processes. After half an hours walking I was seriously in need of a damn good crap! Now such bodily functions are not something I would consider appropriate for inclusion in any journal such as this and in my experience such delicate topics appear to remain generally undocumented in the written word. They are clearly a taboo. Something of which we all know about, intimately, but of which common decency dictates, should remain unspoken and unwritten.
Bollocks!

The satisfaction of a good crap is magnified many times when conducted in the great outdoors and this particular crap was deserving of a mention. Probably because there is so much scope for mishaps a successful outdoor poo can be all the more fulfilling. It is probably fair to say that this particular bowel evacuation was particularly satisfying. The conditions for such events must of course be right and in this respect the venue is extremely important. In the vast arena of the great outdoors very often the chosen latrine inevitably ends up as a poor compromise when you are caught short, especially in the mountains. There's nothing worse than a high level crap on a cold, draughty damp mountainside where your main concentration is focused on not pissing on your undies as you balance precariously, hunched in a ball, whilst straining not to fall on your arse. No such compromise was required on this occasion. I was able to select the perfect location. It was almost purpose built. All it lacked was a roof and flushing water.

My ideal Pyrenean outdoor WC was located just off the path amongst an area of rocks and boulders and its existence and exquisite suitability as a loo was not at all apparent when viewed from the path some 30-40 yards away, however the layout of the terrain first alerted me to its potential and that it may merit further investigation. It was clear from the path that it provided the necessary privacy that is absolutely essential in any toilet visit for outdoor No 2's and I was to find that upon closer inspection I could not have been more impressed with the facility. Having lain down my pack alongside the path I headed off to investigate the suitability of this potential bog. Upon rounding a limestone outcrop probably no more than six feet high which hid me from the path I entered a sort of narrowing mini ravine where the rocks on both sides eventually merged some 10 metres or so back. However, just before the rocks came together there was enough space to wedge yourself into the remaining gap and be able support you weight comfortably on adjacent shelves of rock. It was the most sublime natural toilet I had ever encountered. As I sat emptying the not unsubstantial contents of my insides onto the dusty ground below, buttocks lightly parted and partially supported by the converging rock either side, further assisted by the presence of chest level shelves of rock either side, on which I could place my arms and further support my weight, and the toilet tissue, I admired the unrivalled view that confronted me up the valley to Pic du Midi d'Ossau, the only spectator to my early morning dump. I was most impressed by the exclusivity of my grand surroundings and remained perched there for several minutes longer than was necessary just simply taking in the view on this warm and sunny Pyrenean morning. I would probably still be there now had I not started attracting flies. Michael clearly thought I had gone insane when I returned to the path and rambled on about the virtues of my bog with a view. He was happy to take my word and passed upon the opportunity for a personal viewing. In his defence I don't envisage it would have quite held the same attraction second time around!

Suitably relieved we continued down past herds of sheep grazing the lower pastures of the valley and soon after passing the Cabane de Pucheaux crossed and re-crossed the Gave de Pombie before entering a dense forest. Some half hour later we emerged in an open valley above the Gave de Brousset just beyond which was what would be our last encounter with tarmac until Gavarnie. The D934 was the last pass across the Pyrenees for some 50km as the crow flies but 7 days walking away for us on our contorted passage through the mountains. We crossed the river and rested in the shade against a massive boulder. It was hot in the full glare of the sun and the ascent from this our lowest point of the day was something neither of us relished. We lingered for some 30 minutes or so, munching snack bars and drinking tea, both reluctant to move. We faced a straight 900m ascent up a long valley to the Col d'Arrious.

Despite the desire to tarry we set off once again on our 3000ft slog up the Arrious valley. There wasn't too much to commend the ascent. It's difficult to appreciate your surroundings fully when you're grinding out every last inch and your vision is focused on the ground at your feet. I'm sure the scenery was fantastic but my attentions were concentrated upon my aching limbs and the soreness in my shoulders from the ever-present burden of my pack. The ascent to the col probably took us some 2 hours or more, I don't know I wasn't really timing it. I felt the effort of every single step up that path and all other walkers left us far behind in their wake as successive parties romped past us and disappeared out of site up ahead. Part way up the valley we encountered the beginnings of construction of a small building, possibly a refuge, and Michael was intrigued at how they had managed to transport a small bobcat excavator to such an inaccessible place. We agreed that it could only have got there by helicopter in the end although it did seem rather heavy for such means of transportation. The guidebook mentioned the presence of a cabane, the Cabane d'Arrious, at around 1775m altitude but we didn't spot it. We were constantly on the look out for such landmarks as they marked a milestone, another step along the way of our marathon journey, but today we were reduced to a metrognomic state focused entirely on upward progress, retreating into our own little worlds and private thoughts. Breathing was our only utterance as the effort of conversation became too much effort and we puffed and blowed our way up this never-ending valley. We stopped on numerous occasions for brief rests to allow our aching limbs and straining lungs some respite but our progress seemed interminably slow. It was eventually with great relief that we reached the

Col d'Arrious which was once again marked by a finger post.

We were both quite exhausted and although our ascent for the day was far from over we decided to stop at this point for lunch, both very much in need of sustenance. Our energy levels seemed somewhat depleted for some reason today and our progress had been particularly slow up the Arrious valley. I think we were also missing the company of Charlie and Sue and were feeling somewhat gloomy. Lunch comprised of the remnants of a somewhat sorry looking and dried up baguette with the customary everlasting chorizo sausage with our equally everlasting mayonnaise, which I must acknowledge, in hindsight was one of Michael's better ideas. We were rather apprehensive about the afternoons' section of walk, knowing we were about to encounter the dreaded Passage d'Orteig. The Col d'Arrious offered the last opportunity to avoid this ordeal via a detour down, around and then up to rejoin the HRP at the Refuge d'Arremoulit, adding some 600 feet of further ascent and descent to an already demanding day. There was no decision to make. The prospect of that additional effort discounted it as an option.

Lunch over, our journey took us south east, uphill and we soon came upon the wild and beautiful Lac d'Arrious, trapped in a hollow between towering pinnacles of bare rock. The HRP didn't go down to the lake, which was no more than 50 feet below us but skirted above it and then over a shoulder where we were finally confronted by the intimidating prospect of negotiating a precarious way forward across the Passage d'Orteig. Further progress appeared impossible. The path we were following just seemed to drop off the edge of the mountain. The mere suggestion of any 'path' across an almost vertical face of mountain seemed ludicrous to say the least. As we crossed the shoulder our path was funnelled towards the edge of a precipice. Within a few metres we were balanced on a ledge no more than 5-6 feet wide and 600 feet above the shattered rocks of the valley below. The trekking poles we were carrying now became an encumbrance and we delicately packed away each other's poles in slow and careful movements as we freed up our hands for the more important role of clinging on for dear life. Michael was clearly unperturbed and relishing his traverse of this wall of death. I was feeling distinctly nervous and most apprehensive as I surveyed the route ahead. Vertigo is a most unwelcome companion in the mountains and for the most part was not something that particularly troubled me, but faced with the prospect of this narrowing ledge across a vertical cliff face my palms were beginning to sweat and I could feel my legs trembling and stomach tightening. Upon stowing the trekking poles we pressed on along the increasingly narrowing ledge until we reached a point where we were faced with a short scramble down, probably no more than 5 or 6 feet, where the ledge then continued, accompanied after several metres by a thick steel cable that was bolted to the rock face. I peered down at the steel cable and could not comprehend why on earth it didn't start some 10 feet sooner where we were now standing. "Whose bloody idea was it to start the cable over there? I've got a good mind to write a strongly worded letter to somebody over this!" I asserted trying to maintain my sense of humour as my knees began to knock. As my nerves began to get the better of me I somehow assumed the poise and elegance of a baby elephant as I stooped down and bungled around looking for handholds to secure my descent to the ledge below. As I faced into the rock searching for suitable footholds I became all too aware of the terrifying drop behind me and I could do nothing to prevent a feeling of panic welling up in my stomach. Whilst I dithered and dallied on the edge of this precipice Michael scooted down the rock alongside me as though he was descending the stairs at home and standing on the ledge below cruelly jibed, "Come on dad, shape up. You're moving like woman!"

"Shut it you, smart arse" I retorted immediately, ignoring the sexist thrust of his cruel remark.

I mentally shut out the terror I was feeling and focused my attentions on what I needed to do to negotiate this impasse. My heart was pounding and I was reduced to a gibbering, mindless idiot, incapable of rational thought as I teetered nervously on the ledge above Michael. I was now on my knees, which any climber will tell you is not the most stable of positions from which to proceed further, whether up or down. The additional three and a half stone of my cumbersome backpack further unbalanced my stance and served only to unnerve my quaking form still more. It's all very much a blur now but I somehow made it down. There was certainly no finesse about my manoeuvre to the ledge below. My short descent was conducted in a manner more akin to a raw egg sliding down a wall.

"You wuss!" Michael mocked again.

"It's Mr Wuss to you buster. Have some respect!" I countered, as I turned to survey the next stage of our tightrope walk.

Our further progress along the Passage d'Orteig was uneventful in comparison to the inauspicious start I had made, and as my nerves settled I began to quite enjoy the thrill of the scramble along the narrow ledge across the cliff face. The difference made by the presence of the steel cable and the reassurance that provided made for an entirely contrasting experience to that of my faltering introduction at the start of the Passage. There were short gaps in the cable in places but that tended to be where the 'path' was wider and less exposed so didn't really pose any serious difficulty. Michael was in front for most of the traverse and soon left me behind with my more considered foot placements and careful but steady progress in comparison to his confident, almost hands in pockets stride. Towards the end of the Passage the rock above became less steep and more broken and allowed me the opportunity of sweet revenge for Michael's cruel tauntings earlier. I scooted up a section of rock to a point where I was some 20 feet or so above Michael and waited for him to discover my disappearance. He soon stopped and turned around to an empty path. After a few seconds of peering down across the precipice he surprisingly, and somewhat disappointedly, seemed unperturbed by my sudden vanishing trick and turned around and continued walking.

"You looking for me by any chance," I shouted.

He looked up with an expression of mild contempt and just said, "what are you doing up there you stupid sod? I knew you'd be hiding somewhere!"

"Too predictable aren't I? You kids are no fun anymore. I used to prefer it when you were little!"

"Yeh, well I'm 18 now and it doesn't wash no more!"

"No bloody fun!" I replied, disgruntled that my ruse hadn't worked.

From the end of the Passage our route led down over folds of bare igneous rock, that resembled layers of molten toffee, each one overlaying the next, to the delightful setting of the Refuge d'Arremoult, which nestled beneath the towering mass of Palas. Alongside the refuge a small concrete dam held back the clear blue-green waters of the largest of the Lacs d'Arremoult. There were a number of walkers and climbers gathered on the terrace fronting the refuge taking drinks and snacks. These were probably part of the contingent that had passed us earlier on the way up the Arrious Valley. The dam wall formed the path of some 20-30 metres, which led us across to the refuge and I boldly stepped onto the wall, which was level with the ground at the west end of the dam. As I strode across the ground fell away to my left and the water of the lake deepened to my right. The wall itself was probably some 18 inches wide at the top and took a number of right-angled turns half way across. By the time I reached the first turn in the wall I had become distinctly aware of the fact that I was some 30 feet above the ground on my left and that the water of the lake on my right, the level of which was probably some six feet below the top of the wall, was by now around 20 feet deep. Some 30 pairs of eyes scanned my every move from the front terrace of the refuge as I teetered along the dam wall. The ninety degree right then left turns completely unnerved me as I began to shuffle along like some house bound geriatric, scared to step out lest I lose my balance. Michael laughed and sauntered along behind me like he was walking down the street. I contemplated dropping to my knees and crawling the rest of the way but my dignity won out and I remained on my feet as I shifted direction first right, then left, left again and then finally right again, eventually stepping back on to terra firma at the east end of the dam, somewhat paler of complexion and in need of the toilet. I believe it is physically possible to be sufficiently frightened to a point where you can actually shit yourself. On two occasions in one day I had tested my tolerance levels in this respect and survived with my both bowels and underpants surprisingly intact!

The Refuge d'Arremoult was marvellously situated and we would both have been more than happy to spend the night there but our journey that day took us on to the Refuge de Larribet, some 4km further east where we had already booked beds and evening meal. I was very much aware that we still had 2 high passes to cross, which were over a thousand feet above Arremoult. We needed to keep on the move or would soon be running into the dreaded late afternoon and the now customary thunderstorms. Resisting the temptation of an afternoon break, we pressed on beyond the refuge to a point where the route headed off up some steep rocks to our left. As we approached the point where the path struck off up this awkward little wall of rock we had to step aside while two young men descended towards us on our intended route. The rock was quite steep and certainly required the assistance of hands as well as feet to enable safe progress, so I was somewhat surprised to see one of the young men bounding down with his hands in his pockets. Initially I was impressed by such confidence until when, as he came closer, I noticed that the laces of his boots were undone and threshing around his ankles. His boots were barely hanging onto his feet. He was cocky and exuded a youthful arrogance and clearly believed he was indestructible. He almost paid the price for his stupidity when, at a point some eight feet above the ground on which we were standing waiting, he stumbled on one of his dangling laces and in the split second he had to choose a landing spot in amongst the rocks and broken ground at the foot of the wall next to us, somehow managed to pick out the only square foot of flat ground within miles. He hurtled through the air and landed, on his two feet with an almighty thud, sprung up again, two footed, like some manic frog as the impetus carried him forward and then danced across the tumble of rocks and stones, arms, legs and laces thrashing about wildly until he regained his balance and came to rest some five or ten metres away on more level ground below. Clearly pleased with his somewhat fortuitous though quite impressive performance, he curtsied and turned away in the direction of the refuge, hands back in his pockets and laces whipping around his ankles. His companion followed, gesturing to us with a finger to the temple, that his friend was indeed insane. Not that we needed convincing.

We clambered up the rock wall making full use of our hands and soon ascended into a sort of hanging valley out of site of the Refuge d'Arremoult. The path pushed on upwards and entered a rocky wilderness where we encountered our first snowfield. We were now at our highest point of the walk so far at over 2400 metres or 8000 feet and were entering an area of wild and rugged mountain terrain where, what paths there were, were faint and little frequented. The snowfield was only relatively small and we soon passed over this wet and sugary blanket, which actually made for quite easy walking compared to the rough ground which surrounded it. We passed a young couple on the way up the snow who seemed somewhat unsure of whether they should continue or not and were happy to let us go first. The snow didn't present any problems although I was aware of the possibility of hidden voids or crevasses hollowed out by melt-waters below and tried to stick to the edge alongside a northerly facing rock wall. Some half hour or so after leaving the refuge we arrived at the Col du Palas on the French Spanish border. It was 3pm and our arrival at the col heralded the first rumblings of distant thunder away to the east.

We were alone. Since passing the couple on the snowfield below the mountains had become deserted. The col was an intimidating and fearful place for us that day. Not a place to be caught in a thunderstorm. Directly ahead of us, across the deep valley at our feet were the steep ramparts of the first of the 3000m summits of the Pyrenees, Balaitous. All around we were hemmed in by soaring sheer faces of rock interspersed with boulder fields and treacherously loose scree slopes. The path petered out at the col and we were cast into a harsh and unforgiving environment of rock and stone. There didn't appear to be any obvious path so we descended slightly from the col as suggested in the guidebook. Our route was supposed to take us northeast in a rising traverse up to our next col, the Port du Lavedan. That direction led across some extremely steep and precarious ground that we soon discovered had been the scene of numerous rock avalanches in the not too distant past. The prospect of progress in this direction seemed highly unlikely and as we began to level off and traverse across the steep slope I started feeling really doubtful of our route. There was no sign of any path or any trail at all and the slope was becoming steeper the further we went. This was a level removed from any of the previous sections of the HRP and I could scarcely believe that it was the prescribed route of such an eminent long distant 'path'. I should have known we were headed into some inhospitable terrain from the deterioration in the depiction of the path as defined on our French map from bold dashed line to faint red dots. This same method had been used to mark the 'path' of the GR20 where it passed through the Cirque de Solitude in Corsica where we were reduced to hanging onto steel ladders and cables bolted into the rock some years previous. After our initial descent of probably no more than 100 feet from the Col du Palas we began to traverse ever-steepening scree slopes. I kept stopping to try and select the line of least resistance. It wasn't easy. With no path to guide us and no markers or cairns, it was by no means obvious where the intended line of the route lay. Ahead of us was a steep slope where rock fall had virtually stripped the mountain bare. We stopped to survey the mountainside beyond this unstable rock slide. Some fifty metres away a rib of steep rock that ended in a vertical cliff some 100 feet below us barred our route forward. There appeared to be only one conceivable way through this barrier along a slanting shelf of broken rock and vegetation more or less on a level with our current position. It looked a highly dubious way through the otherwise unyielding rock band on what appeared a rather treacherous, sloping and previously un-trodden line of weakness in the otherwise unbroken barrier. I looked up and down the mountain and could conceive of no other possible way forward past the rock band, so stepping gingerly onto the loose gravel and soil of the rockslide in front of me I slowly picked my way on our precarious route over to this slanting shelf. It must have been bad because Michael actually expressed his fear of the ground we were on as we sent stones and rocks skittering, sliding and bouncing down the steep slope below. The ground was unnerving and very unstable, threatening to collapse beneath our feet as we nervously negotiated this latest obstacle on this our toughest Pyrenean day so far. We crossed the rockslide having sent several tonnes of mountain thundering down into the valley in the process and stood at the entrance to the passageway that would lead us up to Port du Lavedan.

The sloping shelf of spiky grass and rocks was quite a hairy ride and we picked our way slowly across it with vertical cliffs immediately below. It amazed me that such a route even existed and I began to wish we had opted for the more obvious and less tortuous GR10 or GR11 as a more pedestrian passage through the Pyrenees. At times such as this I found that my concentration was so intense that I sometimes almost forgot Michael was with me. I have to say that when faced with such mind focussing situations the tendency was to exclude all other thoughts and to concentrate on survival and little else. Hence the buzz I suppose! Michael was undoubtedly far more confident than me in such terrain. We negotiated the shelf reasonably easily after which we faced a section of steep ground where we began to ascend again. I resorted to grabbing large tufts of spiky grass and vegetation in the absence of any other more sensible handholds and slowly made my way up, sometimes on all fours, onto easier ground.

You forget your tired when your adrenalin is pumping and once the slope eased and my fear began to subside I realised I was puffing like an old steam train and my heart was pounding away in my chest. I sat down for a breather and watched Michael saunter up towards me.

"Bit steep that weren't it?" he said, as he approached.

"Yeh, it was a bit," I responded simply as I contemplated the degree of his understatement. After a short breather we continued upwards across a field of large boulders and fallen rock to a notch in the skyline, the Port du Lavedan. The final hundred feet up to the col were quite a scramble as we were funnelled into a narrow gully choked with rock-fall. We emerged at the top, alone in a world of rock. Our highest point so far at 2615m. Our brief engagement with Spain over as we gazed down northeast into

French territory once more. The darkening sky closed in on our lofty perch and a deep rumble of thunder echoed up the valley towards us from Larribet. We were walking directly into the arms of our next encounter with a Pyrenean thunderstorm.

The next hour was a race against time as we scampered down the lonely Larribet valley accompanied by increasingly louder peels of thunder from a black and ominous sky ahead of us. The rugged wildness of the landscape and beauty of the numerous moody deep grey lakes we passed were lost in a vagueness of haste as we dashed headlong into the maelstrom that was consuming the land and sky to the north and east. We landed breathless on the doorstep of Larribet as bolts of lightning blitzed the steep slopes of the Crete Fachon, some half-mile further east from the refuge. Large drops of rain began to splatter on the rocks outside the hut as we dived inside past a gathering of spectators, oohing and aahing at the firework display across the valley. These close encounters with death by electrocution were becoming a bad habit for us.

Our deliverance was celebrated with two beers each. Justified reward for the efforts of the day. The CAF (Club Alpin Francais) refuges were a welcome shelter on these evenings of wild mountain weather. The prospect of wrestling with a tent and then lying there inside listening to rocks being blasted asunder from above and wondering whether you were going to be next to be atomised was not the most inviting way of spending the night. We bumped into our friend Gerry once again who was in the next bed in the hen coup of a refuge. He impressed us further with his amazing language skills by translating the Arabic tattoo on Michael's leg. I was beginning to wonder if he was an MI5 agent! We enjoyed another superb refuge meal at Larribet and crashed straight to bed afterwards, both completely exhausted.

# Day 15, Sunday 16<sup>th</sup> July, Larribet to Wallon

Up at 6am, amazingly Michael first, and after a meagre breakfast set off at 6.45am on a bright and sunny morning down into the Larribet valley below. After the initial steep descent it was once again a pleasant start to the days walk, as we entered a leafy green landscape of birch wood and small pastures through which the Larribet stream tumbled gently towards its distant rendezvous with the Atlantic. The talk the night before at dinner had been about bears that had recently been seen in the vicinity although the prospect of actually encountering a Pyrenean brown bear is, I had been assured, extremely remote. I told Michael that the bear would eat him first as he was young fresh meat, to which he replied that I was slow and fat and easily caught and that after eating me they wouldn't need to eat anything else for about six months.

"Anyway, they're vegetarians," I retorted.

"So they'll enjoy chewing on an old cabbage like you then won't they," he replied smugly.

"Mmm, definitely gonna have to start teaching you to show a bit more respect, you're getting far too bloody smart" I chastised.

The Pyrenean bear population had been seriously under threat over the last 100 years, largely from over-hunting or direct persecution. In 1900 there were 150 bears in the Pyrenean range whereas in 1990 the population had collapsed to 10 in the Western Pyrenees. In 1996 and 1997 the French government managed the experimental reintroduction into the Central Pyrenees of 3 bears (2 females, 1 male) originating from Slovenia. At the time of our trip the brown bear population throughout the Pyrenees was still only around 15 with efforts to increase this partly frustrated by fierce opponents of the reintroduction of the bears. There are strong views on both sides with the anti-bear lobby consisting largely of farmers concerned for their livestock. For the most part I would support their reintroduction so long as they didn't want to share any of my food or living quarters.

We didn't spot any bears that morning. I dare say they knew very well the areas to stay away from in order to avoid humans. We exited the

Larribet Valley at an unmanned refuge, the Cabane de Doumblas where we stopped at a small stream to do some of our laundry. We almost caught up with Gerry who had left Larribet before us. He was just disappearing over the crest of a hill some 200 metres ahead as we stopped to wash our clothes.

The next stage of our walk was on a well trodden path up the Vallee d'Arrens to the border col of Port de la Peyre-Saint-Martin. The path was well defined and cleverly constructed with gentle gradients and the extensive use of zig-zags to avoid the steeper climbs. With our early start and the fact that we were ascending the eastern side of the valley we spent the majority of the morning in the shade of the steep ridge that struck south from the summit of the exquisitely named mountain Soum de Bassia du Hoo. The benefits of staying out of the full heat of the sun were immense. It was so much more comfortable not having to wear a hat all the time and it wasn't until near the top of the pass where the surrounding gradients lessened that we ended up undefended from the fierce direct heat of the sun.

As was often the case we stopped for a mid-morning snack part way up the valley and decided to treat ourselves to porridge as well as the customary mug of tea. Michael was particularly hungry for a change and, unusually for him, devoured an enormous bowl of the stuff. There were numerous other walkers heading up the same path that day though they all seemed to disappear down into Spain once we reached the col. A col normally heralded a point where ascent turned to descent but not this time. Some hundred metres or so before passing into Spain we took a sharp left turn up the mountainside, kindly marked by another sign-post, almost doubling back on ourselves. We were headed for yet another col, the Col de Cambales, and yet another altitude record of 2706m.

This path was not so well defined and could have caused significant difficulty in any mist. After about five minutes ascent the path split in two and our route headed off up a steep rocky ridge in a series of short zigzags. Soon after, we rounded the end of the ridge and entered a high corrie of rocks and boulders where the route was anything but clear. The inclination was to head up the corrie towards the obvious col on our right. This must be the Col de Cambales? The guide book didn't help much. It did say "climb east" which in the end was actually the telling factor, because the col we were peering up at was more south than anything and must have been the Port d'Azun. The confusing thing from the guide book perspective though was that it specifically said at the point where the path had split a few minutes earlier, "don't follow the white-red-white marks". There were a series of white-red-white marks heading across the corrie, which comprised a large boulder field. They made off across the corrie towards the end of another ridge, which turned out to be the north westerly arm of the Pic de Cambales guarding the entrance to the corrie we needed to be in. After a few minutes of deliberations with map, guidebook and compass we opted for the correct route and followed the white – red – white markers across the boulders and into the corrie below the Col de Cambales. Upon entering this corrie it was still by no means clear we were on the right route. There was no path to show the way and the corrie was wild and rough and gave the appearance that humankind seldom ventured this way. The col was still some 600 feet above us and there was a semicircle of crags guarding the upper half of the corrie. These crags, probably no more than 60 feet in height, looked impassable. Michael pointed out that there appeared to be a sort of ramp breaching the crags at the northern side of the corrie so we made for this. He was right. An obscure little path started to materialise as we made our way towards the weakness in the otherwise unbroken barrier of cliffs. I marvelled once again at the thin thread that was the HRP. It wound itself through a maze of shattered rocks and boulders to maintain its onward easterly course with little concern for its terrified passengers. The ramp that breached the crags was steep and exposed and required 100% concentration as it threaded its way up, over and beyond this latest obstacle. Ten minutes later we stood atop the Col de Cambales looking down east into a valley of lakes, rock and snow.

The guidebook referred to an "initial very steep descent", which made me rather wary since it had not deemed it necessary to make special mention of some of the previous significantly severe descents. I wondered just how steep it would have to be to merit such a particular reference. We proceeded with some apprehension only to find that the descent was most straightforward with no difficulties at all. In fact it was patently easy which once again made me wonder if we were actually in the right place. It turned out that we were. I have to say that the author's description at this point was, well, a little overstated shall we say. Mmmm… no… it was just bloody well wrong. It wasn't steep at all. In fact it was a comparatively gentle slope. I can only assume he must have got his notes mixed up and had been referring to somewhere else entirely. After a short while, where we entered a large boulder field, the path became lost and we made our way down as best we could amongst a jumbled scrap-yard of rocks and boulders. We could see below us a series of snowfields that offered an easier passage through this harsh terrain so we made for the edge of the highest patch of snow. It did indeed make for smoother progress. They also had one further unexpected effect. For the one and only time on the whole trip Michael was clearly unnerved. Upon reaching the edge of the first snowfield I prodded my walking poles into the firm but wet and sugary surface. It seemed solid enough to walk on but soft enough to yield to the imprint of our boots so I stepped out onto its smooth surface to test its load bearing capacity. Michael remained glued to the rocks at the perimeter of the snowfield, nervously contemplating his next move.

"Come on you big scaredy cat, what's up?" I chided.

"Couldn't there be crevasses under there? He questioned.

Mmmmm…let me see…errrr…No. Its not a glacier it's just a snowfield.

"Sure about that?" he questioned again.

"Yeh, of course, come on it'll be fine."

He stepped gingerly onto the snow like a nervous cat stepping onto ice for the first time and we set off down the slope, slipping and sliding, using our trekking poles as improvised ski sticks.

"Tell you what though," I interrupted after some fifty feet of descent.

"What," Michael snatched immediately.

"There's probably gonna be all kinds of voids and caverns beneath here as melt waters wash away the underneath of the snow on their way down the valley."

He looked at me closely to see if I was winding him up.

"I'm serious…listen, you can hear the sound of running water somewhere below our feet."

"Oh my God, you can too. This is a suicide mission. You're trying to bloody kill me aren't ya!" he yelped.

"Don't tell me it's taken you over two weeks to work that out!"

"After you Michael," I gestured, "I only brought you along to test the snow. Walk lightly and you'll be ok."

"Mad bastard," he snarled and set off downhill like Wile. E. Coyote stepping on eggshells, walking as lightly as anyone could.

In reality there probably was some risk of voids on these snowfields although I wasn't really sure of just how serious that was until several days later when we encountered a stream emitting from the mouth of an enormous ice cave at the foot of Vignemale and the folly of our current amblings took on an entirely different perspective.

Anyway, the tables turned for a change, we carried on from one snowfield to another careering rapidly down the valley, stumbling, skidding and sliding like two Bambis on ice until the snow ran out. It was at this point that Michael began to complain of pains in his left thigh, which must have been bad because he never complained about anything, except dodgy snow! It was clearly troubling him and he began to slow up significantly. As we descended into the valley, leaving the boulder fields and snow behind, a path began to materialise. This led us past a series of small lakes until, upon reaching the largest of these, the Grand Lac de Cambales, we stopped for a late lunch. Dark cumulonimbus had been bubbling up all afternoon and threatened to overtake us once again in the now customary daily thunderstorm as distant rumblings moved closer. As Sods Law dictates, with the contents of our rucksacks spread across the ground at our feet, the heavens finally opened and we were consumed in a deluge of water. The small rock face at the base of which we had been sitting, was transformed into a wall of water and threatened to wash away our belongings as we hurriedly donned our waterproofs and stuffed our kit back into the packs, abandoning any idea of lunch.

The rain came down in sheets turning the paths into streams and the streams into raging torrents. We were soon soaked through. The combination of being tired, wet and hungry is a sure-fire guarantee to dampen the spirits and we were feeling pretty sorry for ourselves. To add to our woes, by some strange quirk of fate, I too started to develop a sore leg. It didn't occur suddenly as a result of some violent impact or stumble, it sort of just crept up on me until I became aware of this nagging pain in my left thigh. The pain resembled that of a dead leg. Like two ill shod and dishevelled beggars we hobbled on down the path which took on the guise of a small river as the rain lashed down mercilessly. We still had some two miles distance and 1500 feet of descent before reaching the Refuge Wallon, somewhere in the grey/black gloom below. The distant rumbles of thunder began to close in and our stuttering progress became even less assured as lightning flashed across the ridge of Pic de Bernat Barrau some 1500 feet above us to the north. As the threat of becoming part of yet another light show increased, my eyes scoured the terrain either side of our route in search of suitable refuge points where we could shelter from the storm. Each prospective shelter became a psychological stepping-stone along the way. As the tempest confined the worst of its onslaught to the high ridge above to our left, dumping just its rain on us, we hobbled onwards and downwards, swinging on our trekking poles like crutches like a pair of manic Long John Silvers.

This was a low point for me, and probably Michael too. The throbbing in my leg became quite debilitating as each step produced its own fresh pain. Michael seemed little better and we both soldiered on in a wet and silent misery. Confined to our own little worlds within the solitude of our rain lashed waterproofs. We renewed our acquaintance with each other upon the crossing of the storm-gorged river that emitted from the Cambales valley. Wet feet were of little consequence for our already sodden forms as we waded knee deep through the torrent, which threatened to sweep us away. Upon stepping safely onto the opposite bank we resumed our dour and miserable trudge down to Wallon. Upon crossing a second river the previously isolated pine trees became more numerous and we soon entered the forest that adorned the lower slopes high into the upper reaches of the Vallee du Macardeau. Our introduction to the forest was strangely comforting and although it was sparsely populated with scrawny weather beaten pines it heralded our approach to the refuge. Its baldy intermittent canopy also provided some psychological shelter from the ravages of the lightning, but very little physical shelter from the rain, very similar to our experience a few days earlier with Charlie and Sue after meeting the goat herder in the Valee d'Aspe

Our eventual arrival at Wallon was a welcome relief. We were both struggling with our oddly coincidental leg pains, which only got worse the further we walked. The refuge, one of the largest in the Pyrenees, was a grey 2 storey stone building with a corrugated tin roof and red steel shuttered windows. The building actually comprised of two separate refuges, one unmanned and free and the other one manned. At first, just to get out of the rain, we dived into the nearest entrance, which so happens, was the unmanned refuge. This was a dank and dark hovel of a building that served only to deepen our gloom. What little light there was inside, revealed a couple of dark figures hunched over the blue flame of a camping stove that enveloped a small steaming pan of what smelled like soup. Despite the alluring aroma of the soup this was a soul-less and characterless place of cold and damp stone that fortunately only detained us for seconds in its miserable confines.

The wardened section of Wallon was thankfully somewhat more hospitable. Drier, brighter, warmer and generally more cheery. Simple comforts for which we were most thankful. The hostel was quite full and bustling with activity. Everyone was inside evading the weather. The sleeping quarters were upstairs and could aptly be described as a chicken coup for humans. Still we appreciated the shelter that the refuge provided as we listened to the thunderstorms bombarding the mountains outside. As we were being led to our dormitory we hobbled past our friend Gerry who was resting in one of the bunks. Due to being at the far east end of the building, the route to our dorm took us through door after door into a series of partitioned rooms, cluttered with sweaty boots, wet packs and cagoules and hikers in various stages of undress. Except for the narrow passageway between the ends of the camp beds there were virtually no other visible areas of floor. Every last square inch was taken over by wet clothes and the spewed out contents of peoples' packs. It didn't smell very nice. There were no showers, hence the pong,  so we had to make do with a rub down with our postage stamp size camp towels before changing into dry clothes. As with all CAF refuges the evening meal wasn't served until late, usually around 7.30 or 8pm so, like many of our co-habitees, we spent the remainder of the afternoon resting. It was cool inside the dormitories with no means of heating, except the body heat of all the occupants, so we were forced under our sleeping bags to stay warm. We both dozed off until several hours later the increase in activity around the dorm heralded the much awaited feeding time.

We descended to the ground floor dining area where little name tags had been set out on the tables to mark everybody's places. The dining room was warm from the heat of the kitchen where the presence of a large stove, in full production preparing a meal for 80 guests, had been belting out heat all afternoon akin to a steel furnace. The evening meal, as usual in the refuges, was a substantial affair with three courses, supplemented by plenty of bread and red wine to wash it all down. We were sat at the end of a table for six people, with a Danish family, comprising father, mother, and son and daughter of around 10 and 12 years of age respectively. They all fortunately spoke reasonable English and we were able to at least converse at a basic level until we eventually exhausted the limited topics of conversation and both parties reverted to the comfort zone of their mother tongues and we talked amongst ourselves. Once again however we managed to find some English guests in the form of a middle aged couple on the adjacent table who had walked up the valley from Port d'Espagne in France that day. We chatted about our respective plans and exploits. They were probably in their early fifties and had visited the Pyrenees on numerous previous occasions. They were planning to walk over to the Oulettes de Gaube refuge and then ascend Vignemale the following day. We would pass the Oulettes de Gaube refuge on our next days walking on our way to Baysellance. We agreed to defer our decision whether to walk tomorrow until the morning to see if our legs had mended!

# Day 16, Monday 17<sup>th</sup> July, Wallon

At 6.20am my sore leg and I got out of bed. After walking 2 steps I turned to the lifeless lump encased in a sleeping bag in the bed next to me and said I wouldn't be walking today as I needed to rest my leg. I'm not sure whether I received a response or not but I decided it would be wise not to disturb the lump any further just to let it know it could have a lay in! I descended to the dining area in some pain and with the substantial assistance of the walls either side of the staircase. Whatever it was that was affecting my leg began to worry me and I contemplated whether a days rest would be sufficient to resolve the problem. I partook of the breakfast of bread, jam and coffee that I would have had had we been walking and asked Gerry, another of the early risers, who was moving on to Baysellance that day, to let the warden there know we would be a day late. I bade him safe journey as he left at around 6.40am. Our paths didn't cross again.

The refuge was buzzing with activity as walkers set off early to their destinations, no doubt in an effort to avoid the now customary mid afternoon thunderstorms. I felt detached from their exclusive club. Just a spectator to the hubbub I felt envious of their positive objectives as I pondered how I would fill the day. Enforced inactivity is not something I was particularly comfortable with and the prospect of a whole day-full of nothing in particular, whilst most welcome in respect of the rest and recuperation it would provide, served only to make me restless. Michael was clearly having no difficulty in this field, having managed to embrace the whole concept of a rest day whilst still remaining in a state of total unconsciousness. I on the other hand thrived on activity and found it difficult to spend the day sitting around doing nothing.

As the morning wore on and the refuge became deserted I busied myself with the washing of clothes which had deteriorated once again to a state of decrepit putrescence beyond proper description. Socks and undies were the most notable items, having acquired the redolence of an open cess pit and in truth should not have been handled without protective clothing, including rubber gloves and full breathing apparatus. My t-shirt, having accumulated 3 days worth of Pyrennean sweat and grime had fermented sufficient of its own microbes to be considered as a chemical weapon of mass destruction. They all took some washing I can tell you as bowl after bowl of water acquired a scum reminiscent of a major oil tanker disaster.

It was a bright and sunny morning and after hanging out my revitalised clothing on the metal rails outside of the refuge I wandered down to the river to subject my leg to further pain. My theory was that if I could immerse my sore leg in the cold waters of the river it would assist in the healing process. I had long been a committed believer in the ice pack treatment for injuries and had experienced the benefits of such treatment in reducing swelling and pain when I had suffered with an achilles problem some years previous. I found a suitable pool, some 3-4ft deep and positioned myself on the adjacent slab of rock, immersing my legs up to the groin into the freezing waters of the river. I wasn't convinced this was doing any good but stayed there until I could bear the pain no longer and emerged from the water with two purple/blue legs that no longer felt like they were connected to my body. Some five minutes or so later when I could actually feel my toes again I repeated the process. I was hopeful that this self flagellation would also help in reducing the swelling to my knees which had taken on the appearance of two footballs following repeated punishing descents of the last two days since leaving Pombie. When I eventually emerged from the ice pool all circulation in my legs had ceased and I felt like I was in the latter stages of frostbite with no sense of feeling below the knee at all. I sat by the river and thawed in the morning sun until life returned to my lifeless limbs and I was able to walk again.

Michael could have slept for England had it been designated an Olympic sport. He was still flat out when I returned to the dorm at 10am. I went off for a wash and shave. As best I could I took a full body wash in a cubicle with a wash basin and a dividing plastic curtain. During a sequence of gymnastic contortions which incorporated dangling my bits over the basin whilst retaining just one foot on the floor, I managed to reach all the parts that needed attention. It was at this stage that I was somewhat rudely interrupted as a young lady entered the washroom and threw back the curtains and for one stunned moment, stood aghast and rooted to the spot, clearly in a state of shock, like a rabbit in the headlights. I was in no position to do anything much other than offer a pathetic grin and a statement of surprise,

"Er, this one's taken!"

She spluttered what I assume was an apology, in what I think was Dutch or German, before fleeing in an embarrassed fluster of discomposure into to an adjacent cubicle no doubt scarred for life. For the remainder of the session I whistled Ravell's Bolero in order to alert any further potential users as to my presence. I didn't clap eyes on the poor young lady again that day. She probably spent the rest of the day avoiding me at all costs. I understand the she is responding well to therapy although she still suffers with the nightmares and continues to wake up screaming in the middle of the night, even now, years later!

Returning to the task in hand so to speak, I concentrated on the next item of ablution; shaving. It was at this stage that I became aware for the first time that part of me was missing! I would guess at least a stone worth anyway. My cheeks were noticeably sunken and cheek bones distinctly pronounced compared to the fuller face I was accustomed to seeing looking back at me. With 3-4 days worth of whiskers I took on a gaunt and rather haggard appearance. It reminded me of a scene in the movie Papillon where Steve McQueen on his first day confined to his cell in the hell-hole prison in French Guiana, sticks his head through a small feeding hatch in the cell bars to be confronted by a row of similar heads of his fellow inmates. The guy in the next cell turns his scrawny, toothless and decrepit face to McQueen and asks, "How do I look?" McQueen looks at him obviously thinking well if I'm honest mate you're not much longer for this world and says, "You look fine." The next day the McQueen looked on sombrely as they carted his cellmates' body out of the prison. In the film, some years later, the tables were turned and McQueen became the hapless and pathetic skeleton who having resorted to eating cockroaches in order to supplement his meagre diet turned to his neighbour and asked the same question and was himself given the same throw away lie he had used some years earlier, "You look fine". I gazed in the mirror and this thin man looked back at me.

"Fine my arse, you're wasting away Taylor. There won't be enough of you left to finish this walk at this rate. You'll just be a trail of salt from evaporated sweat droplets spattered on rocks between Hendaye and Banyuls!"

Michael was eventually forced from his pit when one of the staff came in to the dorm to clean the place. We spent the rest of the day relaxing in the sunshine outside and treating Michaels blisters, including a ridiculously large one on his big toe that made the toe appear deformed. Of greater concern was a large angry looking blister on his left heel which we cleaned up and covered with Compeed. I admired his stoicism as he dismissed the blisters as a minor inconvenience when clearly they must have been causing him some pain. On the plus side the sore leg that had troubled him the previous day had eased off. Sixteen hours in bed clearly brings with it considerable healing qualities! However I wasn't faring quite so well. Whilst the pain in my thigh was not so pronounced it still affected my walking and I had nagging doubts about whether I would be fit the next day. Some 18 months previous I had contracted a viral infection known as phlebitis where the veins in my left thigh had become inflamed and I spent several days in quite some pain before anti-biotics had taken effect. I was now experiencing a similar pain and in exactly the same place, the only difference being that there was no rash on the skin surface this time. I kept these thoughts to myself and went and dunked my leg in the river again.

We were eventually forced indoors as the afternoon deteriorated in to more thunderstorms. We enjoyed this latest display from an entirely different perspective. Peering through windows and remaining safe and dry in the comfort of the refuge. Most visitors had arrived by the time the rain started no doubt well accustomed to the familiar daily pattern of Pyrenean weather. The day dragged out for me. Whilst the rest and the chance to restore clothing to a wearable state once more was most welcome, the enforced inactivity was a form of slow torture. At dinner we were surrounded by non English speaking guests and so were confined to small talk by our own limited linguistic skills. Bed was a welcome release from the tedium and mundanity of a boring day.

## Tuesday 18ᵗʰ July, Day 17 Wallon to Baysellance

Up at 5.45am, in the dark, to face our day of reckoning. The legs seemed ok so we decided to press on to Baysellance, the highest manned refuge in the Pyrenees at 2651m, almost 8700 feet. Breakfast was its usual meagre offering of coffee but with dry biscuits replacing the more normal French bread. Not the sort of sustenance needed for such a tough day ahead, including 1400m of ascent incorporating 3 high mountain passes.

We set off from Wallon at 6.35am and ambled down to the river. This was a gentle introduction to what turned out to be a most demanding day. We crossed the Gave de Macardau by a sturdy footbridge and then moments later a similar bridge took us over the Gave d'Arratille. The path then ascended steadily through pine trees and upon leaving the trees behind, it twisted on an unlikely and contorted journey up through a barrier of towering rock polished bare by ancient glaciers, before then emerging onto a grassy plateau. We crossed the Arratille River once again, now little more than a small stream and soon arrived at the Lac d'Arratille where some hardy fisherman were casting their lines into the shimmering waters. A scattering of tents marked their fragile homes in this remotest of angling venues.

We pushed on up rough and steep ground where the path was frequently lost on sections of bare rock before arriving at the Col d'Arratile on the French /Spanish border. My leg seemed to be holding up and we were even 40 minutes ahead of the guide book schedule, probably for the first time ever. The path dropped down a short way into Spain and then traversed high up around the head of the Valle de Ara. In places there had been rock avalanches that had swept the path away into the valley below making progress particularly awkward. Previous walkers had since re-established there own replacement lines of 'path' which tended to be extremely narrow and somewhat precarious. Our boots crunched into the loose scree of tenuous footholds sending endless stones skittering down to the valley floor hundreds of feet below as we balanced on the tightrope of these newly formed paths. Without mishap we passed all the areas of rock fall and eventually ascended to the next pass, the Col de Mulets on the French/Spanish border again, now almost 1hour and 15minutes ahead of schedule still with no reaction from my leg. That was soon to change. The col was a popular spot with numerous hikers gathered and taking brief respite from their labours with an array of different drinks bottles on display. We rested for some ten minutes or so taking in the impressive scenery. Reluctant to concede our hard gotten time advantage we rose to our feet sooner than we would have liked, to begin a steep descent back down into France, and the Vallee de Gaube. Within a couple of minutes, what began as a twinge soon deteriorated into a debilitating cramp in my left thigh and my progress stuttered almost to a halt. Without the heavy reliance upon my trekking poles I would have been reduced to sliding down on my backside. By the time we had descended the 1500 feet into the Vallee de Gaube I was in agony and could barely lift my leg. The stunning scenery of the north face of Vignemale and its glacier were lost on me as I struggled across the myriad of rivulets that fanned out from the mouth of the glacier, washing across the flat valley floor. I cursed at every stumble as my leg became a dead weight and I dragged it across the rock strewn terrain towards the Refuge des Oulettes de Gaube which sat at the foot of a bluff at the end of the west ridge of the Pic d'Arraile some 300-400metres across the valley. The final stream taking the melt waters down the valley was wider and deeper than the others and after a momentary pause and teetering attempt at keeping my feet dry I slipped off a rock into the icy water up to my knees then stumbled angrily to the opposite bank cursing my newly acquired incapacity for walking. I grimaced against the pain as I limped slowly to join Michael who was sat on the wall outside the deserted refuge. I sat down alongside him in the morning sun feeling thoroughly sorry for myself, massaging my painful thigh and rueing my wet feet. To add to our woes Michael announced his leg was hurting too.

We sat and contemplated our predicament. We could book into the refuge here. Even if it was full I'm sure they'd make space for a couple of invalids. (Not PC I know but only two good legs between us sort of brought us into that category) It was still only 10.15am. Our early start had meant we were two thirds of the way through the days walk with only half the morning over. I didn't relish the prospect of sitting around for the rest of the day waiting for my leg to get better again. I'd sooner die trying than die of boredom which was entirely possible if I had to face another day of frustrating inactivity. How long would we have to rest anyway? There was no guarantee my leg would be any better after a days rest. We had a further 550m of ascent (about 1850 feet) and only 80metres of descent. The latter statistic being more to the point so far as my leg was concerned as it seemed to be the descent that troubled me most. We decided to continue on to Baysellance.

After some 15 minutes or so rest we got to our feet and began the cruel final ascent of the day. I groaned, winced, whinged, whined and swore myself to the col at Hourquette d'Ossau, where, after an hour and a half of torture, I plonked myself on a rock and sat in silent and painful triumph. We could see our goal, Baysellance, no more than a few hundred metres away. Almost touching distance! We sat and rested, admiring the impressive scenery all around. Another altitude record at 2734m.

There were quite a number of other hikers and climbers around and after a few minutes we were joined by a Dutch bloke who sat nearby and introduced himself as Bernard Joos, which he proudly announced was pronounced 'goose'. He was walking the HRP in the opposite direction to us, having first walked the GR11 from the Atlantic to the Mediterranean; this being his return leg in effect. I was duly impressed. He had set out from Hendaye on 28th April and must have been walking continuously since. He noticed I was massaging my thigh and enquired whether there was a problem. I explained the difficulty I was having to which he simply replied

"Well you have to have a leg for it to be sore."

A simple philosophy which appealed to my sense of humour and made me realise maybe I wasn't so badly off after all.

Bernard was a jovial chap probably in his late fifties I would guess, of sinewy build, although his weight when he first set out from Hendaye may well have been 25 stone if I was anything to go by. He had a tanned, leathery, weather beaten complexion like he spent his whole life wandering the mountains. We chatted for some ten or fifteen minutes before he skipped off and down towards Oulettes de Gaube refuge. I hope he made it back to Hendaye! Shortly after his departure the English couple we had been speaking to two nights previously at Wallon descended down towards us from the ridge which ascended up to the Petit Vignemale, clearly pleased with their exploits. They had ascended Vignemale earlier and were returning to the refuge at Oulettes de Gaube. Their tales of adventure made me wish we had time to spend exploring the Pyrenees far more. Although our route took us through the very heart of the mountain range it was never enough. It simply whet the appetite for more adventures. There was so much more beyond the narrow path that we trod from coast to coast.

We eventually set off down to the refuge and I chuckled to myself as I pondered Bernard's remark about my leg as we limped down to Baysellance. We arrived at the refuge at 1.30pm. For the first time we had managed to complete the days walk within the scheduled time assigned by the guide book, despite the handicap of only 2 good legs between us. Unsurprisingly, we had lost the time we'd gained earlier though as a result of our laboured hobble since Oulettes de Gaube. One thing I was grateful for though was that we had managed to avoid the thunderstorms for a change. We sat outside along with numerous other walkers and climbers and enjoyed a leisurely lunch in the sunshine. It was nice to eat lunch and not have to face any more walking for the afternoon even if the lunch in question was less than appetising. Rubberised cheese and teeth breaking toast-breads ably lubricated with our everlasting mayonnaise. As we sat idling away the early afternoon we tried our mobile phones with the intention of updating the folks back home as to our progress but once again there was no signal. As clear an indication as any as to the wild terrain we were crossing. After about an hour lazing in the sun our siesta was rudely interrupted by the distant rumbles of thunder behind Vignemale. The build up of dark cumulo-nimbus cloud brought a chill to the air and made the inside of the refuge a far more appealing proposition than the outside.

Inside Michael confirmed the booking that our friend Gerry had made the night before on our behalf before we retired to the dorm to continue our siesta in earnest. The storm raged outside with what sounded like a couple of direct lightning hits on the refuge hut which shook under the impact. Needless to say sleep was not possible but the rest was most welcome. The refuge started to stir around 7pm as people made their way down to the dining area downstairs. There was quite a mix of nationalities at Baysellance that evening with the usual contingent of French and Spanish interspersed with German, Dutch and I'm pleased to say a fair representation of British. Everyone gravitated to like language groups and the dining room became a cacophony of noise akin to a hen house at feeding time. The thunderstorms raged on unabated outside with frequent explosions of lightning strikes which brought about momentary breaks in the tumult of conversations as everyone looked around nervously to see if this was the bolt that was to finally blow the hut to smithereens. On each occasion, following a breath holding hush of maybe 2-3 seconds, the chatter would resume, safe in the knowledge that we continued to enjoy the shelter of an unbreached roof and four walls.

Dinner was the customary 3 courses accompanied by wine and most welcomed after the scant remnants of supplies we had relied upon for lunch. After several very tasty bowls of soup the main course of beef stew arrived. At least I think it was beef. It looked really good and the aroma tantalised the occupants of the room as   steaming pots were laid out in front of us on each table. But that was as good as it got! The meat was very tough and the stew tasteless. It never lived up to the promise. It tasted of…well, nothing at all really. One of the English lads who was sat with us thought it was marvellous and devoured 4 plates full of the stuff but Michael and I only managed only one helping each, which was punishment enough. Despite 2 weeks of endless chewing on indigestible saucisson our jaws were still not sufficiently developed to tackle this grizzled shoe leather that was part of the stew that night. What it lacked in flavour and tenderness it made up for in durability. The cheese and chocolate mousse dessert that followed (that's two separate desserts, not one), whilst very tasty, was not sufficient to make up for the disappointing main meal.

The dining room remained full after the meal was finished as people sat drinking their water and finishing the jugs of wine. As the conversations rolled on I became more and more preoccupied with a build up of severe abdominal wind and began to shift most uneasily in my seat. I was hemmed in with my back against the wall in the middle of a bench with eight people. There was no escape without disrupting the whole dining room. I was trapped, just like my flatulence. The muscles in my bum were in overdrive trying to contain my wind. Holding back this gas was akin to the travails of King Canute. I sat patiently waiting for some indication that the diners at our table would disperse but the social intercourse went on and on and on. After some ten or fifteen minutes and with no sign of any break up of the after dinner chatter, the pains in my stomach became too much. My insides were contorted and twisted with pain and no amount of squirming in my seat could alleviate my discomfort. I decided, 'to hell with it', I could contain this gas no longer, so, choosing my moment carefully to coincide with a particularly noisy spell I let rip the

loudest rasping fart probably ever witnessed in the Pyrenees. The bench I
was sat on vibrated with the impact. Even I was stunned by the thundering
tumultuousness of this cacophonous explosion of wind. I had of course
depended, rather naively, upon the noise being drowned out by the
general hubbub which engulfed the room. No such luck. My fart was like
a clarion call from the summit of Vignemale and resounded around the
room. It brought about the same hush that descended following each clap
of thunder outside. The instantaneous silence that then consumed the
room was even more deafening. Halted in their tracks by my impromptu
thunderbolt the attention of seemingly every one of the 50 or 60
occupants around the tables was suddenly focused in my direction. Their
gazes of collective disgust made me want to slide under the table and
crawl out of the door. In an act of open defiance I raised my glass to the
onlookers,

"Cheers!" I remarked.

They each in turn resumed their respective conversations, none the
worse for this rude interruption, and with roof and walls still intact
Michael gazed upon me with a new aura of respect.

Soon afterwards I was released from this involuntary incarceration as
people dispersed outside into the methane free cool evening air. Wandering
a safe distance from the hut I proceeded to fart at will taking full
advantage of my liberation. I was lost in thought, and wind, admiring the
silhouettes of surrounding peaks in the last remnants of twilight, and
contemplating the barmy notion of somehow harnessing the energy
producing capacity of my flatulence with a view to supplementing the
solar panels on the roof of the refuge.

"Dad, you're a bloody embarrassment," Michael interrupted, as my
train of thought considered whether there would have been enough
energy in that one fart to cook tonight's beef into submission.

"Sorry about that son," I said sheepishly.

"I couldn't have held on any longer…I was in pain"

He shook his head in resigned acquiescence.

The thunder and lightning had stopped but the evening sky was grey
and sullen. For a change the end of the storm had not heralded a return
to a blue cloudless sky. The forecast posted on the wall of the refuge
referred to "gross degradation" for tomorrow. I wasn't sure exactly how
that translated but it didn't sound good. My leg was still sore but it had
improved from when I had arrived at the hut earlier that afternoon so I

was hopeful for our walk tomorrow. We ordered a 5.30am breakfast and headed off to bed early, just after 9pm.

Normally I would sign off here and resume my account the following day however on this occasion I was provided with more subject matter which I believe merits inclusion in this journal. The additional material came in the form of an over amorous and rather ageing French couple in the adjacent bed. Our dorm comprised of 10-12 bunk beds and unfortunately for me my bed was placed transversely across the foot of a double bunk that was to be the venue of some nocturnal hanky panky. The lights went out at around 10pm by which time I was already half asleep. That was the signal for the balding Charles Aznavour look-alike and his insipid female partner in the adjacent bed to commence their night of passion. At first their activities were relatively subtle with just the occasional light groan or muffled gasp. Well as subtle as you can be confined to a 15ft by 20ft dormitory with 10 other sweaty hikers. Emboldened by the shroud of darkness and oblivious to their reluctant but captive audience they moved on to louder groans and the occasional, 'je t'adore' and je t'aime.' Things were obviously progressing nicely when consumed by an overwhelming tiredness I could stand it no longer and let out a cry of, "For God's sake!"

There was a momentary lull, followed by a few suppressed sniggers, and then silence. Proud of having once again tonight brought the occupants of a room to a silent standstill with my intervention I turned over with the intention of going to sleep. Undeterred our rampant Casanova and his willing sex slave resumed their activities a few minutes later and succeeded in keeping the whole dorm, (except for Michael), awake until the early hours of the morning. It's not easy trying to get to sleep when the couple in the next bed are merrily bonking away I can tell you. I was both angry and quietly impressed by their staying power. At some stage another English voice interrupted with the suggestion that may wish to continue copulating outside so the rest of us could get some sleep but that offer wasn't taken up.

They eventually, thankfully ran out of steam and I was just dropping off when a male occupant of another bed returning from the lavatory decided to open a window. It was stuffy and hot in the dorm so I was pleased that someone had taken the initiative. However, it didn't meet with the approval of our Casanova and an altercation ensued that seem to be resolved by the intervention of a couple of calls of 'ouvrez le fenetre' from across the room. So it stayed open. Initially anyway! Some ten or fifteen minutes later our amorous Frenchman got up and shut it again. I was too tired to take up the fight and soon dropped off to sleep. The window was open when Michael and I got up at 5.15am that morning.

## Wednesday 19ᵗʰ July, Day 18, Baysellance to Gavarnie

At 5.15am this was our earliest start, motivated primarily by a desire to avoid the "gross degradation" in the weather and partly to allow for any injury induced delays. My leg actually felt ok and the pain that had so impacted upon our progress the previous day had disappeared. It was still quite dark when we left Baysellance at 6am to begin our long descent to Gavarnie, and within a few minutes it started raining. It was cold, damp and windy. Not since leaving Roncevalles had we experienced such a gloomy commencement to our day's journey. The one remaining advantage was that it was all downhill.

We lost height quickly as the stony path zig-zagged steeply down towards the sheer sided Ossoue Valley. After 20 minutes or so we came upon the somewhat curious sight of a series of 3 man-made caves that had been hewn out of the rock face. The Grottes de Bellevue. These peculiar features had been brought about by the labours of one man, the pioneer Count Henry Russell (1834-1909). Russell's exploits had elevated Vignemale to a mountain of almost mythical proportions. Born in Toulouse of a French mother and Irish father he spent a lot of his time in the Pyrenees. Whilst he climbed extensively throughout the Pyrenean mountain chain and wrote several books and articles about his adventures, it was his focus on one mountain that made him famous: The Vignemale. He is reputed to have climbed it some 33 times and spent 150 nights on the mountain. In order to allow him more time on and around the mountain Russell and his friends carved a series of grottoes as shelters. As well as these three, which were created one for Russell, one for his guide and one "in case a lady should arrive," there were several others on the mountain. Three more, The Grottes Russell, were located near the Col de Cerbilona, at 3195m, just above the Glacier d'Ossoue, and a single cave, The Grottes de Paradis just below the summit where one might presume from this reduction in accommodation facilities he had abandoned the somewhat limited prospect of randomly encountering a female.

We deigned not to investigate the caves more closely having been informed at Baysellance that their primary use now is more of a toilet than a shelter, and anyway we were keen to descend out of the murk and gloom of the dismal weather that surrounded us. My leg seemed to be holding out well so far. I was very conscious that it was yesterday's descent from Col de Mulets which had resurrected the problem with my thigh and this path was no less steep. Our route traversed above the Barranco d'Ossoue, a precipitous gorge that held the the River Ossoue in it's tight jaws some thousand feet below. Once again the HRP wove an unlikely and delicate line above the yawning void below taking on a winding descent that seemed impossible from above. We cut across a series of glacial streams, including one that emitted from the mouth of a ravine packed with snow and ice. The melt waters spewed from the mouth of a huge ice cavern some 30 feet high at the mouth of the ravine leaving a rather precariously perched and very thin ceiling of snow and ice above, before tumbling down into the barranco below. This provided us with a new perspective on our antics a few days previous when sliding down the snowfields below the Col de Cambales, when I'd joked with Michael about the potential voids beneath our feet. It didn't seem quite so funny now.

The path continued downwards until having descended some 750m we arrived at the flat valley floor of the Oulettes d'Ossoue where the river, released from the grip of the gorge walls, fanned out into a series of small streams before rejoining to form a man made lake, contained at its south eastern end by the Barrage d'Ossoue. The weather had improved as we escaped from the mountains, which still harboured ominous black clouds, and we stepped out into a land of sunshine. It was here that my leg once again began to protest. We took a break at the dam and brewed up a cup of Earl Grey whilst I sat and massaged my thigh in the vain hope of banishing the pain. It didn't work. After our morning brew and a couple of snack bars we pressed on, opting to forego the official HRP in favour of the rough track that descended more directly to Gavarnie on the northern side of the Gave d'Ossoue. Whilst I was concerned that we were diverging from the prescribed route I felt vindicated in the decision to do so by virtue of the injury to my leg.

The area around the dam was accessible to vehicles via this track and numerous 4x4's, and land-rovers, the first cars we had seen for 4 days, were parked all around. Amongst their likely passengers there were numerous boy and girl scouts that were scattered around a large encampment nearby, who viewed us with a certain curiosity as we set off down the track. I certainly seemed to generate some interest as we headed off down to Gavarnie. My sore leg gave me a pronounced limp and relying heavily upon my trekking poles for support my progress through the gathered throng of teenagers certainly provoked some second looks and a series of comments beyond my translation skills. I soldiered on and smiled at the puzzled onlookers, gritting my teeth against the pain. As we left the campers behind I began to find that I could barely lift my left leg which in turn resulted in my kicking numerous protruding rocks scattered on the path. Each stumble was accompanied by a searing pain surge in my thigh and I cursed every time but could do little to avoid the trips on my faltering passage down the track. A recurring distraction from this spiral of pain was the constant accompaniment of the numerous communities of marmots that whistled their alarm calls as we approached and scurried off down into a labyrinth of burrows and tunnels that festooned the surrounding hillsides. There were hundreds, probably thousands of them. The whole valley was a marmot enclave. These brown furry rodent-like creatures were about the size of a large domestic cat and sunbathed on rocks and boulders before our presence disturbed their morning siestas. They were apparently reintroduced to the Pyrenees in the 20th century having been caught in the Alps and released here. It was certainly clear that they were thriving in the Ossoue valley.

After a few miles the stone track improved to a metalled single track road which did make for easier progress but by this time I was in agony and could barely lift my leg. Every step was an effort and every footfall brought a new pain that soon combined to become a throbbing wall of endless torment. My jaws ached as I continually gritted my teeth in anticipation of the pain resonating from each repeated impact of my boot against the tarmac. On one steeper section of road I had to stop on several occasions to obtain some brief relief from the constant pain. Michael looked on with concern etched on his face. I knew this was serious and there was no way I could continue walking whilst this injury persisted. I concentrated on the task in hand, reaching Gavarnie, and continued to step through my pain barrier.

We eventually arrived at the village of Gavarnie at 11am, which, strangely, considering the difficulties with my leg, was half an hour within the guide book time. For some reason I seemed to move faster on one leg! Back in civilisation for the first time since Candanchu and the Col du Somport our first priority was an early lunch. We were both famished and eager to partake of some "real" food after several days of camp rations and dubious beef stews. We sat down at a table at a little roadside café and very quickly devoured a couple of cheese and tomato baguettes. It was only upon finishing the food that I really began to notice our surroundings. Gavarnie, a busy and very touristy little village at the head of the Gave de Gavarnie ou de Pau valley, which stretched up into the Pyrenees from the town of Lourdes, was buzzing with visitors. They were arriving by the coach load and pouring out onto the main street which ran through the village. I'm sure this had once been an attractive little hamlet tucked away up this cul-de-sac valley quietly getting on with its predominantly rural way of life. That was no longer the case now. It was a like a miniature Blackpool, crammed with gift-shops displaying all manner of tourist tat, including curious whistling marmots that contained sensors which detected movement and subsequently wolf-whistled at all of the passers by. The hustle and bustle of this tourist trap in the peak of summer was in sharp contrast to our surroundings of the previous week and it took some adjustment on our behalf to become accustomed to our new environment. We didn't look like the majority of other visitors to Gavarnie and we certainly didn't smell like them.

After this early lunch we headed down to the tourist information centre in the village square in search of accommodation. We were ready for the luxury of a proper bed, good food and comfortable surroundings. It wasn't to be. All the bloody tourists had taken every last guest house. Everywhere was full so once again we resorted to camping. We trundled up through the village and booked into a small campsite on the southern outskirts of Gavarnie for a reasonable 6euros/night. The campsite afforded us excellent views of probably the main tourist attraction of Gavarnie, Le Grande Cascade and the Cirque de Gavarnie. The Cirque presented a formidable wall of rock which defended the Spanish border and incorporated a series of 3000m summits. In the midst of this impressive crescent of vertical cliffs the icy waters of the Grand Cascade plummeted over 1000m in a single leap. I sat and admired our impressive surroundings and massaged my sore leg as Michael erected the tent.

From our earlier enquiries at the TIC the nearest doctor was located in the town of Luz-St-Sauveur some 10-12 miles further down the valley and if my leg required medical attention then I had been advised to use the mountain rescue centre some 100m down the road from the campsite. After a shower and freshening up we headed down to the MRC. I don't know just what sort of response I was expecting but I certainly wasn't prepared for what happened next. I explained the situation and described my symptoms in a combination of broken French, English and a fair degree of elementary sign language and gesturing which they relayed onto a doctor over the phone. Upon finishing the conversation I was immediately ushered into a wheelchair and told not to move. I learnt later that my reference to possible phlebitis had raised some concern with the doctor as it is recognised as a form of thrombosis which can ultimately lead to blockage of the arteries and subsequent instant death. I was somewhat bemused by the fuss and, along with Michael, found the whole situation far too hilarious for me to be remotely concerned. Some time passed before an ambulance turned up. I was being taken to hospital in Lourdes. Perhaps the divine intervention of St Bernadette was to be called upon to heal my troubled leg. Michael almost fell about laughing as three burly Frenchmen and a diminutive female, eyeballs bulging, huffed and puffed as they hoisted me and the wheelchair into the waiting ambulance. I did offer to walk to the ambulance myself but I was no longer in control of my own destiny and my incumbent bearers insisted upon transporting me to the ambulance bed despite my protestations. They had no intention of allowing a big fat 17stone Englishman to die on their premises and were insistent that I should be carried and I think relieved to see me off their hands so to speak. In the ambulance I was immediately strapped to a bed and had an oxygen mask slapped over my face.

As the ambulance sped off my first thought was, 'Oh my god, what's my little lad gonna do? Despite the initial amusement he's gonna be worried seeing me whisked off in an ambulance, on oxygen whilst he's left stuck on his own, in a tent on a campsite in a foreign country!' I just resolved in my mind that he would have to fend for himself. He was 18 and big enough and daft enough to do that. Wasn't he?

As we sped through the village, sirens blaring, heading off to Lourdes some 60km away I felt somewhat disarmed by the language barrier and was sure they were making a big mistake in their prognosis of my sore leg. I was frustrated by my inability to communicate these thoughts, which was even more difficult through an oxygen mask, and just had to go along with things.

As I lay on my back, gazing over my oxygen mask at the roof of the speeding ambulance as it ripped down the winding, twisting, undulating and narrow mountain road towards Lourdes I soon began to feel nauseous. Being bounced around in a metal box, with no indication of when the next bend, dip, hill or oncoming vehicle is approaching is akin to riding a white knuckle big dipper blindfolded. After 5 minutes of this I was on the verge of puking. My demeanour and desire to sit up caused some alarm in the attendant paramedic. I was trying to tell him that I needed something in which to throw up and I also needed to release some of the straps pinning me to the bed so that I could see out of the window and gain some perspective of my surroundings in order to reduce the feeling of nausea. I'm sure he was convinced that I was having some sort of seizure and kept pushing me back down on the bed and replacing the oxygen mask back over my face. We battled for several minutes as I tried to convince him that I was just feeling bloody travel sick and wasn't experiencing the advanced stages of a pulmonary embolism. As the colour no doubt drained from my face and beads of sweat trickled from my forehead I managed to at last make myself understood as I beckoned to him for a container in which to throw up as waves of nausea washed over me. He passed me a cardboard basin and my cheese and onion baguette made its reappearance as I regurgitated the contents of my insides.

After puking up my lunch I was forced to lie down again as my attendant spoke to the driver via an intercom, I think urging him to speed up and get us to hospital before I popped my clogs. "Non, non lentement s'il vous plait," I pleaded, but to no avail. We hurtled ever faster down the road and I gave up my appeal and just concentrated on deep breathing and trying not to vomit again. My attendant was clearly convinced I was at death's door and fussed over me all the way to Lourdes, insisting I keep the oxygen mask on and continually asking if I was ok. We eventually arrived without me having to part company with any more of my lunch.

After submitting to a blood test and scan of my injured leg (which incidentally was feeling much better for the imposed rest) I was discharged several hours later having been told that there was no phlebitis or thrombosis and that what I was experiencing was probably muscular. It seemed an awful lot of fuss just to be told I had a strained muscle. I was almost disappointed. My big problem now however, as I wandered down into Lourdes was that I was some 40 miles away from Gavarnie, it was 7.30pm and the last bus to Luz had left at 7pm. I contemplated staying the night in Lourdes but after a visit to a cash dispenser opted for a taxi ride back up to Gavarnie. An hour later and 104 euros lighter I rolled back into Gavarnie in serious need of some sustenance. What food I had managed to eat since 6am this morning was probably now designated as clinical waste and on its way to an incinerator somewhere in southern France. I NEEDED FOOD!

Michael was sat in the tent looking rather forlorn and was both surprised and I think pleased to see me. I have since speculated what would have become of him if my ailment had resulted in more serious consequences. I can just imagine the conversation between him and my wife now.

"Hi Sue, it's Michael,"

"Oh my god Michael where have you been for the last 2 months?"

"Well…I've been staying in my dad's tent in Gavarnie since he left the village in an ambulance on 19th July. I haven't heard from him since so I thought I'd better ring you and see if he'd been in touch."

"Michael its 14th September, why didn't you ring before now?"

"Well I was ok at first but I've ran out of food and money now and the camp site I'm on is about to close for the winter and the farmer wants me off his field because he needs it for winter grazing for his goats. Did dad say when he was coming back?"

"Oh Michael, I'm so sorry I've got some really bad news for you."

"What?"

"We cremated your dad last month after flying his body home from Lourdes hospital. We tried to contact you but nobody knew where you were."

Silence…

"Oh no…what happened? Did he die because of the problem with his leg? The doctors seemed to think that was serious."

"No. On his way to hospital the ambulance he was in left the mountain road and crashed a hundred feet down a ravine into a raging torrent. The driver and the paramedic escaped with minor injuries but your dad was strapped to the bed and couldn't get out of the ambulance which was swept down the river."

"Oh no, that's terrible, what happened then, did he drown?"

"No, he managed to release the straps and escape from the ambulance before it was swept over an enormous waterfall."

"So he escaped yeh?"

"Well initially he did but he couldn't escape from the ravine and had to jump off the waterfall 250 feet into the river below."

"Oh my god, he can't stand heights. What then?"

"Well he got swept 3 miles down river in the raging torrent, battered against rocks and boulders on the way. By the time he managed to get out of that river he had the sort of injuries that would have killed a lesser man; a broken leg, fractured arm, 6 broken ribs, a fractured pelvis, dislocated shoulder, severe concussion and he lost 4 teeth, although one of them was the plastic one he had in the front. You know the one he'd knocked out when blind drunk on his 20th birthday when he fell flat on his face in the street!"

"That's terrible, is that what killed him?"

"No, he survived all that and suffering with advanced hypothermia he dragged himself out of the icy glacial melt-waters of the river and scrambled up the treacherous cliff face 200 feet up to the road above."

"That's incredible."

"Yep, that's your dad for you. He was a tough old nut."

"Did he die later of his injuries then?"

"No, when he reached the road he collapsed with exhaustion and was run over by a second ambulance that was speeding up the road to a reported traffic accident."

"Jees! He never did have much luck did he?"

Fortunately for me of course this particular scenario did not materialise and Michael and I were re-united that evening and enjoyed the luxury of a restaurant meal with plenty of beer and wine to assist digestion. This went some way towards compensating for the six previous days of occasionally ambiguous and consistently insufficient refuge and camp cuisine. Just when we were getting in the mood to make a night of it the restaurant closed and ejected us out on to the street and into the midst of a torrential thunderstorm, the third that day in Gavarnie apparently. Returning to the tent we were entertained by another 2-3 hours of battering rain and thunder and lightning dancing across the mountain tops that surrounded the village. Witnessing such powerful forces of nature from the confines of a tent is not exactly conducive to sleep and we both lay there until the rumbles of thunder diminished somewhere in the far distant Spanish mountains to the south when sleep overtook us.

## Thursday & Friday 20<sup>th</sup>/21<sup>st</sup> July 2006, Days 19/20, Gavarnie

Medical advice from the doctor at Lourdes was for me to rest, so rest is what we did. Michael needed no encouragement or professional advice to engage in his favourite pastime of extended sleeping and general lounging around. It was a skill he had perfected during his limited years on the planet and something for which he required no further training or tuition. These two days were spent mostly in relaxation in and around the village with a bus trip down to the town of Luz-St-Sauveur on the Thursday for some shopping and a much needed visit to a launderette. Luz had probably been about the point on the road at which I had become re-acquainted with my lunch the previous day in the back of the ambulance. The existence of only two public buses per day in each direction extended our stay in Luz beyond what we would have chosen and we spent most of the day sat at a pavement café stretching out food and drinks to pass the time whilst watching the world go by.

The campsite comprised a small field on a west facing hillside above where the river, the Gave de Gavarnie, is crossed by the narrow tarmac road leading up the valley from the village. It was a busy little site with most of the available flat sections of ground occupied by generally smaller type tents. The upper part of the field was segregated by a single wire electric fence which partitioned the campers from grazing cattle which were particularly noisy, especially in the mornings.

Most of the campers were French but we did become briefly acquainted with a Scottish couple upon encountering them at dusk one evening returning from an epic 13 hours ascent of Le Taillon. They both looked ready to drop and reminded me of how we had felt at Belagua some 11-12 days previously.

One notable aspect of our stay at Gavarnie over these two days was the absence of thunderstorms after 8 consecutive days of 'les orages terrible.' We certainly enjoyed our rest, sitting around in the sun, and my leg seemed to be on the mend with only the occasional slight twinge. I was apprehensive as to whether it would stand up to the next stage of the walk over the high pass of the Hourquette d'Alans, en route to the tiny hamlet of Heas. However, after much procrastination I decided I was fit to resume battle with our adversary, the HRP on Saturday. In retrospect I know now that I should maybe have waited a few more days. At the time however I felt ok and lulled into a sense of blind optimism from 2 pain-free days saw no reason why the injury to my leg would return. It was an impossible decision though. My leg had had felt ok on previous occasions after rest but had flared up again after resuming hard exertion. How was I to know how much rest was enough? Anyway, I was bored. The fine food, drink and relaxation were no compensation for the imposed inactivity and I longed to resume our quest. Despite the comforts it brought I was beginning to find the tourist environment of Gavarnie a source of irritation and an intrusion into our world of former mountain solitude and tranquillity.

## Saturday 22<sup>nd</sup> July, Gavarnie to Heas

Was I destined to vanquish the demon of my injured leg or would it return to haunt me? This was my day of truth. We were up at 6am and packed up and walking by 8am. After an initial gentle stroll up the valley we struck off east up the steep pine clad slopes towards the high pass, Hourquettes d'Alans, in the narrow, rocky ridge that joined the summits of Pimene and Grand Astazou. We had initially planned to ascend Pimene along with a number of other summits in the Gavarnie area but our unscheduled rest days at Gavarnie had deprived us of that opportunity. We had a strict timetable to keep to if we were to arrive at Banyuls in mid August as initially planned.

The well defined path was a succession of interminable zigzags up through the forest as we rapidly gained height. As we ascended the trees slowly began to thin until a point where we emerged into a high Alpine meadow, the Plateau de Pailla, laced with a silvery web of tumbling mountain streams fed from the glacial melt-waters of snowfields trapped high beneath the north facing cirques of Grand Astazou. Our progress was laboured today. It seemed the excesses of the previous few days had induced a lethargy in the limbs that could not be shaken off. Clearly pizzas, red wine and French beer do not constitute good "hill food." We toiled up stony paths that weaved left then right easing the otherwise steep gradient until, two hours after leaving Gavarnie we arrived at the Refuge d'Espurgettes, where we both flopped down on the grass and stretched what would normally have been a short rest into lazy 45 minutes of tea drinking and snack bar munching idleness.

Our languid state persisted after the morning break and upward progress was laboured as we trudged into the high reaches of the mountains towards the Hourquettes d'Alans. As the path zigzagged up towards the pass Michael dropped behind me by some distance despite my somewhat modest pace. It was here that my leg gave out again. Over the course of just a few metres I felt first just a twinge and then the full numbing pain that had so plagued me before Gavarnie. I stopped and rested, perched on a boulder at the side of the path whilst massaging my thigh in the forlorn hope of somehow kneading away the pain. I could see Michael some couple of hundred feet below me, clearly struggling under the load as he slowly plodded up, up, up the path. He stopped at each turn in the path leaning heavily on his walking poles and I could almost feel the pain of his aching limbs. The magnificence of our surroundings were at first lost on me as I contemplated the implications of this nagging injury and the threat it posed to the success of our expedition. As I sat and pondered the hopeless prospects of any meaningful onward progress I was overcome with an air of dejection that drained me of all my long held optimism. I felt like crying. The wretched realisation of our futile predicament dawned stark and unforgiving. I knew I could go no further whilst this pain in my leg persisted. I was overcome with a deep despondency that crushed all my previously held confidence in seeing this adventure through to the end. How could it be that all our trials and tribulations over the last three weeks were to fizzle out in such a muted fashion all because of some pathetic muscle strain? Fate had dealt such an unfair hand. I got to my feet, driven by the compulsion to continue and gazed around at the spectacle of grandeur that surrounded me. How could our efforts reach such a miserable end in such a spectacular setting? This was not how it should be!

My eyes were drawn to the peculiar notch that was chiselled into the rocky skyline of the Cirque de Gavarnie some four to five kilometres distant, the Breche du Roland. It's presence amongst the sweeping curves and pyramidal peaks of its surroundings, was, like the nagging pain in my thigh, an aberration. It was unreal; man made, as though it had been air-brushed onto the landscape. It didn't conform with the otherwise majestic and almost feminine curves of its neighbouring summits of Le Taillon and Pics des Gabietous and Saradets. It was as though some mighty blade had sliced through the border arête renting a great vertical gash in the rock.

I turned away and hobbled lamely up the last few hundred feet to the col where I sat down feeling deeply sorry for myself. I was in the company of several other parties of walkers and our gaze was captured by the towering cliffs and the new horizons of the Cirque d' Estaube. The adventure was over for Michael and I. It only remained for us to descend to Heas and civilisation. Our objective was no longer the distant shores of the Mediterranean but the humble surroundings of the Auberge de Refuge at the tiny hamlet of Heas where I had pre-booked our accommodation. All my focus was now upon reaching this objective. I couldn't think beyond our day's destination.

Some fifteen minutes later Michael appeared at the col obviously toiling under the weight of his monstrous backpack.

"Pull up a rock and come and join me and my gammy leg," I announced cheerfully.

My remark was lost on him at first as his focus was concentrated upon disengaging from the clasp of the hip and shoulder straps of his pack. He emitted a colossal sigh of relief as he lowered his pack to the ground.

"God I feel like I could fly when I take that off," he declared triumphantly.

"That could be a useful asset right now," I responded.
He looked at me and I could see that my previous comment had just dawned.

"It's gone again," I said rubbing my thigh. "I can't walk on this any more until it has fully recovered and that could take weeks. It's very painful when I walk and reaching Heas is going to be difficult for me. It's always worse downhill." I asserted.

"What are we going to do? He exclaimed like some little boy lost.

"I don't know son. Let's just concentrate on getting down this mountain eh. We can think about our next move when we reach Heas." Anyway, less about me, you're very slow today, what's up?

"I'm just knackered. I don't seem to have any energy," he said.

"Too much easy living in Gavarnie I reckon!"

The descent from Hourquette d'Alans was quite steep and once again I was forced to make extensive use of my walking poles to the point where they were more like crutches and absolutely vital to my continued progress. Each step brought its own excruciating pain as the impact of my boot striking the ground reverberated up through my thigh. Slowly but surely lowering myself down the mountain on these two thin sticks of carbon I found myself repeating under my breath on numerous occasions, "thank God for these trekking poles," Michael was well out in front now as my tortuous hobble could not keep pace with his rejuvenated young legs. The tortoise like progress of my ponderous descent down to the Gave de Estaube was probably best measured by my repeated encounters with what I can only describe as the most enormous lady I have ever encountered whilst walking in the mountains. She was travelling in the same direction as us and on the same path. I would have guessed she was probably in her mid forties but more importantly, and somewhat remarkably, she must have weighed in at somewhere between 25 – 30 stone. She was truly massive and certainly not built for mountain walking. However, here she was, undaunted by her obvious physical handicap, some 7000 feet up in the Pyrenees, tottering along as though she was simply walking down the street. We spent probably an hour and a half passing and then re-passing each other dependent upon the terrain, each time with a nod and smile of acknowledgement as though we had developed a mutual understanding of the each other's impediment. Our shared struggle gave me a different perspective and certainly helped me cope with the pain in my leg but I could eventually compete no longer when she and her walking companions finally passed us for the last time just before we reached the Lac de Gloriettes. With a knowing smile she teetered off down the path and out of sight and took with her, a good deal of my respect for her sheer determination and tenacity.

The Lac de Gloriettes, with a tarmac road up to it's northern dammed end was clearly a much sought after and accessible venue for picknickers and day trippers and a reminder that we weren't too far from civilisation in this popular region of the Pyrenees. I suppose the name Lac de Gloriettes itself conjures up images of almost biblical splendour. We took a rest on the westerly bank of the lake and it was here, whilst gazing down onto the deep, still, blue-green waters that I began to formulate a plan to enable us to continue our long distance odyssey. I figured I needed to give my leg probably around a week to recover fully from what I increasingly suspected was a muscle strain and nothing whatsoever to do with phlebitis or any inflammation of the veins. My notion that a week would be sufficient time to recover was not based on any sound medical theory just an instinct that a week would be enough for the strained muscle to mend and not fail again upon resumption of any strenuous exercise. The trouble was we didn't have a week to spare. The guide book recommended that 42 days was sufficient time to complete the whole of the HRP and we were currently on day 16 in the guidebook (Day 21 since leaving Hendaye). So, with 26 walking days remaining and allowing for 1 day of rest per week, we needed 37 days in order to complete the walk and allow a week of injury recuperation. This would mean us not completing the walk until 28th August. However, at the end of our walk we had planned to meet our respective partners, Sue and Haley at Pineda de Mar on the Costa del Maresme on Wednesday 23rd August for a weeks relaxation and holiday. In order to meet this deadline we needed to find 5 days from somewhere. The guidebook schedule was very demanding and it was difficult to see where we could begin to make up that sort of time based on our experience so far. I felt one rest day a week was essential in order to recover from the aches, pains and strains of the trail.

The only options remaining were to either:-

Stay in Heas and rest for a week and so finish the walk short of Banyuls, probably around the Col de la Perche on the N116 road (Day 35 in the guidebook). We would probably be able to pick up public transport at this spot to take us down into Spain.

Omit the next section of the HRP between Heas and Salardu (8 days of walking), travel to Salardu by public transport and rest there for a week, resuming the walk from Salardu, (Day 25) thus allowing us to finish at Banyuls.

Neither option was ideal. The mere thought of either alternative meant we were abandoning the very principal of walking from coast to coast. I knew that such a diversion from the original objective was always going to detract from the overall sense of achievement and would probably gnaw away at me forever. Oh what a bloody dilemma! I put the options to Michael, who, I was most surprised to discover, had all but conceded that in the circumstances we would have no option other than to return home. Despite my earlier despondency I had never truly considered abandoning the whole walk completely. Such a notion was unthinkable. It had been 6 days since my leg first gave out above the Refuge Wallon on Sunday 16th July and we had walked on 3 of those intervening 6 days. This was hardly conducive to proper rest and recovery. I felt I had to at least give us a fighting chance by allowing myself and my troublesome leg a long rest and the reasonable prospect of full recovery.

After some discussion we went for option b). The prospect of at least finishing at the recognised finish point of the HRP gave the whole trip some definition. It seemed wholly inappropriate to end what for us was the adventure of a lifetime at some inconspicuous pass in some quiet unknown backwater of the eastern Pyrenees. At least Banyuls was an obvious terminus and would provide a fitting conclusion to such an epic journey. The trouble was we were giving up on the highest section of the HRP, including the prospect of climbing Pic d'Aneto, at 3404m or 11,172feet, the highest summit in the Pyrenean range. Furthermore the next 8 days of the HRP, from Heas to Salardu included the highest point of the walk, the Col Inferieur de Literole (Day 21) at 2983m or 9791ft, as well as passing through the highest mountains of the Pyrenees where we would probably be required to utilise crampons and ice axes in order to cross the numerous glaciers and snowfields. We were losing a lot in turning our back on this section of the walk and it was with great reluctance and heartfelt misgivings that this decision was taken but what the hell else could I do? I could barely walk! There had to be some sacrifice in order to give us a fighting chance of completing the remainder of the HRP.

Upon resuming walking and reaching the barrage, or dam at the end of the lake the remainder of our journey that day was on tarmac roads, which made for slightly less painful progress than the rough ground since the Hourquette d'Alans. We slowly descended the access road to the dam down into a valley of pastures and wild flowers to the Pont de l'Arriele where we encountered a Danish family collecting wild strawberries. As inviting a prospect as it was to join them I was keen to arrive at our days' destination so I could rest and bring about some relief from the pain in my leg. We pressed on up the valley over gentle gradients to the tiny hamlet of Heas where we had booked 2 beds at the Auberge le Refuge. Our accommodation was in a converted barn but comprised of the usual 'demi-pension' or dinner, bed and breakfast and benefited from the ever welcome facility of hot showers. Another bonus was that all the beds were of the single variety which was a positive luxury after weeks of imposed close confinement in tents and Alpine bunks. Michael seemed pleased too.

We had arrived relatively early and it was still only 4pm when I emerged from the bosom of a reviving hot shower. Since dinner wasn't due to be served until 7.30pm I took the opportunity of a siesta and in the soft and gentle comfort of a sprung mattress was soon lost in strange dreams of fat ladies, strawberries and communal sleeping arrangements.

Dinner was excellent and comprised 3 courses, each of them substantial, including gallons of hot soup, and home-made bread, several large lamb steaks with absolutely tons (or should I say tonnes) of new potatoes and finally a home-made fruit flan, which I think was mostly blackcurrant, all served outside on the stone terrace on the most pleasant and warm of summer evenings. The food was served with a seemingly endless supply of the most soporific red wine, after which, duly anaesthetised, I could have slept for England that night and think I pretty much did!

## Day 22, Sunday 23rd July. Heas to Bagnères de Luchon

We didn't know where we would end up that day we left Heas. We were headed for Salardu in the Vall d'Aran in Spain but with no notion of whether we would be able to get there in the course of one day. As I said to Michael though it didn't really matter too much. Like travelling snails we had our home on our backs and plenty of food to sustain us. After the usual modest but pleasing breakfast which we'd pre arranged for 7am, we headed off at 8am back down the road we had walked up from the Pont de l'Arriele yesterday. Our immediate destination was the village of Gedre, a distance of some 4-5 miles, mostly downhill, where we were aiming to catch the Gavarnie to Luz St Sauveur bus that we had used a few days previously. From recollection the bus left Gavarnie around 10am so would pass through Gedre probably some 10 minutes later and even with a gammy leg I figured we would be able to cover the distance in the available time. The intention from Luz was to take a further bus, probably down to Lourdes, again, and then out of the Pyrenees completely, possibly onto Tarbes where we could pick up a train travelling east. Beyond that our plans were rather vague.

It was so difficult to abandon the H.R.P. As we departed the refuge I gazed mournfully up at the narrow stony path that was the next section of the Haute Route, threading its way up the mountainside on its journey over to Parzan across the border back into Spain. This should have been our route today. This felt like betrayal. We were abandoning a trusted companion and taking the easy option. My leg actually felt ok again, as was very often the case in the morning. Perhaps we could rejoin the route and I could persevere and somehow get through despite my leg strain? Real adventurers had suffered far worse and prevailed, why couldn't I? It didn't seem too far a stretch of the imagination to contemplate continuing walking through the pain. After all what was it? It was just a muscle strain. It wasn't like I'd broken a leg or something, and I'd managed to complete 3 days of very demanding terrain with the injury so why not the rest of the walk? These were the feelings of guilt that I churned over in my mind as we continued down the road. Over the course of the next half hour or so as we moved further down the valley and away from the sight of that narrow path up the hillside I rejected the ludicrous prospect of further progress on the HRP. I knew that continuing with the walk was not a realistic prospect and to confirm my decision the pains in my leg returned after a mile or so of relatively gentle descent on a tarmac surface. To have attempted to continue the walk could have resulted in some sort of permanent injury to my leg which I would be a fool to risk and would no doubt regret forever.

We continued down the road to Gedre and my limp became more pronounced the further we got, especially on the steep shortcut path which avoided the zigzags of the road as we approached the village. We arrived at 9.45am, in plenty of time to catch our bus to Luz-St-Sauveur on which we bumped into the Scottish couple we had met in Gavarnie some 2–3 days previously. The bus connection from Luz to Lourdes was not until early afternoon so once again we had an enforced stay over in the village where we made a second visit in three days to the launderette to try and make our presence in public slightly less objectionable. I became a source of some mild amusement for some of the other customers as I took the opportunity to clean everything except the pair of underpants I was standing up in. This tendency to exhibitionism was, I can assure you, not something which I practised on a regular basis. At least not until I came to the Pyrenees anyway! My semi-nakedness went mostly unnoticed and we managed to escape the launderette without coming to the attention of the local Gendarmerie and embarked on the bus to Lourdes. Our visit there was even more brief than my last one as we were dropped at the bus/rail interchange where, following a brief consultation with the map, we dived almost immediately onto a departing train to Tarbes, from where our journey continued on a further train bound for Toulouse. After a journey of some 40km through a mostly rural landscape in the foothills of the Pyrenees we alighted at an obscure halt on the outskirts of a small town by the name of Monterjeau.

As the trained pulled away from the platform and we re-engaged with our backpacks we became aware of a solitary coach with its engine ticking over in the station car park. Otherwise the area was deserted. A number of other train passengers had made for the coach so we followed and before we knew it we were soon travelling south on this coach headed for Bagnères de Luchon. This wasn't really our intended destination but it was either that or end up left standing on our own, abandoned in the station car park whose solitary link to the outside world was this bus. After a conversation with the driver, who refused to take any fare for our journey, we were advised to alight from the bus at a small village called Marignac, close to the Spanish border. There were apparently no cross border buses and the best way to get into Spain, apart from walking, was to jump a taxi from Marijnac to the Spanish border some 10km distant. As it happens this didn't quite work out.

I don't know if it was because this was a Sunday but the village of Marijnac seemed deserted. After alighting our free bus, we tramped along the main street of the village and didn't see a soul, except for the driver of the occasional car that passed along the road. There had been two German lads who had got off the bus ahead of us and who gave the appearance of knowing where they were going, so we followed them. After some fifteen minutes they stopped at a bar, seemingly the only bar in the village, or the only one open anyway, where they disappeared inside. Upon reaching the bar we dropped our packs at a couple of tables outside and I went inside to order a couple of beers. I got chatting to the German lads who were also trying to get to Spain and were enquiring upon the availability of any taxis that operated in the area. After agreeing to share a taxi with them I went back outside to Michael with a couple of beers and we sat in the afternoon sun awaiting arrival of our taxi. A couple of beers later the German lads joined us outside and informed us that all the local taxi drivers were drunk and were not available for business. Not relishing the prospect of a rather long walk into Spain with my dodgy leg we decided to head back to the bus stop to see if we could catch a later bus up to Luchon.

By this time we were feeling rather hungry and surprisingly managed to find a pizza restaurant which was just opening on the outskirts of the village close to the railway station where we had been dropped off by the bus earlier. After gorging ourselves on made to order pizzas the owner kindly directed us to the official bus stop which seemed the most unlikely spot, off the main road, on some dusty back street surrounded by empty and boarded up buildings. The whole place had the atmosphere of a ghost town and the only two places where there was any sign of life, the bar and the pizza restaurant, stood in stark contrast to their deserted surroundings. I wondered how these two oases of life sustained a business. There was nobody around to eat or drink anything!

When the bus didn't arrive on time we started to doubt whether we were in the right place. There was nobody around to ask. The streets were empty. It seemed highly improbable that any bus had ever been down this particular road in this quiet backwater suburb at the edge of the village. Just as we were about to head back to the pizza restaurant the bus arrived, six minutes late at 18.55. It was the same bus and the same old guy driving it, who still wouldn't take any fare off us, although he did accept payment from the two German lads, which made me feel rather awkward at the time. I guess some old wounds run deep. Half an hour later we got off outside of the railway station in Bagnères de Luchon and crossing the road booked into the first hotel we came across, The Hotel de Sports. After a shower we headed off into town in our clean bodies and clean clothes.

Luchon, despite being quite a big place didn't initially seem to amount to much. Just more run down, half empty properties, deserted streets and an air of neglect. Tired old buildings, testimony of a foregone era of a prosperity that had long since ended. That was until we turned into the main tree lined boulevard, the allée d'Étigny, in 'downtown' Luchon. What a transformation!

This was where everybody was hiding. All those drunken taxi drivers from Marijnac were here in Luchon wining and dining. The centre of town was a bustling hive of activity with pavement bars and restaurants competing for custom. A long, wide and elegant boulevard, shaded by mature lime trees, stretched into the distance. The whole place had an air of opulence and grandeur that you would associate with the Victorian era, but with a modern and fresh appeal. Hemmed in by 2000m summits on all sides Luchon had established itself as a spa town as far back as in Roman times although it had undergone a revival in the latter half of the 18th century. We walked the length of the allée d'Étigny past the Thermes or hot baths, to the Parc des Quinconces just taking in the atmosphere of the town. This was a whole new experience in comparison to our earlier adventures in the Pyrenees. We sat at a pavement bar enjoying a few drinks where we couldn't help but admire and appreciate the relaxed ambience and sophistication of this most cosmopolitan of spa towns.

"Not quite like Liverpool city centre of a weekend is it?" I remarked to Michael.

"What, you mean the streets aren't full of scantily clad scrubbers?"

"Well you could put it that way I suppose."

It occurred to me that this was probably the sort of street scene that municipal planners in the big cities of the UK craved to recreate but I couldn't help but think that they were destined to failure. First and foremost we just don't have the climate and secondly our towns and city centres at night are predominantly the habitat of young and often rowdy revellers. The people in Luchon that evening were a diverse group with a wide age range. Our drinking habits in major British urban conurbations were born in a working class background of street corner ale-houses dominated by the spit and sawdust environment and smoke filled bars whose sole purpose was that of serving working class men. Our inner cities now seem to have evolved downwards to what is possibly an even lower common denominator of catering for youngsters whose sole objective is that of achieving mental oblivion in the fastest possible time by getting completely rat-arsed. It is difficult to envisage a family friendly culture of gentle evening leisure activity developing in such a harsh environment.

There were no scenes of drunken loutishness in Luchon that night. It was a relaxing way to spend an evening and a million miles away from the toils of our journey. We eventually sauntered back to our hotel around eleven o'clock, my left leg reminding me on the way that it would not take to kindly to anything more than gentle exertion.

# Day 23, Monday 24th July. Bagnères de Luchon to Arties

The luxury of a hotel bed was something we had not experienced since the Basque village of Lescun and it would have been easy to have remained in this comparative comfort for the rest of the week. However, our wallets would never have coped with the strain and we decided to continue our journey to Salardu, over the border into Spain, and head for a little campsite shown on our map on the outskirts of the small village of Arties about a mile or two down the valley from Salardu. The awkward bit was deciding how we would get there. To climb the 2000ft over the Col du Portillon and down into the town of Bossost in the Valle d'Aran was hardly conducive to the rest and recuperation needed for my leg. The non existence of cross border public transport gave us the sole option of hiring a taxi, which we duly arranged over breakfast with our host. For the princely sum of €40 (around £28) we ordered what turned out to be a mini-bus which already contained several passengers when we joined it outside of our hotel. It then proceeded to collect numerous other travellers from various gîtes and hotels around Luchon before heading off up the snaking strip of tarmac that led out of Luchon via the Col du Portillon and over into Spain with a full load of a dozen or so passengers.

Once we had left behind the last straggling outposts of Luchon the road steepened and our minibus laboured loudly up through mountainsides of open pine forest. I was conscious that the landscape was more Mediterranean in appearance than the mostly temperate and green pastures of Gavarnie and with the exception of the Col d'Annaye, most of the earlier sections of the Pyrenees. However, what most caught my attention though were the endless and inescapable slogans painted repeatedly all the way up the road to the pass, "MORT A L'OURS!" (Death to the bears) "NON A L'OURS!" I learnt later that some two months prior to our visit on Saturday 6th May 2006 there had been a large demonstration in Luchon by people protesting against the introduction of Slovenian bears to the Pyrenees following the death of Canelle, the last ethnic Pyrenean bear, killed by a hunter in November 2004. Apparently the demonstration and march comprised of some 1300 protestors, 35 tractors and 1200 sheep. I for one can understand the feelings of the sheep who were no doubt alarmed by the prospect of slipping one notch further down the food chain. Seriously though I would have thought it possible to reintroduce the bears, as the majority of French people apparently wanted, and yet compensate the farmers in the event of loss of livestock? It was a subject for which local feelings obviously ran high.

We passed over the col and into Spain leaving all of the bear protest slogans behind. I was glad we hadn't chosen to walk over to Spain because the descent into Bossost seemed endless as the narrow road switched back time, after time, after time, with the valley floor below never seeming to get any closer. We were eventually dropped off in the town at a bus stop in an avenue of trees alongside the River or eth Garona. We didn't have to wait too long for the bus which travelled up and down the Vall d'Aran from Les, near the French border to the village of Tredos just above Salardu and back again throughout the day. Our journey to Arties, some 12 miles away, at the exorbitant fare of 85cents, was somewhat better value than the 40 euros it had cost us to travel less than half the distance from Luchon, and we had the added bonus of listening to a local radio station on the way which had a seeming fixation with English Sixties music. I felt I'd stepped back in time.

The bus trundled its way up the Vall d'Aran alongside the lazy and partially dry eth Garona, passing through numerous attractive little villages and hamlets each with their own Romanesque church. The peculiar aspect of this valley was that the river flowed north into France to become the Garonne and empty into the Atlantic, yet we were in Spain. It seemed strange that the Vall d'Aran (which apparently translates as valley of the valley) should be on the north, or French side of the Pyrenees and yet was part of the Catalan region of Spain. We arrived at Vielha, principal town of the Lleida province, a once attractive and remote outpost of the Catalan region that had clearly become bloated by the influx of mass tourism. Outside of its old and quaintly attractive town centre were a collection of ugly concrete developments comprising of largely sixties and seventies apartment blocks incorporating endless winter sports shops and cheap holiday apartments.

The Vall d'Aran, once cut off and remote from the rest of Spain had even developed its own language, Aranese, which, since 1984, has become regularly taught at local schools. A measure of its detachment from its mother country was demonstrated by the fact that Spanish Republican guerrillas controlled the area until 1948, well after the cessation of the Spanish Civil War in 1939. The area had depended upon the C28 road which passed over the high col of the Port de la Bonaigua, which at 2072m was completely cut off from Spain during the winter months. The construction of the Vielha road tunnel in 1948 opened up the area and brought an end to this last fortress of republican defiance, and so began the venture into tourism which now dominates the economy of whole valley.

Our bus continued beyond Vielha to our destination, Arties, a small village where we found our campsite on the banks of the rushing infant Garona. I let Michael do the talking at reception. He seemed to have grasped Spanish far better than me. My Spanish frequently descended into concoction of incomprehensible jibberish that served only to confuse the listener. We booked into the site for a total of six nights at 15euros/night and duly set up our tent at the edge of the site alongside the gurgling waters of the river. The site was quite busy with other campers and caravanners and was blessed with the luxury of showers, a small camp shop, a bar/restaurant and, the 'pièce de résistance', a small outdoor swimming pool. One of my immediate observations as we pitched the tent was that the ground on which we were camping was hard, very hard. No doubt compacted by the continuous presence of years of previous campers. It was impossible to force the tent pegs any more than an inch into the ground, which beneath a skimming of topsoil seemed to comprise of solid rock. I didn't relish the prospect of sleeping on such an uncompromising surface with only three quarters of an inch of inflated bed mat between me and it!

After setting up our home for the next week we ambled off to take a look around the village. It was a quiet and attractive little place but for the most part it gave the impression it was shut. It was almost completely deserted. Where were the people? As we meandered through the narrow cobbled streets it became clear that this was not a village in the conventional sense. It had lost touch with itself having pandered to the lure of tourist cash. There were extensive areas of pristine newly built properties, which I have to say, whilst they were largely in keeping with their surroundings, comprising of local stone with rustic timber balconies and exposed beams and eaves, the place was soul-less. The majority of the buildings were empty holiday homes, awaiting the onset of a winter season when the whole valley would be deluged with snow and wall to wall skiers. The village church looked forlorn and abandoned and in imminent danger of collapse with a crooked and tilted spire. We managed to find a small café open in the village square where we had a lunchtime snack before wandering back to the campsite where we spent the afternoon lounging by the pool in the hot afternoon Spanish sun.

During an afternoon of total abject laziness and with little meaningful to do I sent a text to Keith, who was due to meet us in Salardu on Sunday, submitting a shopping list of provisions to see us through the next and reputedly toughest section of the HRP. It went like this, "Hi Keith, lookin' forward to seein' ya Sunday at the Refugi Rosta, Salardu. Michael wants a book on the Royal Marines and a crate of ice-cold Budweiser. Can you get us 10 dehydrated camp meals and puddings and I'd like a drop-dead gorgeous blond Swedish masseuse in her mid twenties, with warm hands, plenty of patience and a good sense of humour please. Thanks, Steve."

His reply was brief.

"Got Michael's book and the food, see you Sunday."

He was never one to waste words.

We returned to the tent early evening and I immediately went in search of some chairs. The ground was not the most comfortable place to sit, unless your arse was made of granite, and when I returned with two white plastic chairs that I had noticed earlier, partially hidden behind one of the nearby empty caravans. We were the envy of the camp site, especially the pampered French teenage lad in the next tent, to whom I had taken an instant dislike I have to say. That evening we took advantage of the on site café bar for dinner and both enjoyed a rather large spaghetti Bolognese and several San Miguels to help it down.

# Day 24, Tuesday 25<sup>th</sup> July, Arties

When I could no longer bear the pain of continuing to lie on the camping equivalent of concrete I crawled out of the tent and after a visit to the loo I returned and sat in the comparative comfort of one of 'our' plastic chairs. It was 7.50am. The great advantage of camping in this part of the world was the ability to sit outside in warm sunshine most days. It was a sunny and peacefully pleasant morning and I sat in quiet self contemplation with the gurgle of the Garona tumbling over rocks behind our tent and admired the sweeping lines of the surrounding mountains high above the Vall d'Aran as a pan of water came to the boil.

Michael eventually surfaced at around 9am and we shared a pan of porridge sweetened with honey, a bottle of which I had carried since leaving Liverpool. We got chatting to a couple of Canadian lads who had dropped down to Arties from the Restanca refuge on the GR11 in order to stock up on food, an indication of the difficulties of walking these mountain routes and the practicalities of ensuring you have sufficient supplies to sustain you to your next shop!

The day was typical of our stay at the Arties campsite with time spent cleaning clothes, eating and generally lazing about, especially by the pool, which we virtually had to ourselves. Following the heat of the day it was inevitable that the afternoon would bring the customary thunderstorm and sure enough it arrived at around 5pm. It forced us into the tent and an imposed extended siesta for about half an hour or so. We secured our neighbours tent (the ones with the stroppy teenage son) after the strong wind preceding the thunderstorm threatened to uproot it at one stage. Our reward was a selection of anti-inflammatory creams and pills for my leg after they returned and I explained the reason for our enforced rest.

For tea I decided to experiment and put together an unlikely concoction of mash potato, paté and chicken stock. Not out of a particular passion for this dish but more to simply empty our packs of the 'never likely to be used except in a crisis' provisions that would probably have remained unused forever had it not been for this concerted effort. We didn't anticipate the extent to which this ill considered culinary disaster would assault our palates, only previously bettered by the fish soup at the Bagargui refuge a few weeks previous. It was totally disgusting. The reconstituted mash had the consistency of wet cardboard and the paté was something more suited to hanging ceramic bathroom tiles. It possessed an aroma akin to my walking socks after a week of unbroken confinement inside my walking boots. It was truly putrid and was in no way enhanced by the chicken stock which was a ridiculous and futile attempt to supplement the flavour of this ghastly meal. We treated ourselves to a bar of chocolate each and removed the lingering taste of this unfortunate repast with a welcome mug of Earl Grey tea.

After our meal we were entertained by the couple camped opposite who spent best part of an hour trying to fashion a makeshift flysheet out of a tarpaulin, a few clothes pegs and the assistance of a nearby tree. I would have offered to help but I wasn't really sure just what they were trying to do? They attempted a few variations, none of which looked like they would withstand a sneeze let alone a moderate breeze, until in the end they settled on their preferred design. Their efforts were most commendable even if their homemade tent was somewhat Heath Robinson and we duly applauded the finished product, much to their amusement.

Our evening was spent in the bar where we sampled the local draft beer and I added the word cerveza to my somewhat limited Spanish vocabulary. The beer was cheap at 1.20euros as was the local brandy (same price) that we also sampled later. I was puzzled by the way customers settled their bills and couldn't seem to pay for our drinks as the waitress seemed to display complete disinterest once she had poured the drinks and I was beginning to think the beer was free! No such luck, we paid before leaving after persuading the waitress, with some difficulty, that we did actually owe them some money. It was typical of the manâna attitude that pervaded the populous of the Spanish Pyrenees and something that, whilst most welcome and therapeutic, took a little getting used to coming from my mad world of deadlines and "want it yesterday!"

We returned to the tent where unfortunately my alcohol consumption was not of sufficient quantities to anaesthetise the body enough against rigours of our 'bed of nails.'

# Day 25, Wednesday 26<sup>th</sup> July, Arties.

At 7.35am I conceded to the pain that wracked my body through sleeping on concrete disguised as grass and crawled stiffly out of our Vango Storm sarcophagus. I felt like I'd just stepped out of the boxing ring after a good hiding rather than risen from a nights 'sleep.' As the blood stopped flowing to first one limb then another I had spent the night in permanent motion trying to find some comfort but to no avail and it was a relief for this torment to end. Once again it was a pleasant morning with high cloud and the temperature somewhere in the low 70's.

Our day comprised primarily of gentle relaxation, although we did take a trip up to Salardu on the bus mid morning to book our accommodation for three at the Refugi Rosti for Sunday night. We took the opportunity of walking the two miles back to our campsite. I hadn't had any problems with my leg since Sunday night and I thought a gentle stroll, all downhill, on easy paths would be well within my capabilities. Fortunately, I was right and there was no reaction, which was pleasing. On the way back we passed the both sad and curious site of a bear enclosure on the outskirts of Arties. The two internees looked particularly melancholy and so dispirited that it was impossible not to feel sorry for them. Their loss of freedom seemed a high price to pay for the brief and questionable satisfaction of a limited number of passing people that would ever encounter this obscure little enclosure tucked away on the outskirts of a deserted village high in the Spanish Pyrenees.

Following another afternoon alongside the pool we took advantage of the site bar/restaurant once again for our dinner. I became mesmerised by the TV in a corner of the bar which flashed out pictures of a new conflict between Israel and Lebanon. Rocket launching jet fighters, tanks and the bullet riddled buildings of Beirut amidst a scene of smoke filled streets of rubble and crying mothers played across the screen. A reminder of world outside of our own that continued apace on its path to self destruction. We were detached from this world of war and suffering, even more so than would normally have been the case in our comfortable suburban habitat. It was as though we had stepped onto a different planet. This conflict seemed almost fictional and I wondered at first whether it was and old news reel. It wasn't. A new fight had broken out once again in this war torn region. I couldn't really make any sense of the broadcast, being in Spanish, but the pictures told the story and there wasn't any sense to be made from it all anyway.

Despite increasing my alcohol intake to include wine, beer and brandy, in not insignificant quantities I was still unable to sleep.

# Day 26, Thursday 27th July, Arties

I arose once again at 7.35am when I could bear the pain no more. Each night I was slowly being crushed to death by my own weight, which had probably diminished to somewhere around 16 stone by now. After Michael got up, without any prompting whatsoever I may add, we decided upon a walk down to Vielha that day, 6km distant, using another less conspicuous long distance path, the GR 211.1. It just didn't quite have the same ring to it! The French couple whose tent we had secured a couple of days previous offered to lend Michael a bike and he decided to take them up on the offer whilst I opted for a return trip on the bus.

We pottered around throughout the morning, washing dishes and clothes and whilst in the course of our daily chores, befriended a British couple, with a little French dog, the three of whom had turned up late Wednesday and pitched their tent a few yards away from ours. I knew the dog was French because it couldn't understand me and growled whenever I approached the next tent. They were apparently living in Tarbes, which they described as a beautiful city which belied the impression we had come away with from our brief encounter with the graffiti strewn railway sidings.

Our social circle really expanded when we were invited to a barbeque that evening whilst being overheard talking at the kitchen area washing dishes. Our hosts, Graham and Wendy were a couple in their mid forties I would guess and were on holiday with their young teenage daughter Sarah having stayed at Arties on previous occasions. Anyway we now had an additional reason to venture to Vielha, meat and beer!

It was late morning on another hot day in the Val d'Aran as we set off through the village down to Vielha. We were grateful that the initial few miles of our journey was in the shade of the trees and hillside on the north facing south side of the valley. After a half an hour or so we crossed the river at an old stone bridge, the Pont deth Garona and entered the small village of Garos where we almost immediately lost our way amongst the tangle of narrow alleys and cobbled streets. After accidentally stumbling across the village church, this distinctive fixed point enabled us to find our way out of the village via a cobbled lane which soon became a narrow grassy track which led off up the hillside. This in turn became an even narrower, partly overgrown and little used path which skirted the upper edge of meadows up high above the valley floor. I wasn't at all certain we were still on the GR211.1 but we continued to travel in the right direction and anyway the prospect of becoming lost seemed mildly appealing. We had all day and not a care in the world. I was also pleased with the fact that my leg seemed to be holding out, so much so that I even ran for a short section of this most pleasant morning amble in the warm sunshine.

We arrived in Vielha through the back streets of Betren, another village of holiday homes, and feeling rather peckish and quite thirsty picked up a melon the size of a football from the small market on the outskirts of town. We sat down on a nearby wall and cut up the melon into quarters, with my small camping knife. It was truly delicious, although we could have done with eating it in a bath. Michael only wanted one quarter. After about 15 minutes of endless slurping and dribbling I finally finished off the last of my three quarters after which I felt I didn't need to eat for a week. It felt good to have enjoyed such a massive helping of fruit having been mostly deprived of such luxuries for so long. After a brief shopping trip to a small supermarket where we obtained beer, wine and meat from a mad butcher who was a rabid Bill Haley fan, we went and sat at a the terrace of a bar in the town square.

If the waiter who was serving had got his way then that's all we would have done, just sat there. After numerous fruitless attempts to gain his attention, culminating in almost tripping him up and after he had served everybody on every table in the vicinity, except us, and after waiting half an hour for some service I gave up and wandered inside the bar and ordered our drinks from a stunningly attractive Spanish barmaid. I don't know what the waiter had against English people but his efforts to ignore us eventually became blatant and truly obtrusive. Anyway, I successfully submitted my own order of "dos zumo de naranja con heilo, por favour" from this delightful Spanish waitress who was most entertained by my infantile efforts at speaking the lingo. Who needs a snotty and ignorant Spanish waiter anyway, stuff him! I'd much sooner flirt with this dusky, dark eyed and raven haired Iberian beauty any day!

Service apart we spent a pleasant afternoon relaxing in Vielha before returning back to Arties via bus and bike. Michael said he only realised how much lower down the valley Vielha was from Arties when he realised from riding back how much higher up the valley Arties was from

Vielha. I renewed acquaintance with the seemingly one and only local bus driver for the third time in four days after a wait of and hour and a half. He had the sort of features and accompanying gruff scowl that you might associate with a Mexican bandit and if he had said anything at all, which he didn't, it would have been along the lines of, "Hey Gringo, leave da money on da counter, ok!"

The barbeque was a really lavish treat in comparison to our usual fare, with steaks, sausages, burgers and chicken with numerous buns, rolls, baps and baguettes and loads of salad, and not forgetting the beer and wine. Besides Michael and myself another family joined us, a Scottish bloke named Dave who was rather brash and at least mildly uncouth but nevertheless endlessly amusing. He was accompanied by his quiet and more reserved Swiss wife, who's name I didn't catch, as well as their son, Robby and daughter Serine. It was a coming together of people whose paths would probably never cross except in the leveller that is camping! Their upbringings were clearly worlds apart. Dave had numerous amusing tales to tell and every one of them made liberal use of a wide range of expletives, including numerous 'effin this and effin thats' spread liberally throughout his dialogue, at the end of which I though Wendy was going to be physically sick. She smiled a polite but cringing smile at the culmination of each tale which barely disguised her obvious unease and clearly found Dave just too much. She kept disappearing into their caravan on the pretext of having some other pressing duty when she could see Dave was working himself up to the next profanity. I have to say I did feel a bit sorry for her but in a Billy Connolly sort of way Dave was an undoubtedly funny guy and I laughed as much at the uneasiness of the situation as I did at his effin' tales of mirth.

Dave and his family apparently lived in Switzerland and his wife and children both spoke French as their first language although they did have a basic understanding of English which was demonstrated in a hilarious way when at one point of the evening Robby, who was football mad, accidentally kicked his football into the middle of our table full of food and drinks. His dad, angry at his son's clumsiness whirled round on him demanding an apology.

"You stupid pillock, what do you say?"

The poor lad stood there lost for words and then held out his hands and said, "Sheete" in a questioning and apologetic tone, clearly accustomed to this obligatory response from years of witnessing his dad's response in similar scenarios. I roared with laughter while Wendy's mouth dropped open and her hands clasped her face in shock.

"No, not 'shit.' You say sorry! Retorted Dave.

"Oh…sorreeee!"

He was clearly his father's son!

When I had managed to stop laughing we all helped to clear up the devastated table and soon finished the remainder of the food. After a short rest Robby cajoled all of the males into an impromptu football match with another half a dozen assorted footballers from around the campsite. It was a stern test for my leg despite the game only lasting some 20 minutes or so. Michael and I were on the same side and came out victorious by 4goals to 3 following the significant intervention of our super-sub, a young Danish lad of around 11 or 12 years of age who lashed in the winning goal shortly after it had been declared that "the next goal is the winner!"

The rest of the evening was spent sat outside of Graham and Wendy's caravan telling tales of our death defying exploits and interspersed with regular sessions of eating and drinking. It was a most pleasant evening spent in the company of an interesting and diverse bunch of people, which quenched our thirst for the social intercourse we had been so lacking since Charlie and Sue had left us some two weeks previous.

The profusion of alcohol still didn't help me sleep I'm afraid. It just meant I needed to pee in the middle of the night. That terrible decision process which takes place when sleeping in a tent where the pain in your bladder slowly but inextricably invades your slumber, eventually to reach a point where the balance is tipped and the need to relieve your bursting bladder exceeds the desire to remain in the warmth of your sleeping bag. You know that there is no way you are going to last until morning so reluctantly, extricating yourself from the womb that is your bed you find yourself fumbling for invisible tent door zips and stumbling in the dark over abandoned pans, cups and assorted camping paraphernalia, waking the whole campsite in the process, stepping onto dew soaked grass to finally piss all over your already wet feet until, at a point where you are completely and utterly awake and have no realistic prospect of any further sleep until the following night at the earliest, you return to your sleeping bag and await the onset of dawn.

# Day 27, Friday 28<sup>th</sup> July, Arties to Restanca (and back)

The main feature of this day, our fifth at the Arties campsite was the decision to accompany Graham, Wendy and Sarah up to the Restanca refuge, located high in the mountains some 6-7km south of Arties at an altitude of 2010metres. Restanca was on the HRP and would have been one of our overnight stops had we continued our walk onto that section. More importantly it would prove a stern test for my leg with 500m of relatively steep ascent and more importantly, descent.

We were able to forego part of the walk by virtue of the fact that Graham was able to drive the majority of the distance along a narrow single track road that wound its way up the Val Arties to a car park at the head of the road at the Plan de Nera, from which we commenced our walk of 3km up to Restanca. We set off along a dirt road that climbed gently up the valley to a point where a finger post marked our departure on a narrow winding path up through a green swathe of forest and dense rock garden of low shrubs. I was so pre-occupied by the prospects of my leg giving out that I barely noticed any aspects of our walk that afternoon. I remember emerging from the trees into a land of bare rock below the Restanca barrage.

The Refugi de Restanca was dour looking 3 storey grey stone building that stood at the eastern end of the dam that held back the picturesque blue-turquoise waters of the Estany de Restanca. It was a busy and popular placed with dozens of walkers congregating outside. We purchased some cans of coca cola from the refuge and sat amongst the crowd outside. As we sat sipping our ice cold drinks a young woman with a rather large pack approached along the dam and sat alongside us. Her name was Katrina and she was walking the HRP alone after initially having set off with a friend from Hendaye. Her friend had abandoned the walk after the first two days and she had continued alone, which I found most impressive having experienced much of the route she had travelled. The fact that she had walked so far as a 19 year old girl on probably the toughest recognised long distance route in Europe demonstrated a depth of fortitude and resilience beyond her tender years and I have to say, beyond her 'little girl lost' demeanour. She was clearly a tough cookie!

We sat and chatted with Katrina for some time and it was the source of some mild amusement that her primary fear and concern was the presence of bears in the Pyrenees. She had camped a lot during her five weeks of walking in order to keep the costs down and had spent numerous sleepless nights listening to mysterious noises close to her tent, convinced that she was about to be devoured any minute. I tried to reassure her by pointing out that there were many creatures which inhabited the Pyrenees, none of which to my knowledge considered humans as part of their staple diet, and the likelihood of these nocturnal noises emanating from one of the very few bears that remained was extremely unlikely.

I think we were all more than impressed by this inspirational and determined young lady and immediately resolved to help her in whatever small way we could. She had said she was running short on food so Michael and I contributed a diverse collection of deformed snack bars that we had carried all the way from Liverpool whilst Graham was able to administer a large Compeed dressing to a particularly angry looking blister on her heel. We wished her luck and departed Restanca back to the car in the expectation of possibly meeting up again with Katrina once we resumed the HRP at Salardu in three days time. We never did. I hope she made it!

My leg withstood this latest test with no suggestion or hint of the muscle strain that had plagued me since Wallon. Michael similarly had not experienced any further problems with his leg strain and we were both looking forward to resuming our adventure on Monday. Our return to the campsite heralded another late afternoon thunderstorm so after a shower we retired to the tent for a rain induced siesta.

## Day 28, Saturday 29th July, Arties

This was our last full day at the Arties campsite before heading off up to the refugio at Salardu to meet Keith. We were both restless and eager to resume our walk. This enforced inactivity, lazing around the campsite and pool was becoming tedious. Although this was to be our last opportunity to enjoy such relaxation for many weeks to come we just wanted the time to pass. We had an overriding objective to which we were compelled to return. Our inertia dragged every second from a reluctant clock and made each hour seem endless. This ponderous passing of time doing nothing in particular at all was most tiresome. I felt like Gary Cooper in High Noon, just witnessing the clock tick ever so slowly down, watching a distant horizon and waiting for that train to arrive. Our inevitable fate awaited our arrival in Salardu at dawn on Monday. "Do not forsake me oh my darling"

The afternoon slowly ebbed away and upon discovery that the camp bar was closed on a Saturday night we found a restaurant in the village, El Pollo Loco (Mad Chicken). It was far too posh for us but my attitude in such places is that my money is just as good as the next mans so I am just as entitled to dine there. Opting for the red meat once again I spent the next half an hour in a closely fought contest with a steak which had the consistency of a Wellington boot. We were well matched that steak and I and both of us fought like demons but my determination won through in the end. I came out ahead on points, with an aching jaw having spent a few rounds on the ropes! It would appear that cooking is clearly a concept that is yet to penetrate these high mountain villages. A 'medium' done steak is a piece of meat, both sides of which has had the briefest of encounters with anything resembling heat. There would have been less blood at the table had I opted for a heart bypass as opposed to a medium sirloin.

On the positive side we discovered a local concoction, Licor de Miel, a very drinkable blackcurrant and honey flavoured firewater which I dare say, due largely to the quantities we consumed that evening, induced my best nights sleep under canvas in a month.

## Day 29, Sunday 30<sup>th</sup> July, Arties to Salardu

After limboing out of the tent around 8.30am, followed by a visit to the loo, I began the ritual and so often feverish morning search for the T bags accompanied by a mock David Bellamy commentary that soon had Michael in splits. No matter how organised I may have been the previous evening the T bags were always certain to evade my attention the following morning.

"Here, in the deep dark depths of this mountain fastness we find the alien species Homo Scouseiens engaged in a frantic foraging hunt for the basic nutrients that will help sustain him throughout the day. Just watch as, like a forgetful squirrel that's lost his nuts, he searches desperately, returning time after time in a frenzied exploration of the hidden cache, known to us as a backpack, seeking that elusive sachet of dried, chopped leaves that are so crucial to his very survival. Driven by an unyielding instinct to seek out the life sustaining leaf referred to as "Earl Grey" all else is cast aside in a mêlée of whirling limbs as pans and dishes are scattered asunder. Here on this planet called Earth, this is what passes as "intelligent life"! How did they ever come this far?

Eventually the T bags put in an appearance and we sat on our borrowed camp chairs and enjoyed a relaxing breakfast in the warm morning sunshine. Our last day of freedom! We took our time packing up camp and after lunch set off on the gentle, but uphill 2.5km to Salardu, reintroduced once again to our monstrous packs. It was a hot afternoon and despite the relatively modest nature of this short walk we struggled after our week of lethargy. We trudged into Salardu village square in a lather of sweat and being too early for the refugio had no choice but to spend the rest of the afternoon sipping cold beer at a deserted pavement bar.

Keith arrived around 6pm at which stage we all went and booked into the refugio. It was good to see him and the new supply of foods that he'd brought along although I was disappointed the he had seemingly disregarded my request for the masseuse! The evening was spent chatting and planning the resumption of our trek, first over dinner and then back at the bar in the village square. The next section of the HRP from Salardu to Hospitalet pres l'Andorra is described by Ton Joosten as "by far the hardest of all", and we were soon to find out why. It was to turn out to be a section of the walk without compromise in wild country with little in the way of civilisation and only one manned refuge, Certascan at the end of day 3. As we were to discover the opportunity to replenish food stocks was certainly limited, however we would at least have the benefit of Keiths' support for the next 2-3 days. This would allow us a relatively gentle reintroduction to the HRP as he would be able to transport the majority of our kit while he was around, allowing us to travel light with just 'daysacks'. This would really help with my leg, lessening the load and strain on my thigh. With all of this in mind we slept well in real beds for the first time in a week that night, content in the anticipation of our 'return to action'.

## Day 30 Monday 31st July Salardu to Alos de Isil

Our day dawned grey and misty at 5.45am. We set off with our unbelievably light back packs up through the deserted alleys and streets of Salardu. Our trek today entailed a total of 1500m of ascent and a similar amount of descent and ranked as one of the toughest on the trek, even by HRP standards. It passed through pathless sections of remote and mountainous terrain, including a particularly large and awkward boulder field.

A grey mist filled the Aran Valley that morning as we slowly made our way up and out of Salardu on stony tracks and through farmstead pastures towards the small hamlet of Bagergue which stood guard on the hillside overlooking its larger neighbour. The blanket of mist shrouded the landscape and our passage was soon lost behind us denying us the prospect of the no doubt fine views back across the Aran valley.

The directions in the guide book were good and the mist presented no real difficulties with navigation as we passed through the sleeping Bagergue onto the open hillside high above the villages of Tredos and Vacqueira in the upper Aran hidden somewhere below our feet in the damp, grey murk. This was a gentle introduction to the days walk with easy loads and a steady ascent on mostly good and well graded dirt tracks. All was going smoothly until our track crossed the strip of tarmac road leading to the ski resort of Plan de Beret where we encountered a sign informing us that the next section of path was closed due to an avalanche. We could always resort to using the road. Both it and us were heading to the Plan de Beret, but hey, we were here for adventure and negotiating a landslide devastated path seemed to fit that category, so, ignoring the sign we pressed on regardless. Anyway, the road clearly zig-zagged too much, flattening the gradient, ok, but increasing the distance fivefold.

It wasn't long before we encountered the section of path the signs had been referring to. A large slice of the hillside had fallen away to the river, some hundred feet or more below, taking some 30m of path with it, exposing an extremely steep and what appeared a very loose and unstable slope in its wake. A huge scoop of hillside both above and below the path had parted company with the rest of the mountain and left a yawning void behind. It looked quite intimidating and we hesitated on the last remnants of stable path before stepping forward. Immediately I sent a cascade of rubble, earth and stones tumbling down to the water below and it was only the use of my trekking poles that prevented me going with them. I froze, awaiting the onset of some secondary landslip, but it didn't happen and slope settled down again after what seemed an eternity. We resumed our passage across the void and after relocating what were probably several tonnes of rock and gravel further downhill in the course of our stuttering traverse we managed to reach the other side without serious mishap. Pebbles continued to skitter downwards behind us as we stepped back onto the more stable path.

Continuing upwards we soon rejoined the tarmac road we had crossed earlier and as the gradient eased we followed its meandering course across the flat and featureless Plan de Beret. It was here where we broke through the mist which had enveloped us all morning and the day was transformed into one of uninterrupted blue sky. This could hardly have been better timed since we were about to enter a pathless wilderness which certainly did not need the added confusion of impenetrable mist in order to bring about the disorientation of those who ventured therein.

The road ended at a large car park containing the vehicles of a handful of day trippers. From there our route became confused amongst the paraphernalia of ski tows, chair lifts, deserted bars and empty buildings of the winter resort of Baqueira-Beret through which we threaded our way and soon found a short stretch of dirt road referred to in the guidebook. After probably no more than a hundred metres of this last remnant of human influence we abandoned the track and stepped into a different world. A vague line of flattened grass disclosed our route straight ahead and into the mountains. We pressed on uphill and soon lost sight of the last signs of civilisation below. The path became faint and intermittent on the rough and sparsely vegetated stony ground as we made our way up the valley of the Arreu Malo towards our next landmark, the dam of the Estany de Baciver, where we took a long overdue rest after three and a half hours walking so far. The dam containing the Estany de Baciver had been constructed in the summer of 1990 extending a formerly natural, smaller glacial lake into the large reservoir that now filled the valley floor.

The day had become hot and dry since the earlier dispersal of the mist and we took the opportunity to break out the camping stove and brew up a couple of mugs of our now customary Earl Grey tea. The muesli bars we snacked on provided a much needed energy boost but I personally could have easily eaten ten or more. We would get used to sparingly eking out our provisions over the next few weeks. Burning twice the calories we consumed. It was the 100% guaranteed get-slim, fat loss diet but I couldn't see it catching on some how!

We still had over 500m of ascent before reaching the days highest point, the Tuc de Marimanya at 2662m. It may not sound much but 500m of ascent is a long way up when viewed from below. We couldn't see Marimanya from our resting point at the dam but the surrounding summits of Tuc dera Lanca and Cap de Vaqueira were of similar height and towered above where we sat. Resumption of the walk saw us ascending through an area of rough scrub of stunted rhododendron interspersed with an ever diminishing scattering of native pines. The path, as was, had become more and more intermittent until finally giving out completely just before we reached a large basin containing a beautiful collection of small tarns, including the two larger Lacs de Nant de Baciver, referred to as the Estanys Rosari de Baciver by Mr Joosten, where the vegetation was reduced to a basic ground cover of grass and low level shrubs. Beyond the lakes our onward progress was barred by a wall of rock and stone that enclosed the basin to the north, south and east. According to the guidebook the recommended route was to pass alongside these two lakes, keeping them on your left and then make straight for the summit of Marimanya over rocks and very steep scree with no path. The prospect of this direct route seemed most improbable from our position some 1000 feet below. In fact the east face of Marimanya looked vertical and completely out of the question. The absence of any path reinforced my doubts and I soon dismissed this as a viable option.

I pointed out to Michael that there appeared to be an easier option whereby we could ascend far less steep grassy slopes immediately to the east towards the Collado dels Estanys de Rosari. This would take us onto the south ridge of Marimanya which we could follow to the summit. An obviously simple and straightforward option. No bloody chance! This was yet another Taylor shortcut in the extensive and much maligned journal of the same name. The trouble I've caused over the years with my bright ideas of "lets go this way, it looks easier, shorter, better, more interesting, etc, etc." This normally translates as more difficult, longer, worse and only more interesting if you happen to be a thrill seeking adrenalin junkie. For the rest of us "more interesting" bit can be replaced by downright bleedin' dangerous, and this was to be no exception.

Following the promised easy and straightforward ascent onto what was a broad and rounded but rough and stony ridge we turned north to ascend the final few hundred feet to the summit. As we approached the summit cone it became apparent that further progress was not going to prove quite so easy. We found ourselves faced with a narrow ridge of shattered rock supported by steep angled slopes of loose scree. Without comment we started a nervous ascent of this latest HRP hurdle, which partly comprised a series of precariously balanced blocks of stone, each of which appeared to have progressively less contact with the rest of the mountain. Some huge blocks rattled and wobbled upon contact, upon which we quickly retreated in search of an alternative route to save bringing the mountain down on our heads. Sometimes there was no alternative and we would clamber on gingerly, stepping on eggshells, fearful for any sign that our foot and handholds would not support us. On occasions we would top out on the apex of the ridge to face maybe ten metres of tightrope walking only to find we had climbed to a false summit from which we must descend once again. We were both so grateful for the light packs we were carrying that day. Our normal loads would have made this section of ridge all the more daunting.

In between the scrambling on bare rock we were forced to follow indistinct stony trails which crossed below vertical slabs beneath the crest, usually to the eastern side of the ridge, and led into cul de sacs from which we were compelled to then escape upwards via dubious loose and shattered rock faces. One of the difficult decisions was whether to stash the trekking poles. They became an encumbrance on the sections of scrambling but then were so vital on the sections of exposed ridge-top walking and on the numerous goat tracks across the east face. We stashed them in our packs after a particularly awkward scramble where it was clear they presented a serious hazard, dangling from our wrists and clanking against the rock and generally getting under our feet as we tried to climb. We wandered all over that bloody ridge as we sought the line of least resistance until suddenly and almost without realising we stepped up onto a point where the ground fell away in all directions. The summit! We were never going to find a better lunch spot.

Peculiarly the HRP, despite its name, does not seek out many Pyrenean summits on its journey from the Atlantic to the Med', preferring to stick mainly to the cols and passes. But here was a summit to savour. The panorama was most stunning and we had it all to ourselves. To the north the nearby border mountains of Mont Vallier and Tuc Mauberme dominate the horizon whilst to the east the mountain we were to skirt tomorrow, Mont Roig, captured the eye. My gaze though was drawn back west towards the high summits we had missed. The Maldeta Massif ,including Pic d'Aneto, the highest in the Pyrenees and its extensive northern glacier could clearly be seen no more than some 30-40km distant, but 4 days walking in HRP terms. It was an area to which I knew I was compelled to return one day. This walk would never be complete without this missing link. (That's a reference to the section we missed out, not me!) But even then the whole principle of starting at one end and finishing at the other and completing everything in between in one go, a single attempt, had been compromised. Our efforts would, in my eyes anyway, remain forever tainted by omitting this High Pyrenees section between Héas and Salardu, and there was only ever one way that I would be able to satisfy this niggling disquiet.

Lunch and sightseeing over we picked our way down the steep easterly ridge of Marimanya, trekking poles once again to hand. After a short descent we re-ascended a further satellite top of similar but slightly lesser elevation to Marimanya. On this confined and narrow connecting ridge there were the occasional hints of the passage of previous footfall but upon descent of this second summit we entered an open and featureless stony terrain devoid of any signs of a path. We were now abandoned to find our own way as best we could in a trackless wilderness. The next landmark was the somewhat indistinct Col d'Airoto. When we got there it was clear we had arrived at the col but the absence of any paths, waymarks, cairns or indication whatsoever that anyone had ever been there before us was unnerving but in one way quite exciting. The continual lack of evidence of previous human presence lent an air of mystery and adventure to some of the wilder sections of the HRP. We had already encountered this atmosphere of a remote wilderness on previous sections of the trek, especially during the first week. It was something we were to come up against on many more occasions, especially over the coming week in travelling though this wild Arierge region.

We descended steeply south from the col and stopped to top up our drinks bags at a small stream that formed the outflow from a series of pools that occupied a flat area containing a number of freshwater springs.

We had been consuming water at a rapid rate in the heat and exertion of the day. As we descended further our way ahead was now blocked by an immense boulder field spanning some square kilometre of mountainside. Defended from above by a vertical wall of crags beneath the summit of the Tuc de Bonabé and below by the waters of the Estany d'Airoto there was no option other than to head straight into its midst. At the far south end of the lake, probably a mile distant, stood a manned refuge, avoided by the HRP and ignored by Mr Jooosten. This would have provided a welcome end to what had already been a long and demanding day but didn't figure on the itinerary probably because it was slightly off the main path and wasn't at a convenient position to fit in with the following stage of the route, leaving an otherwise impossibly long day for tomorrow. Anyway the Airoto refuge was not on our programme for today but the Airoto boulder field was.

Boulders of every shape and size were scattered in a random meleé before us and forward progress became extremely tortuous. Every 100m covered on the map was matched with probably four or five times that distance on the ground as we laboriously negotiated up, over, around, under and through this frustrating rock maze. Sometimes we would clamber to the top of an enormous slab only to be confronted by a ten foot drop and have to retrace our steps and find an alternative route. For some reason we found ourselves separated as we each sought to find the easiest line through this rock jungle. Although we were probably never more than about fifty yards apart there were long periods when we completely lost sight of each other for minutes on end. I would liken it to being in a very small boat in a tempestuous ocean where at the top of each wave (boulder) you may briefly have some notion of where you were and in which direction you were headed before dropping into the next trough and being surrounded by anonymous grey walls of water (rock) once again. My paternal instinct kicked in and I would stand on some prominent point waiting for Michael to re-appear from some nearby hidden rock canyon, gripped with an irrational fear that he may have fallen into some bottomless crevasse between the rocks. Each time I was reassured when I caught sight of his brimmed hat bobbing up from behind some slab in an entirely different position to where I had anticipated he would appear. This game of cat and mouse continued for well over an hour.

It was a relief to eventually emerge from the clutches of the seemingly endless boulder field onto the side of a rocky ridge, just below the Collada del Clot de Moredo, where we were looking for yet another "rather vague track", according to the guidebook. We continued upwards towards the col and did eventually encounter our vague track which had an appearance of what seemed to once have been a well constructed path which over the years had fallen into disuse. This vague track led us over the col and down into the Moredo valley until its vagueness reduced to a point of complete oblivion. Nevertheless the route finding was straightforward as we headed down to a tiny tarn called La Basseta from which the outfall disappeared below ground beneath a narrow valley choked with rocks. We followed the valley gently downhill the beneath the white limestone cliffs of the Pic de Quenca on our right and the path slowly re-established itself until it became clear. The Barranc de Moredo eventually reappeared at the surface tumbling away over rocks to our right and the gradient of the ground steepened as we exited the narrow confines of the barranc and the valley floor broadened out beneath us.

We began a steady descent down towards Alos de Isil, our days' destination on an improving path where we were treated to a scintillating spectacle of nature. The hillside sprung to life with a profusion of colourful butterflies and moths and what appeared to be a sort of gliding bright red grasshopper or cricket which whirred in to the air at our every footfall. Each step induced an aerial display of sound and colour as the ground came alive at our feet. The myriad of blues, reds, yellows purples and every shade of every colour in the spectrum was a wonder to behold.

The entertainment unfortunately ceased upon our arrival at a dirt road which zigged and zagged in long sweeping curves at a gentle gradient downhill towards a small gathering of farmhouses at Bordes de Moredo below us. After enjoying the initial easy gradient, which was far less punishing on the knees, we grew impatient at the dirt roads reluctance to descend and we took a short-cut down through the long grass of the open hillside once again releasing hoards of dozing fritillaries into the air. For some reason I had made the assumption that this dirt road would take us all the way down to our destination of Alos de Isil. Lulled by the warm afternoon sun into an air of complacency I not consulted the guidebook in detail and upon reaching the buildings of the Bordes de Moredo was abruptly awakened from our leisurely amble down this easy dirt road when it stopped and dumped us in a pathless field some 430metres above the village of Isil. A brief consultation with the guidebook confirmed that we were pretty much now expected to make our own way down the now very steep hillside from here. Following the directions we found ourselves on a very steep ridge between two ravines, picking our way as best we could along a series of narrow parallel cattle tracks which we threaded together in a home made descent route until they led steeply down into a dense and tangled forest of small broadleaved trees to emerge at the more northerly of the two ravines. We crossed this almost dry streambed and picked up one of a number of further cattle tracks which just became lost amongst a maze of terraced fields and dry stone walls with the remnants of the occasional long ruined building and livestock pens scattered amongst the wooded hillside.

According to the guidebook we were supposed to find an obvious path near a small dam. We didn't even get to the river, let alone find a dam, as we were diverted across the hillside by walls and impenetrable hedgerows of thorns. The closer we approached Alos de Isil the more elusive it became and I was convinced that we were probably trespassing as we resorted to clambering over numerous stone walls in a now aimless meandering search for something resembling a path. After endless 'dead ends' and changes of direction we eventually gravitated to the lowest point of the valley and stumbled upon the 'obvious path' that had so long eluded us. A few minutes later this duly decanted us into the deserted village of Alos de Isil. More by luck than design we had once again reached our intended destination. We wandered into an empty village square where we rested in the shade beneath a sort of timber shelter, gorging ourselves on fresh cold water from the nearby fountain whilst awaiting Keith's arrival.

I began a series of gentle 'warm down' stretching exercises, pleased in the knowledge that my leg had survived the rigours of the day on this our reintroduction to serious walking. This had been a regular routine throughout the walk which I found reduced the stiffness that would otherwise take over my limbs following such exertions. One of the exercises was to gently pull the heel of each foot up to the backside which had the effect of stretching the thigh muscle. My thigh clearly wasn't ready for such a stern test and immediately let me know.

"Aarghh" I screeched as sharp pain shot through my left thigh. I let go of my foot immediately and stood there frozen awaiting the onset of the muscle strain that had plagued me previously…nothing.

"Oh my god, I won't be trying that again in a hurry."
Michael looked on concerned.

"You OK?"

"Yeh, I must have just twanged something but it seems to have gone now," I responded.

"You're such a drama queen!"

"Thanks son."

Keith soon turned up after having ventured miles further up the tarmac road that threaded its way north up the Noguera Pallaresa in search of our exit point from the hills. Our communication skills were questionable at times and this was typical of the sort of misunderstandings which occurred between us.

We had been joined moments previously by a French guy who was also doing the HRP, but by the somewhat different route as prescribed by George Veron. This route had avoided Salardu and stuck to the high ground of the water table passing to the south east of the town and crossing the Port de la Bonaigua, the more natural but ignored border line between France and Spain at the head of the Val d'Aran. The guy was probably in his mid to late fifties, tanned and sinewy and looked like he had spent a long time in the mountains. Anyway the poor bloke was very hungry as he hadn't been able to stock up on any food for several days and asked us if we had any spare bread and cheese. We didn't have any food left at all, having only carried day sacks, but Keith's arrival brought a whole new larder of provisions and we were able to send our fellow traveller away fully laden with several days worth of grub, including the bread and cheese he had asked for and numerous items of fruit. He offered to pay but Keith was having none of it. The look of gratitude on his face was payment enough, as he thanked us repeatedly before heading on his way.

Our intention was to bivvy that night about a mile up the valley from Alos de Isil next to the river. According to Mr Joosten there were apparently "some fine places [for camping] to be found" alongside the road. The availability of the wheeled transport was quite a temptation but despite my tiredness I could not forego the principle of walking the whole route (notwithstanding the bit we had missed before Salardu) and set off up the road. I conceded to having my pack transported ahead of me which didn't feel as though it was too great a compromise but could not have lived with myself had I not arrived at our evenings destination on my own two feet. Michael on the other hand had no such qualms and promptly dived into the passenger seat.

"See ya later sucker," he chided as I tramped off shaking my head at my son's easy surrender to convenience.

Some twenty minutes later I strided into the small field next to the river to find we weren't the first to discover this idyllic little camping spot with three other tents already pitched, each of them with accompanying cars. We pitched our tent on the riverbank while Keith opted for a berth in the car. After a refreshing bathe in the cold clear waters of the Noguera Pallaresa, whose origins derived from flat ground around the Plan de Beret ski resort we had passed through earlier in the day, we took advantage of our transport and drove down to the town of Esterri d'Areu for dinner.

Our destination was the terminus of Le Chemin de la Liberte, an escape route over the Pyrenees for POW's, French men and women and allied airmen and Jewish refugees during World War 2. The starting point was over in France at the town of St Girons from where the high mountain route threaded its way over the Massif de Couserans to the high Col de Pecouche at the border and so on down into Spain and freedom. Official statistics tell us that between 1940 and 1944 there were 33,000 successful escapes by Frenchmen along the entire length of the Pyrenees. Of these 782 escaped over the mountain peaks of the Arierge, the high point being when there were 113 successful evasions along or close to the Chemin de la Liberte.

Several other escape trails were established near St Girons, each one known only to its particular guide or passeur. Neighbouring towns and villages such as Foix, Tarascon, Aulus-les-Bains, Massat, Castillon, Seix and Seintein, all had a network of invisible mountain routes leading upwards to the Spanish frontier.

But at the beginning of 1943, due to increased German surveillance and often betrayal by Frenchmen who worked for the feared and hated Vichy-run paramilitary force known as La Milice, ambushes along many of these trails became more and more common. In all, more than a hundred passeurs were arrested and deported or shot out of hand as they tried to flee across the mountain slopes.

However, even during the years of high surveillance, the Saint Girons-Esterri escape route via the soaring massif of Mont Valier stayed operational and remained so until the end of the war.

I'm not sure just how far our own journey was that evening but the tortuous nature of the narrow and twisting road seemed to drag on for an eternity. It clearly wasn't long enough though because upon arrival at the town around 7pm we were still an hour early for dinner. True to tradition the Spanish evening meal did not start until 8pm, a custom to which my body clock had great difficulty in adjusting. Michael and I managed to procure a pre meal appetizer of a 12 inch pizza, each! They were delicious and had no apparent impact upon either mine or Michael's appetites as we both ordered our customary steaks from the main menu followed by an ice cream dessert as Keith looked on in abject wonder at our capacity to consume food. I did point out to him that we had foregone the official starters.

Back at our campsite the markedly more forgiving ground offered by the soft earth and alluvial deposits of the Pallaresa promised a rather more comfortable night than those experienced on the 5millimetres of turf covered solid granite at Arties. I doubt whether this made any difference to Michael though who slept the deep and uninterrupted sleep of the adolescent male which, from my experience is as close as the human species gets to hibernation. I on the other hand was destined to suffer continuous sleepless nights under canvass. My discomfort sleeping on the ground was seemingly unavoidable but varied in proportion to:-

a) The hardness of the ground,

b) Level of prior alcohol consumption.

Unfortunately there were to be very limited occasions when the pain threshold was ever raised to such a level by b) that it would override the discomfort induced by a). And tonight wasn't to be one of them!

## Day 31, Tuesday 1ˢᵗ August, Alos de Isil to Gruas

By 5.45am the inclination to remain in the warmth of my sleeping bag was overcome by the desire to end my proximity and contact with the not so soft ground, and I was desperate for a piss. Following a frugal breakfast of tea and a couple of snack bars, we set off at 6.55am, once again with our light day sacks, north up the tarmac road with the Noguera Palerosa on our right. After some ten minutes or so we came to a dip in the road where a bridge, the Palenca de la Pena, crossed the river. Beyond the bridge a dirt road zigged its way up the open hillside past a series of barns and farm buildings. Several hundred feet above us a group a four walkers were just disappearing into the woodland above the last of the farm buildings, probably some 10-15 minutes ahead of us. Peculiarly, we didn't see them again that day.

It was very warm once again as we left Keith behind and set off on our ascent into our next mountain wilderness, zagging up the dirt road past the seemingly empty farm buildings. The sun was still hidden in the eastern sky behind the mass of the Mont Roig and Serra de Pilas mountain ranges as we began the arduous 1200metre ascent to our first col of three that day, the Coll de la Cornella. Our ultimate objective was, uniquely for us, some five miles beyond the recommended finish point suggested in the guide book, which ended the day at the remote and unmanned refuge of Enric Pujol. We were intending to continue past the refuge, also known as the Refugi Mont Roig, on down the Torrent de la Roia de Mallas to the small settlement of Gruas, a mile or so and some 500feet below the HRP, to relative the civilisation of a camp site in the valley of the Riu de Tavascan, where we would once again meet up with Keith.

Above the last of the stone farm buildings we soon disappeared into the forest on a trace of a path that threaded its way through a tangle of trees and undergrowth. The route was narrow, faint and obscure at times hinting once again that this was a path in very little use. After about an hour of steady ascent, enclosed within a screen of trees we exited into an open valley of grass and rocks with the Barranc de Comamala on our right. We were alone. There was no sign of the group of people we had observed entering the forest ahead of us earlier. The path all but disappeared completely as we pushed on over open ground to cross the tumbling waters of the Comomala where it split into three streams. The slope steepened here as a re-established path zigzagged up over rocks and through a blanket of pink flowering alpenrose, alongside a plummeting and delightful waterfall. We ascended between rocks, hauling ourselves up having to frequently use our hands to overcome the otherwise big steps that legs alone could not conquer. It was here that I managed to snap one of Michaels trekking poles as it wedged in a hidden crevice. How I happened to be using one of Michael's as opposed to my own poles I can't recall but it was rendered useless. Michael wasn't impressed! I sent a text to Keith requesting a replacement if he happened to pass by an outdoor shop and we pressed on.

The terrain became rough and rocky as we passed by a small isolated tarn. Leaving the last remnants of hardy vegetation behind us we wandered higher and higher over barren expanses of rocks and boulder fields. The path wasn't easy to follow being marked with stone cairns that were sometimes difficult to spot amongst a sea of rocks. The path, as was, twisted and turned to avoid the most awkward sections of rocks and boulders and we had to check our route frequently. Such was the confusion of the terrain we were forced to refer to the compass on numerous occasions in order to confirm we were headed in the right direction. There appeared to be several alternatives so far as passes through the Serra de Pillas ridge was concerned, each of which appeared as difficult and implausible as the next. We were headed for the Coll de Cornella, an unlikely route when viewed from below, which would take us up a very steep slope of what appeared to be quite loose scree. The scree was as it appeared, loose and steep, and we sent endless rocks crashing down to the valley floor below as we skirted the top of the slope beneath a vertical cliff face. As the rocks constantly slid from beneath our feet the trekking poles became crucial in stopping us sliding down with them. As the effort of ascending and the danger of sliding into oblivion increased so did my breathing and heart rate until I became enclosed in my own exclusive world of survival, focusing on staying on my feet and accompanied by the dum, dum, dum, dum of a pulse that echoed around my head and rippled the veins in my sweat drenched temples.

My concentration was abruptly interrupted by our sudden arrival at the col as we stepped up to yet another horizon where mountains stretched into a distant haze beyond vision. We lingered at the col for maybe twenty minutes or so taking in this new panorama. No photograph could ever capture the true beauty of such a scene and our eyes scanned and re-scanned the endless folds and creases of seemingly infinite mountain ranges as we struggled to take in such awe inspiring grandeur from our lonely and lofty perch. The Coll de Cornella was a narrow notch in the ridge of the Serra de Pilas which itself was just one of five mighty treelike roots which fanned out from the summit of Mont Roig to the north. The ground on both sides of the col fell away very steeply which induced a sense of vertigo and our descent route wasn't visible from where we sat. We could however see our next landmark, the Estany de Tartera.

As we descended from the col I once again marvelled at the vision and sheer optimism of the person who had first conspired to designate this as a route where it was somehow possible for pedestrians to tread. Its inception must have appeared inconceivable to most normal folk! The 'path' made a traversing descent east north east across a precipitous mountainside of rock and grass where our hands once again were constantly in use as we picked our way down to the lake.

The Estany de Tartera was located at the head of a remote and unfrequented valley and was a silent and peaceful place enclosed on 3 sides by the towering Mont Roig and two of its five ridges. I had the distinct impression that this obscure and isolated cul de sac didn't receive many visitors other than the seasonal trickle of HRP wanderers who passed by. The waters of the lake were flat and still, reflecting the surrounding cliffs in a perfect symmetry. We passed on by unnoticed and headed up to our second col, the Coll de Curios. We had become so attuned to every step of ascent that we knew immediately that the 35metres referred to by Ton Joosten as the difference in height between the lake and the col was undoubtedly wrong. We felt cheated by such errors. Every inch of altitude was hard won and this so called thirty five metres was more like 100. The unusual thing about the Coll de Curios, as well as the fact that it was more than 35m above the Estany de Tartera, was that we continued to ascend once we reached the top, hence the name? We continued upwards peculiarly passing numerous white cattle along the way. They seemed entirely out of place at some 2400 metres up in such a remote corner of the Pyrenees. The nearest farms were some 1000m (3300feet) down into Spain and at least 7km distant. Were these animals lost? Surely there was equally succulent grass in far more accessible and hospitable sections of the valley lower down? They were unperturbed by our presence and continued grazing as we pressed on to our planned lunch stop at the lovely Bassa de Curios, which at 2490m was only 120m below our highest point of the day at the Col de Calberante.

Upon arrival at the lake we removed our boots and socks and sat at the edge of the cool clear waters, dousing our feet and munching through our much welcomed lunch, in which Keith had delightfully incorporated the luxury of a chicken leg each. Wow, a banquet! Our toes shared the waters with an array of frogs and tadpoles as we savoured the comfort of our sun-bathed picnic spot. Lunch stops were never long enough and the reintroduction of our feet to socks and boots made the end of this one less welcome than most. We hiked up the final rocky but relatively easy slopes to the big open Coll de Calberante where we were surprised to encounter a large group of ten or more Spanish walkers. These were the first people we had encountered in the mountains for two days. I felt a certain indignation at having to share this landscape with others. They were intruding into our space; a world which had been our exclusive playground since leaving Salardu. We didn't linger at the col, despite the fantastic views all around, choosing instead abandon our fellow travellers and to press on down towards the large and distinctly turquoise Estany Major de la Gallina.

It was very hot walking in the full heat of the afternoon sun and the attraction of the lake was too much to resist, for me anyway. My impromptu bathing session was short lived though. The shock of an instantaneous reduction in external body temperature of probably some 30 degrees was rather more than I'd bargained for and refreshing though it was, it was only ever going to be brief in the circumstances! Michael was satisfied to merely spectate once he had witnessed my sharp intake of breath reaction upon resurfacing from my ill conceived plunge into the icy depths of the lake.

After the swim we continued down towards the Enric Pujol refuge over a peculiar landscape of smooth and polished grey rocks. There was no path as such but the profusion of stone cairns made for a web of alternative routes. The Enric Pujol Refugi was located on a bluff at the eastern side of the most northerly of the Gallina Lakes but our way forward was blocked by the deep channel of the outflow from the lake. The opportunities to cross this narrow stretch of water were limited before it entered a narrow and inaccessible steep sided gorge. I would guess it was probably some five to six feet across and a similar depth so it formed quite an intimidating barrier to onward progress. We pondered around the southern bank of this veritable water jump looking for a weakness, a narrow point or a spot where it was shallow enough to wade through. There was no apparent chink in the armour. We eventually opted for the first and most obvious crossing point which involved a standing leap of some six feet onto rough and uneven rocks on a quite steep bank. This sort of gap would not pose a problem on open ground, with a run up and a level landing point but this was rather different. I opted to go first and after what seemed like an eternity I finally leapt across the void and after a slight wobble on landing regained my balance and turned to assist Michael. He decided to toss his pack across first for me to catch in the expectation this would improve his prospects of staying dry. It was probably only around 7 kilos but I would need to catch it due to the steep gradient of the northerly bank. He took up position and we jointly gave a count of three as he swung the pack and I readied myself for the catch.

"One, two…splash!"

"Jeeeese, what the bloody hell did you do that for?" I gasped in astonishment as the backpack bobbed in the slow flowing water, half submerged in the centre of the channel after Michael had seemingly changed his mind in mid throw, and simply let go. He had somehow been gripped by uncertainty at the most inopportune moment.

"I don't know," he stammered.

"I wasn't sure if you meant 1-2-3-throw or 1-2 then throw and sort of had this moment of doubt at just the wrong time."

"Oh my gawd, you bleedin' berk!"

"Hold on lets see if I can reach it with my trekking pole before it sinks completely or gets swept down the gorge," I said.

I managed to hook a trekking pole under the shoulder strap and haul the sopping pack onto the bank as it slowly exuded air and began to sink.

"Let's see if you're a bit more successful than your backpack," I mocked as he stood nervously on the opposite bank.

After a few seconds of dithering he made the leap successfully and we gathered our packs and set off again without further incident, with Michael leaving a slug-like wet trail of water behind him from his wet pack.

We didn't bother dropping in to the Enric Pujol Refugi despite our concerted efforts to arrive at its doorstep, so to speak. Once again I think the extra effort of the fifty feet of ascent up to the hut was sufficient deterrent. Unjustified effort for limited reward! We skirted around the promontory which housed the refuge and headed downhill following a line of stone cairns towards the Estany de Lavera. We had now stepped into Day 27 of the guide book and were chipping away at tomorrows walk, albeit in the form of a generally gentle descent down the valley of the Torrent de la Roia de Mollas. We were headed for a car park marked on the map north west of Noarre where we planned to meet Keith who would drive us down to the campsite at Gruas.

Our avoidance of this remote and unmanned refuge Enric Pujol and the presence of Keiths support gave a different feeling to these first two days of this most wild and inaccessible section of the HRP. Whilst we were both grateful the lightening of our packs and the benefits this brought there was a price to pay for this convenience. We had temporarily avoided the hardships that the Arierge held for those who ventured into its wilderness. We had the benefit of civilisation and restaurant food at the end of each of these two days as opposed to the more spartan existence we would otherwise have experienced. Without the benefit of dispensing with two thirds of the weight in our packs we would have struggled to complete the first day at all, and the likelihood is this second day would have ended at the Enric Pujol, in a remote wilderness beneath the towering ramparts of Mont Roig. Keith's arrival had softened the impact of these first two days of this the most demanding section of the HRP, though I wasn't altogether sure this was a good thing.

It was a pleasant walk down the Torrent de la Roia de Mollas on a predominantly good path with a mostly steady gradient throughout. We encountered a newly built stone cabane, not shown on the map or referred to in the guide, about halfway down the valley. I presume it was to provide refuge for a local farmer in tending the herds of livestock that seemed to wander these mountains. It's presence seemed alien in this otherwise untouched landscape although I was impressed by its construction and wondered how? How had the materials been delivered? Was it stone from the immediate surroundings or was it dropped in by helicopter? Did the builders camp nearby during construction or did they have to walk in and back out each day? There was no vehicle access. The nearest you could get a vehicle was some thousand feet and probably

2-3 miles further down the valley. It remained to us one of life's little mysteries.

As we dropped into the lower reaches of the valley we entered a small forest of mostly pine and birch trees where for some reason my fear of being confronted by a bear returned to haunt me. The Ariege region was one of the areas where the brown bear had been reintroduced and this desolate valley seemed the ideal haunt for them. Perhaps it was the claustrophobic effect brought about by being hemmed in by the trees but I could envisage this forest as being the sort of place where you could round a corner in the path and be confronted by a large hairy mammal with a ravenous appetite. But then that could just as equally apply to the bear!

No bears turned up and we eventually stepped out of the forest into a clearing which led us down to a footbridge across the Reiu del Port which descended from the high pass of the Port de Tavascan on the French border to the north. The path turned south through birch trees and soon brought us to a dirt road which led down towards Tavascan and more importantly to our rendezvous point at the car park some half mile or so down the track. We reached the so called car park where there were no cars and no Keith. A dirt road led down from the car park on a course of sharp hairpin bends on its journey down to the valley floor. There was no tarmac surface up here which was the impression given from the positioning of the car park symbol on the map. It was a car park for 4x4's and all terrain vehicles only at the end of a steep, rough and winding dirt road. Disappointed that our taxi had not arrived we plodded on downhill, weary and footsore, down an interminable series of hairpin bends until we were finally deposited onto the tarmac road in the tiny hamlet of Quanca where we were greeted by a host of barking dogs at a roadside farm. I gave Keith a ring to see if he could pick us up. The road levelled out as we reached the valley floor and we trudged off in the hot afternoon sun along the remaining mile to Gruas. We were both exhausted and after half a mile or so very pleased to see Keith in the car even if we were only some 500m from the campsite at the time.

Much to our delight the Gruas campsite was quite civilised with hot showers and a restaurant and bar. I even took the opportunity to wash some of my smelly clothes which I'm sure was a welcome relief to Michael, having to share a tent with me. Keith had managed to purchase 2 new trekking poles one of which I used to replace the Leki pole I had unknowingly snapped the tip off some weeks earlier. This pole had progressively grown shorter where the soft plastic bottom was eroded at an accelerated rate through its unintended contact with the ground. I don't know how long I had been walking with this un-tipped pole but it wouldn't have lasted much longer in this punishing terrain. As it progressively shortened I probably would have developed a tilt! We enjoyed and excellent meal, with red wine and preceded and followed by numerous beers in the site bar/restaurant. So much so that for once I actually got a decent night's sleep under canvas.

# Day 32, Wednesday 2<sup>nd</sup> August. Gruas to Certascan

Despite an early rise at around 6.30am it took us an age to pack up all of our kit. We had hoped for at least one further days support from Keith but such was the remote nature of the region we were about to enter there would be no more convenient road heads at the end of our walks for at least the next five days. Our destination today, the Refugi de Certascan, was some 250m above and a mile distant from the nearest 'road', and based upon our experience yesterday that so called road may not be something suitable for a normal car. Even so it would have been too much to expect Keith to lug probably 60lb of kit 250m up to the refuge even had he been able to drive to the car park marked on the map below Certascan. Today we would be reintroduced to the dubious pleasure of fully laden backpacks once more. Our tardiness was probably as much down to a reluctance to shoulder these heavy loads once again as it was down to an alcohol induced hangover from the previous evening. We spent the morning consuming endless cups of tea and generally lounging around delaying the inevitable. We eventually shifted ourselves at 9.45am and Keith gave us a lift a mile back up the valley to the start of the dirt road back up to the HRP. We may have shaved some 4 miles and 600m of descent from today's route by continuing onto Gruas yesterday but we had replaced with an additional 200m of ascent on what was promising to be a very hot day.

We parted company with Keith who had a long drive back to Tarragona for his evening flight. We were sorry to see him leave. His support had been priceless but we were on our own now. The remaining fifteen walking days would be unaided. We were about to face the most demanding and by far the toughest section of the trek alone and unsupported once again.

According to our map there was a direct route up to the hamlet of Noarre which would save us retracing our steps back up the rough switchback dirt road to the HRP. Could we find it? Could we hell! We spent probably half an hour dithering around in the valley searching for any hint or semblance of a path. I was convinced that in the absence of a road there must be a reasonably substantial path or track linking the isolated community of Noarre with the valley below, but, if there was it, was not where it was shown on the map and in the end we gave up and reverted back to the known route back up the dirt road. The weight of the packs made an immediate impact. We had 5 days worth of food and of course all of our camping kit once again and I feared the strain would be too much for my dodgy leg. With each step I could feel the strain on my thigh muscles as we ascended up through the forest.

Noarre was a peculiar place in that it was cut off from civilisation by all means except on foot. I was convinced there would be a vehicle track of some description but no. The only means of access was to walk in via the narrow path of the HRP. It was incredible to realise that this little community of maybe ten or so properties had remained isolated from the outside world in such a way. As we wandered past the seemingly deserted stone buildings, some of them recently rebuilt and renovated there wasn't a sign of a single soul. In former times this had probably been a self sufficient little rural community quietly co-existing in harmony with its remote environment, its inhabitants eking out a meagre living from the land. Now, well it was still quiet for sure but I suspect the newly rebuilt stone properties were probably holiday homes. There was no evidence of a rustic way of life being pursued in Noarre any more, it was just too perfect!

As we passed on above Noarre we met a young English guy, Richard, who was miraculously also walking the HRP. Only the third such person we had met in over a month. He was sat upon the remnants of a rather dilapidated dry stone wall routing through the contents of his pack. It became clear immediately he was an avid photographer. Anyone of the frame of mind to lump a tripod up and down these mountains had to be regarded as either mentally unstable or devoted to their cause beyond all redemption. He had spent the night up at the unmanned refugio at Enric Pujol and was headed to Certsacan, the same as us. After a brief chat we left him wrestling with his tripod to enable him to take perfect photos of the perfect Noarre just below as we headed off up the narrow stony path into open birch woodland steadily ascending above the Riu de Noarre. The dominant feature of the morning ascent was the heat. We were both sweating profusely as we laboured onwards and upwards on the well defined path through the tree clad slopes on the sunny western side of the valley. The tree canopy offered some respite from the intense sun but there was no breeze and it was like walking in an oven. The path zig-zagged up away from the river as we slowly gained height. After a morning of hard toil in demanding conditions we emerged from the dreary slog through the woods at a most enchanting little cascade and pool where we stopped for lunch. We lingered long at this most exquisite of lunch stops and removing our boots sat for probably an hour or more soothing our battered feet in the cool crystal waters of this high mountain pool. This was an altitude of some 1900m still some 700m below our high point of the day at the Col de Certascan. We measured every day in this way, by the amount of ascent remaining. I often found myself counting down the metres as we slowly picked our way up mountainsides. This is not to say that I wasn't enjoying what we were doing but there was an aspect of our trek that simply required you to put your head down and grind out the miles. It was at the stops in between such as this lunch where you could then look back and savour the fruits of your labours. As with many mountain journeys I often found that the enjoyment was retrospective. Looking back it is easy to disregard the aching shoulders under a burdensome back pack or the bruised and sore feet that so tormented you at the time, choosing instead to recall the more romantic aspect of your trip.

One thing that did strike me this particular day was that we were now all alone. Keith had departed back to the UK. There would be no supply parties coming out to meet us and share our load any more. The remainder of our trip to Banyuls sur Mer was to be unaided. No feather-light day sacks for us now. We must face the remaining miles of our journey with a full load and relying solely upon ourselves. The thought of that left me with a feeling of isolation, and, despite Michael's company, even a little alone. We were now on the 3rd day of the section of the walk described by Ton Joosten as "by far the hardest of all," and it was now down to our own wit and resilience to see this adventure to its ultimate conclusion.

With some reluctance we departed from our beautiful oasis-like lunch spot and leaving the tree line behind headed up over steep rock and grass onto a high marshy plain where a stream meandered gently in the afternoon sun across a flat field of sedge and grass. The overgrown remnants of an old shepherds cabana which overlooked this tranquil pasture were now home to a gang of sun bathing lizards which skittered away into hidden crevices upon our approach. The route beyond here steepened as we clambered up a steep and rocky slope decorated with the sun-bleached stumps of numerous dead trees before reaching a series of small, remote and lonely mountain lakes. The terrain transformed to that of rough bare rock as we plodded ever upwards to finally reach a small a small gap in the ridge, the Col de Certascan and the wonder of another new horizon. The descent from the col was surprisingly gentle as we meandered our way down towards the azure waters of the large Estany de Certascan. The guy we had met earlier, Richard, had caught up with us while we had rested at the col and we walked and chatted together.

It soon became clear that his obvious enjoyment of photography, as witnessed earlier above Noarre, was actually more of an obsession. It turned out that a few days earlier, when faced with the dilemna that he must lighten his load or fail in reaching his objective of Hospitalet pres L'Andorra, he opted to ditch his tent and cooking utensils in favour of his beloved tripod. On other sections of the walk this would be less of an issue, where the abundance of manned refuges provides endless possibilities for hot food and shelter. In this wilderness of the Arierge I wasn't so sure and I could only conclude that he must indeed be mad, although he was good company and apparently quite normal on the outside.

The remaining 2 kilometres to the Refuge de Certascan soon passed and we arrived to join a throng of other walkers drawn to this outpost of civilisation nestling high in this Pyrenean wilderness. It was 3.30pm. I always found it peculiar that you could walk all day and never see another person in these mountains but you were always guaranteed to joined by dozens or sometimes scores of other wanderers at these remote refuges. Where were all these people during the day? I began to wonder if they actually just lived there for the summer and didn't venture out onto the surrounding hills. The refuge was well kitted out and even had the luxury of hot showers which was a welcome sight after our arduous reintroduction to our full backpacks and went a long way to easing the aches and pains of a tough day.

After a relaxing shower followed by a late afternoon siesta we joined the other refugees down at the dinner table, where we were overseen by the refuge's resident mule who peered through the window upon the diners with a most pitiful and sorrowful gaze. As the bread and soup was served he duly pursued what I am certain was a well rehearsed and productive routine of tapping the window with his nose. He achieved his no doubt customary reward as the window was opened and bread rolls were passed out and consumed with a vigour and appetite of .........a horse. As we sat awaiting the main course, lapping up the jugs of red wine that abound at these mountain refuge mealtimes, I began to fantasise about what we may be served up.

"You know what son, I could murder a bloody big plate of sausage and mash with lashings of gravy!" What d'ya think, any chance?"

"Nah, it'll be pasta again with marmot stew."

"Oh gawd, hope it's nothing like that shite we had a Baysellance. Remember, the guy next to me thought it was wonderful and had about 4 plates full. Bet he's still chewing the bleedin remnants of it now."

I couldn't believe it when dinner was served. We were each served an enormous sausage as big as the proverbial knob on the mule outside, which judging from his aroused state, was also excited at the prospect of this main course and was standing patiently at the window awaiting his next feed and sporting an erection the size of my lower arm.

"Didn't think I'd be eating my dinner whilst peering at a donkey's knob!" remarked Richard.

"Wonder where they get these sausages?" asked Michael.

"I think it's a mule," I corrected.

"Don't care what he is he's not getting my bloody sausage!" declared Richard.

As we continued with dinner it began to rain and the mule and his knob disappeared in search of shelter.

## Day 33, Thursday 3rd August.
## Refugi de Certascan to Refugi del Cinquantenari

It was still raining when we got up. It hadn't stopped all night. It was a grey and miserable morning and the rain lashed at the dining room window in endless, gale driven sheets. This was not the sort of morning to which we had become accustomed. It was cold, wet and windy and we lingered long over the coffee, bread rolls and jam that was breakfast, delaying our encounter with these unwelcome and uncustomary conditions. The guide book did not alert us to the day we were about to encounter making brief reference to a "short wilderness walk" but an otherwise "relatively easy walk without any major difficulties." Humph. Maybe it was the weather that made the difference, but this day was definitely not easy, not by a long shot. Looking back I rate the day we were about to set out upon as probably the toughest we experienced on the whole route. It was certainly the case that the weather played a massive part in making the day the ordeal it became and perhaps without the wind and rain it would have passed off as just another day. We were about to venture into a pathless mountain wilderness in the most miserable of conditions, the likes of which we had not experienced before on our trek to the Mediterranean.

After donning our waterproofs we set off on a well used path downhill in the company of Richard along with another party of some dozen or so walkers who were all heading down alongside the Riu de Certascan towards the un-metalled track that came to within a kilometre of the Certascan refuge some 200m lower down. This was the path that Keith would have needed to negotiate with our extra provisions had he stayed around for a further day. We didn't get as far as the track, instead turning off uphill once again on an obscure and faint little path to cross the ridge of the Serra de Lurri lost somewhere above us in the mist and rain. The large party continued on downwards on the main path and were soon lost from sight in the swirl of mist and rain.

After some half an hour of ascent we passed over the Serra de Lurri and slowly descended eastwards down to what would ordinarily have been a beautiful and remote Estany Romedo de Dalt. It was not a day to linger and we pressed on with the rain driving in over our left shoulders from the north-west. It was in some way re-assuring to be in the company of Richard on this dour and wretched day. Although it was clearly not in everyday use the path was reasonably well defined as it descended gently towards our next landmark, the Estany de Romedo de Baix. The driving rain slowly and persistently started to penetrate through the long since failed waterproof qualities of my old blue gortex jacket to reach every last square millimetre of my skin. There was little conversation between us except to occasionally stop to confirm our direction of travel.

It was to this remote and lonely mountain lake some 64 years previously that a young French lady, Jeanne Agouau, accompanied by her father Jean Pierre, bravely led a group of 13 Jews, who were fleeing for their life from the Nazis in Vichy France, over the Pyrenees to the relative safety of Spain. This is a transcript of her emotive tale in her own words:-

*After my father, Jean Pierre Agouau, had led 2 Dutch Jews to the Spanish border we set out a few days later on December 5 at 3 am with a group of nine – five men, three women and a boy of 12. The group gathered in the shadows by a nearby barn. We could take little with us; a back pack, some food, warm clothes and most importantly good footwear. My father told everyone to keep as quiet as possible, not to use walking sticks to test the way but to follow in each others footsteps.*

*I led the way and my father brought up the rear. Then in the upper village a dog barked but no one stirred and we could make our way up through the shadows, staying out of range of the streetlights. By the Croix du Ruisseau I crossed myself and muttered a prayer for a safe journey.*

*Once we were over the bridge there was less chance of meeting anyone. The stars were out but it wasn't too cold. Leaving Artigou, it was a steep climb but then we came to the path by the side of the waterfall – the Cascade d'Ars – where the path was covered with patches of ice glinting in the starlight and the only way up was to trust your feet to the dark patches where you hoped there was still grass. Later at frozen streams we had to take the party over one by one. All the time we were climbing. A gust of wind brought some drops of rain and worry to my father but the cloud passed.*

*There by the Lac de Cabanas, to our surprise was another group, a family of four. The mother, father, grandmother and 8 month old baby boy, Belgian Jews, had* been staying with the Cabaillés. They had left on the stroke of midnight guided by the man Jean Baptiste Rogalle Matièlot, who later became my husband.

We all stopped there for a short while to rest and eat, but the new day had broken and we couldn't stay for long. The pace was slow. Everyone was tired. The women kept sitting down and begging for a few minutes rest. "We must keep going" said my father, "we can't go back, the Germans are there. Up here we daren't rest in case the weather turns bad."

Arriving at the top of the Troun d'Ars he continued to encourage them, showing them the pass which seemed to be so close, while knowing how long was the path that remained.

We stopped again to gather our strength just before the tumbled boulders near the Guillou pass. Then we had to go from rock to rock while giving a helping hand to those who were exhausted. Jean Baptiste looked after the mother and grandmother of the baby while the father carried him on his chest in a duvet strapped to his neck by a band of cloth. He too was exhausted; so I carried the baby while leading the way to the frontier.

On the col a rock bears the letters F.E. (France-Espagne) and in its shelter on the cropped grass I laid the baby wrapped in its duvet. A few moments later one of the group arrived and I could go back and help my father and Jean Baptiste bring everyone to the top. The sun lit up the rocks but we couldn't wait there, so we climbed down the Spanish side towards the Lake of Romédo. Just above there we stopped for something to eat.

We took out the little that was left: bread, cheese and a few lumps of rationed sugar, while the baby sucked on some milk from a thermos carried by his mother. This little meal and the rest revived everyone. A woman took out a compact and powdered her nose. " I see everything is better" chuckled my father. One of the men asked me how old I was and thanked me for all that I had done for them. It was nearly 3 pm and time to leave. My father showed them the path which leads down to the lake and the track made by the Spanish herds which goes down the valley to Tabescan.

One of the women gave my father a letter that she had quickly written saying that someone would come and pick it up from our house that night. We parted ways; it was 4 o'clock and we climbed up to the Guillou pass. From the col we looked back and our last sight of the group was of them walking around the Lake de Romédo in single file following the well-marked track. "They've got a good start" remarked my father.

We left the pass almost running, leaping from one rock to another. By the time we reached the foot of the waterfall it was almost dark so we had to slow down. At

*Gouettes de Pey we walked down towards the footbridge. My mother had left the shutters open so we could soon see the light of the lamp in our kitchen. We arrived and sat down for dinner when the man who had asked us to take the group came for news. My father gave him the letter. Seated by the fire he read it without translating. "It was a hard journey, wasn't it?" My father told of the 12 hours it took to reach the frontier and then we talked of what was happening, the war and its horrors, of the fate of the Jews, of my brother a prisoner of war in Germany… Trusting us, he stayed for some time. Several days later he came back to tell us that the group had arrived safely at Tabescan and to ask my father to take another.*

*Postscript*

*To our regret, since the end of the war we have not heard any news from those whom we helped cross into Spain. Even today, I sometimes wonder what happened to the baby I carried to a new life.*

*In the 70s some strangers came to the house asking for us, but we were in the fields. "They will be back this evening" the neighbours said but in the evening no one came.[1] – Extract from the bulletin of the Association des Amis d'Aulus et de la vallée du Garbet, no. 17 & 18, published in 2000. Translated by T.Nash*

*After this article appeared, several individuals carried out research in France and Spain and were able to discover the names of all the members of this family. The baby that Jeanne Rogalle helped carry was found : Claude Henle lives in Montreal; his whole family made it to Canada from Spain. He has 4 children and many grandchildren.*

*On July 10 2004 Jeanne Rogalle was awarded the medal of the Legion of Honour in Aulus-les-Bains in the presence of Mr Henle and his wife as well as numerous elected officials.*

*On October 30 2005 she was presented with the medal of the Righteous Among Nations.*

As we came alongside the grey windswept Estany de Romedo de Baix the path arrived at a short and awkward section where we had to down climb a steep gully on very slippy and wet rocks. In normal conditions it would not have merited any mention but the rock surfaces had taken on

*([1] Further information on the story of Jeanne Rogalle can be found on the following web link:- www.ariege.com/histoire/jeanne.html )*

the consistency of ice and the simplest of scrambles was transformed into a nasty and difficult descent where the frictionless rock lay a deathly trap for the unwary traveller. The scramble down of no more than about 20 feet led to a precipitous path that skirted delicately around a cliff face some 40-50feet above the deep waters of the lake. I went first and though the foot and handholds were substantial there was an uncertainty with every placement as I struggled to establish any truly re-assuring holds on the slimy surface. The rain ran down my sleeves as my arms strained to hold me in place as I floundered around blindly for foot-holds. Not for the first time I could feel the beating of my heart as adrenalin pumped through my veins. After what seemed an age of nervous fumbling I eventually reached the ground safely and looked up as Richard then Michael followed, in far less ungainly fashion than I had managed I must add.

As Michael reached the ground his pack caught on rock and his drinks bottle was dislodged from the side pocket. We stood frozen as it tumbled down the rock face towards the choppy waters of the lake only to catch in a small crevice some 10 feet down from the path. Before I could even contemplate the prospect of climbing down to retrieve it Michael was down and back up again with the bottle in his hand.

"That was lucky. I thought we were witnessing a repeat of the tent fiasco for a moment," he gasped.

This difficult little scramble was a good indicator of the perils we were to face later in the day. The entry in my note book for 3rd August starts with the words, "before writing any more I would like to praise the lord for seeing me and Michael through a very demanding day." I know this may seem rather dramatic, but such were the trials and tribulations of this most testing of days.

The path skirted delicately above the lake before descending the meet the dirt track which had contoured its way all around the Serra de Lurri ridge from below Certascan to end here at the remote and desolate Estany de Romedo de Baix. *The same track referred to in Jeanne Rogalle's account as the 'track made by the Spanish herds'.* It was from this point onwards that the route became indistinct and created a deal of indecision amongst us. We crossed the small dam and despite the directions to turn immediately right, where no path existed at all, we were drawn to follow the faint path which headed north around the lake, (*the route of descent in to Spain taken by fleeing Jews in Jeanne Rogalle's account)* looking for some indication of a route that set off in the direction we wanted; east. We could find no evidence of any such path and floundered around rather perplexed for 10 minutes or so until conceding to the directions of Ton Joosten and striking off in an easterly direction through long spiky grass keeping the Riu de Romedo on our right, looking for some vague semblance of a path. Occasionally a path, of sorts, did materialise but would disappear again twenty yards on, leaving us once again to stumble along, searching for the next thread of animal track or remnants of a long abandoned way that we could string together into our faltering route through this wilderness.

Initially the ground was either level or descended gently through this abandoned valley but soon the river we were following turned south and tumbled loudly down into a steep sided gorge to our right. On occasions the 'path' we were following would come upon slabs of bare rock that were ridiculously slippy. Lines of small stone cairns, the solitary mark of previous human passage, led us across these bands of rock on which we could barely keep our feet. I found myself searching out the tiny islands of vegetation that grew from hairline fissures in the otherwise smooth rock and offered tiny refuges of friction for the boots. If the rock was in anyway sloping I found it inevitable that I would end up sliding. This didn't cause too much concern until our route drew closer to the precipice of the gorge on our right at which stage I decided to forego any last vestige of dignity that remained and resort to increasing the friction between myself and the ground by travelling on my arse wherever the need arose. It didn't exactly make for speedy progress but I felt a whole load safer than when I was on foot where I felt like I was walking on a carpet of ball bearings. For some reason Michael and Richard were not afflicted to the same extent and managed to remain upright throughout. God knows how. The hazard was real and not just some nervous imagined perception held only by me. I watched them skid and slide, teetering on the brink of a 300ft precipice above the swollen Riu de Romedo thundering through the gorge below, and they remained unfazed by their gamble with death. It scared the shit out of me and I resisted their tauntings and resorted to my posteric perambulation whenever I felt in the least bit apprehensive.

Half an hour or so after leaving the dam we arrived at a point where the ground ahead fell away in a seemingly impregnable rampart of rock which that completely barred our progress to the valley below. We probed and searched for an alternative easy route but none existed. A slanting shelf of greasy rain drenched granite was the only means of further progress. The prospect of this dreadful and treacherous descent immediately filled me with utter dread. This couldn't be the route, surely. I stood there contemplating the prospect of doing battle with this ugly and terrifying cliff face ahead. In dry conditions it would have been daunting but after some 14 hours of heavy rain it looked impossible. Richard led the way which was an incredible feat bearing in mind that he had one hand devoted to carrying his precious tripod.

"Can't you strap that to your pack somehow?" I suggested.

"No, I'm ok, I'll manage," he replied confidently.

The prospect of tackling this latest barrier on the HRP in such dreadful conditions with 4 available limbs occurred to me as a somewhat foolhardy enterprise. With one hand otherwise occupied seemed beyond the realms of sanity.

As he started out I could barely bring myself to watch. Clambering down the slimy gully at our feet his boots scrambled for a grip on the frictionless rock. After some ten feet or so of faltering descent he reached start of the slanting narrow shelf of rock that angled it's way across the vertical crag. I'm sure I held my breath throughout as he literally single handedly made his way slowly down and across the rock face, the yawning void at his back. At one stage he needed to swap the tripod to his other hand and to this day I cannot comprehend how the hell he managed it, but he did. This manoeuvre occurred in a split second sleight of hand worthy of any professional conjurer. He continued downwards and within a few minutes he was stood at the far end of the crag, still on steep ground but with the main danger behind him, for now!

It was my turn. I decided it was my turn because I didn't relish the prospect of being the last one left at the top and I didn't need any more time pondering as to whether this latest death defying feat was actually a good idea or not. I felt slightly re-assured by having two hands available to cling on for dear life as opposed to Richard's one. The initial down climb of the gully was terrifying. It was like sitting at the top of an enormous water slide and waiting to be propelled into oblivion.

"Jesus Christ, how the fuck did *he* manage to get down here? There's nothing to hold on to!"

I faltered at the top of the gully for what seemed an eternity and the longer I delayed the more frightened I became.

"What I'd give for a bleedin' rope now!" I moaned nervously.

"Michael, if I die today I want you to carry my body to Banyuls sur Mer, ok?"

"You can bog off fatty. If you die today the only way you're getting to the Mediterranean is if that river takes you there! Oh and if you do pop off I bags your posh sleeping mat ok?"

"Thanks son."

"Come on dad you'll have it dark."

"Ok, ok. There's nothing like a bit of moral support is there. And that was…" I tailed off.

I just had to focus. There were limited footholds below me as I began the down climb facing out away from the rock. I wedged myself into the gully and used the large woody clumps of heather that hung down from the side as handholds. Luckily for me their roots were well bedded and it provided the only remotely reassuring handhold there was available in many places. The next ten minutes are very much a blur. I can only recall being absolutely scared shitless. I remember my boots skidding off the rock in a number of places, fortunately never more than one at a time or I doubt whether my arms would have been able to hold on. I kept on questioning how on earth Richard had managed to do this with one hand! Incredible! When I finally lowered myself onto terra firma I found, not for the first time, my heart was pounding out of my chest and beads of sweat had combined with the rain and were running into my eyes making them sting.

I spent the next minute or so allowing my breathing and straining heart to return to normal. In the couple of moments it took to regain my composure Michael had run the gauntlet and was stood alongside me.

"Oh my God, have you got bloody wings or something?" I questioned.

"Come on dad, it wasn't that bad."

"No? …I beg to differ."

We descended towards where the river emitted from the mouth of the gorge below. The rain hadn't stopped all day and the waters of the river were swollen and angry. We had to cross it, there was no option. This raging torrent, innocently described by Mr Joosten as the 'beautiful stream' barred our way forward. We shed our heavy packs and sat on the eastern bank of the Riu de Romedo contemplating this next formidable hurdle and looking for a line of weakness. It wasn't like we could wander up or downstream searching for a safer crossing. The river disappeared into another gorge downstream. This was the only realistic crossing point. We knew we were in the right place because there was no other feasible crossing point in either direction. We reckoned it was probably 2-3 feet deep which in itself was of little consequence. It was the speed with which it was thundering over the rocks that made the crossing so intimidating. The most compelling argument for pressing on through the river though was that we wouldn't have to climb back up the slanting rock ledge again. Incentive indeed!

Feeling brave, and infinitely more confident than minutes earlier faced with the rock ledge, I picked my line and strode out into the stream. It wasn't as bad as it first appeared with the water reaching just above my knees. The trekking poles were invaluable offering another two stabilising points of contact with the river bed. Without too much difficulty I made it to the opposite bank without incident. The other two followed safely upon which we ascended the steep and muddy opposite bank and within minutes disappeared into a dense wooded hillside.

The comments by Joosten in the guide book gave an indication as to the nature of the terrain ahead. *'Find your own way down in a forest (here and there are hints of a path and a few cairns, but you are on your own now) and work your way towards the stream.'* After our initial ascent for maybe 100m over a ridge we found ourselves enveloped in a dense mass of trees and vegetation where any semblance of a path was at best intermittent. The slope was very steep and we stumbled blindly downhill on mossy and muddy slides constantly seeking any signs of the so called path. Trees branches and trunks were used to steady our descent and we soon lost all sense of direction and frequently had to revert to the compass. The tree canopy, no more than 15-20 feet above us was dense and impenetrable but at least provided us with shelter from the persistent rain. The regular checks on the compass confirmed we were heading south, downhill to our next landmark the Pla de Boavi. After probably an hour of fighting our way through this dense jungle of a forest we emerged from the trees onto a rocky promontory some 200 feet or more above the crashing waters of a river held deep within the sheer sided walls of a narrow gorge. It may have been 'our' river, it may not. Who knows? There were four significant water courses shown on the map all heading generally south and this could have been any one of them. One thing I did realise, immediately, was that we were once again on smooth, wet rock that sloped gently towards the edge of the precipice. A rock with all the surface characteristics of polished ice. Once again the other two just strode across with barely an acknowledgement of the treacherous nature of the ground underfoot. I skirted around the perimeter of the rock, shredding my legs on the gorse and brambles as I sought the security offered by the trees along the perimeter of the clearing.

"What are you doing dad?" Michael questioned as though I had taken leave of my senses.

"I'm staying alive, if that's ok with you!" I retorted.

"It's not that bad."

"Mmm, where have I heard that before?"

I scrambled through the last few metres of undergrowth, beyond where the path moved away from the cliff edge and stepped away from the trees and onto the bare rock, where I promptly fell on my arse in a Chaplin-like farcical tumble.

"Not that bad eh?" I griped in a sardonic sneer as I got back to my feet with a bruised bum and dented pride.

"I'm staying clear of any further wet rock from now on."

We continued descending steeply through the woods with the ravine on our left until we emerged from the trees onto a large flat grassy area, the Pla de Boavi. Relieved at our release from the grip of the forest and pleased to be on level ground we sauntered along on the beginnings of a stony track in search of the footbridge, chatting about our adventures on the 'short wilderness walk' before we realised we were soon approaching the end of the grassy plain, without any sign of the bridge we were looking for. I opened my map case and turned to the next page of Day 28 in the book.

"According to the guide it would appear that the bridge is located at the eastern end of the Pla de Boavi where we first arrived."

"I didn't see anything, but then I wasn't particularly looking, I was just pleased to get out of that awful forest," remarked Richard.

We retraced our steps back to where the path began to re-ascend where we found our bridge, or at least the stone buttresses that marked the position where it used to be!

"Wet feet again guys", I pointed out.

"What d'ya mean, *again*? Michael corrected. "They'd have had to have got dry in between for it to be *again*."

"Suppose you're right son, good point."

The river here was wide and deep and the rocky bed was covered in moss. It wasn't as fast flowing as the earlier crossing but it wasn't far short of testicle level and it was cold! Although the prospect of crossing the river was somewhat daunting it turned out to be more uncomfortable than dangerous and we each made it across without any real difficulties, and all with dry nuts. We had been through a most demanding morning and were all looking forward to lunch. The tall canopy of mostly pine trees offered the best shelter we were likely to find so we shed our wet and heavy packs and settled down in a small hollow to have lunch. We were a bedraggled looking bunch, all soaked to the skin from our two river crossings and the continuous rain.

"I don't think there's any part of me that isn't wet!" Michael said feeling rather sorry for himself.

"Really? There's a part of me that isn't wet", I replied.

He looked over to me puzzled, "Is there, where?"

"My mouth!" I announced, dryly.

Richard snorted, not having heard the joke before but after a month of being together Michael probably knew all my one-liners by now, and just smiled politely. It wasn't easy to be happy on this drab and miserable day. I'd heard the Pla de Boavi referred to as a little corner of paradise but it didn't feel like that now. The pervading feeling was that of wetness and we needed something to lift our dampened spirits.

"Fancy a hot chicken soup anyone? I suggested.

"Oh yesssss," was the immediate combined response.

We had powdered soups by the dozen amongst our supplies and I promptly set about assembling the camping stove and soon had a pan of water on the boil. Despite the sheltered nature of our lunch venue there was no reprieve from the all pervading wind which whipped through our refuge amongst the trees chilling our dampened bones, and wafting the blue flame of the gas stove. I provided what shelter I could to the stove using my pack and large boulder on which I was sat. I must have had the appearance of some mysterious hooded wizard as the pan boiled and the steam rose around me. We each in turn cradled our steaming hot mugs of soup in both hands, hunched up in our sodden waterproofs, hoods drawn fending off the large drips from the trees above.

There was no inclination to linger over our repast and with a long way still to go and with the penetrating dampness beginning to chill us to the core, like three drowned rats, we set off uphill through the forest heading for the distant unmanned Refugi del Cinquantenari (also known as the Refuge de Baborte). The path on this side of the river was well constructed and struck up through the trees at a moderate gradient in a series of zigzags. Like many of the paths on the HRP though it had an air of neglect and disuse. The occasional fallen tree had been allowed to slowly decompose where it fell across the path and the carefully placed rocks which had been cleverly constructed to form the path surface were blanketed with decades of tree debris; pine needles, cones, twigs and dead branches. In places the rain had washed narrow channels through this forest litter on its way downhill to meet the swollen waters of the Riu de Broate. The noise of the river, crashing over rocks in the valley below and the wind in the trees provided a plaintive accompaniment to our upward trudge in this remote and desolate corner of the Pyrenees.

It felt like we had completed a full days walking already but the reality was that we still had over 3000 feet of ascent before attaining the high point of the day, the Col de Sellente from where we could look down upon the remote and lonely refuge at Baborte. Our route took us up and eventually above the tree line into the desolate Val de Sellente. Unlike the popular Pyrenean honey pots around Gavarnie, Vignemale and Pic du Midi d'Ossau this region of the Arierge was devoid of other travellers. Testament to this was the forlorn ruins of the Refugi de Sellente high in upper valley, long since abandoned, presumably because it could never be financially viable. Up to this point the path since Pla de Boavi had been distinct, well constructed and easy to follow. However, beyond the ruins we entered the mist that hung over all the summits and had to rely upon the compass for direction as any evidence of the path soon disappeared. The terrain, what we could see of it, was featureless and comprised short grass and ground hugging sedges. Every now and then a stone cairn would loom up from out of the mist to confirm we were still on course. These cairns did offer some reassurance but they could just as easily be marking some ambiguous route to the summit of a nearby mountain as the route to our col.

I've always found when walking in mist that the longer you're dependent upon a compass bearing for maintaining your direction the more you crave the reassurance of some landmark to reinforce your wavering reliance upon a thin sliver of metal aligning itself with the magnetic field of the earth. Whilst I have no reason to doubt the reliability of the compass itself, I do sometimes question my ability to use it properly. Even though I understand the principles and theory of how to use a map and compass, sometimes following a bearing is not so easy, especially on terrain that continually deflects you from your chosen line. Also, another critical element of route finding with map and compass, and one which is probably most prone to human error, is assessing the distance covered. For instance, if you know you have to remain on a bearing for a distance of say 1kiliometre before changing to another bearing then it is quite important to be able to estimate the time taken to reach the point to which you are heading. Failure to do so can result in all manner of confusion. On our ascent to the col the natural grain of the land continually deflected us from our intended line and though we tried to correct this I became more and more doubtful that we continued to remain on course the further we went.

This self doubt was compounded even further when we reached a false col which, because of the limited visibility appeared to all intents and purposes to be the Col de Sellente. It didn't occur to me that we had probably arrived some 10 minutes before we would realistically have expected because I hadn't paid too much attention to distance involved and the consequent time we should take to cover that distance. Believing that we were stood at the Col and still in mist I set a new bearing to descend to our destination at the refuge hut and we set off into the grey murk, for what we believed was to be our final leg of the day down to Baborte. All seemed well, for a minute or so anyway, until the ground ahead started rising. We stopped and I looked at the map again. We couldn't possibly be going uphill if we were where I thought we were. In that case we were clearly somewhere else, but where? I checked my bearing, 90 degrees, directly due east, yes, correct. Eventually, through a process of elimination, I surmised that we must still be on the west side of the col. Once I had accepted this fact, it became reasonably straightforward correcting our mistake although, I wasn't entirely clear just exactly what our position was. Ten minutes later with some relief we arrived at the real Col de Sellente and with the benefit of hindsight I could see where we had gone wrong.

There was a large bank of soft snow on the east side of the col, which disappeared over a convex slope into the swirling mist of the Cirque de Baborte below. It looked quite intimidating. We had no ice axes to arrest any slip and no way of knowing how far the snow slope stretched or what lay at the bottom. I checked the map and guide book again looking for reassurance. The book just said "work your way down..." with no reference to the gradient or possibility of snow. The map gave the impression that the gradient was not too severe with the spacing of the contour lines suggesting a 100m descent over the 500m distance 1 in 5, although this was never altogether convincing on a 1:50,000 scale map. We stepped down onto the snow, prodding it with our trekking poles as we went. Fortunately unlike our approach to the col, our descent route across the snow was well defined by the passage of many earlier boots over the course of the summer and although the slope was initially quite steep our diagonal traversing route across it was relatively straightforward. Our encounter with the snow was brief and we were soon onto wet scree and rocks, where we picked our way down eager to encounter our home for the night. The rain had stopped as we reached the col and within a few minutes the mist and cloud parted and revealed the distinct orange-coloured Refugi del Cinquantenari, a kilometre away beneath us. A more welcome sight could not have presented itself. Ever since our misfortunes at Belagua I always maintained a nagging doubt that these refuges may have been demolished or closed down since the publication of Ton Joosten's guide, but this wasn't to be the case today. We were tired, hungry and very wet, and the comforts of four walls and a roof, basic though they were, were eagerly awaited.

The orange painted hut, held down with metal stays, resembled an old railway freight carriage from the outside and stood high on a promontory above the Estany de Baborte. It was 4pm when we arrived and this most remote of huts was already, and surprisingly, partly occupied by a young French couple and two Spanish blokes, but there were nine beds in total and plenty of room for three more residents. Our first priority was a hot drink and upon arrival we immediately boiled up another 3 mugs of soup. As we sat and burnt our lips slurping hot minestrone Richard announced that he intended to press on down to the manned refuge at Val Ferrera some 6 kilometres further. The prospect of a decent meal, more spacious surroundings and a degree more comfort than the cramped confines of this metal box were an understandable lure and though we were both sorry to see him go Michael and I were both too knackered and absolutely committed to travelling not an inch further on this most demanding of mountain days, to be tempted to accompany him any further. Anyway, I suspected Richard probably relished the prospect of travelling alone once again, a sentiment I could understand from many previous solo trips of my own into mountainous regions.

One luxury I was relishing was the prospect of climbing into dry clothes and immediately after Richard's departure we both changed into dry gear, though in deference to our four hut co-habitees we forwent the option of a change of underpants. We hung our wet clothes on the metal cable stays that secured the hut to the ground. Although the rain had stopped and the cloud was breaking into ragged strips allowing brief glimpses of the sun it was still quite cool in the wind and the prospect of our kit being dry by that evening seemed rather unlikely. This was our first of three consecutive nights where our meals were to be confined to the dehydrated variety. I must say, despite their less than appetizing appearance and reputation, these meals were actually quite satisfying and on each evening we enjoyed a twin course of both main meal and pudding. (The chocolate sponge pudding being the most delightful of the latter, and therefore first to be consumed). There was little to do after dinner, it was too cold to sit outside, so after collecting our still damp clothing from the improvised washing lines we crawled inside our sleeping bags and were both asleep before it went dark.

## Day 34, Friday 4th August, Refugi del Cinquantenari to Etang de la Soucarrane

We were the last up and out of the hut this morning. Michael was particularly tardy and I left him sorting his pack out as I set off to go and find a suitable toilet venue. For obvious reasons hut users are encouraged to travel a distance from the huts for No. 2's. It was cool and breezy, but dry, thankfully. I descended from the hut to skirt around the Baborte Lake where a suitable toilet facility presented itself amongst an area of large boulders. Business over Michael had still not emerged from the hut so I decided to press on to the end of the lake where I would still be in sight of the hut. I continued to look over my shoulder but Michael had still not emerged from the hut by the time I reached the end of the lake so I climbed up onto the shoulder that began the descent down to the Val Ferrera and stood there awaiting his appearance. It was now some half an hour since I left the hut and I was beginning to wonder if he'd gone back to bed or something when finally a small figure stepped out of the hut door, now some 800m away in the distance. I watched him closely as he started down the hill from the refuge and then after a few steps he stopped as if looking for someone, probably me. I whistled and waved but there was no acknowledgement. I suspect any sound I made was carried away towards the Val Ferrera in the stiffening wind.

After a short delay he continued down the hill towards the lake and headed in my direction. It took Michael some twenty minutes or so to walk the length of the lake and it wasn't until he neared the southern end just below where I was stood that he appeared to notice my presence. It was quite cold in the wind and I had resorted to wearing my still damp jacket as I stood awaiting Michaels arrival. He was upset when he caught up with me.

"I couldn't see where you'd gone!" he complained bitterly.

"I thought you knew it was this way?" I said

"No it wasn't obvious, I had no idea which direction you'd headed off in and I was worried when I couldn't see you anywhere. Didn't you hear me shouting when I was by the hut?" he protested.

"Sorry son, no I didn't hear you. I whistled and waved when you were by the hut but you obviously didn't hear me."

"No I didn't!" he asserted.

"Sorry Michael."

For a short moment he seemed vulnerable. I could feel his hurt. He reminded me of a small child who loses his mum or dad in a large department store and I felt guilty for abandoning him.

"You were always in sight you know," I added defensively.

He could see my remorse and chided me with his next comment.

"Neglect and abandonment is a form of child abuse you know. You should be ashamed!"

"Child abuse!? You're bleedin' 18 for God sake. Behave yourself!"

"Adult abuse then."

We set off together downhill, friends again, towards the Val Ferrera, passing a group of half a dozen French walkers heading uphill on the way. After passing a high cabana we left the open pastures of the higher hills and entered a deciduous forest. The path threaded its way through the trees remaining well above the river, the Noguera de Vallferrera which we could hear but not see somewhere below us. After a couple of hours walking, mostly downhill, we arrived at a bridge, Puenta de Molinassa, our lowest point of the day at 1800m above sea level.

After crossing the bridge we had the comfort of a dirt road to walk on for a short spell. This was a reunion with our long lost companion, the GR11 which we hadn't encountered since Candanchu some three weeks ago (13th July). It was a welcome relief to be able to stroll on an even and foot-friendly surface after the rigours of the wild country through which we had passed over the last few days. Some 10-15minutes later we passed a sign for the Refugi de Vallferrera, Richard's destination the day before. He would probably be well ahead of us by now. The dirt road deposited us at another high plain, the Pla de Boet, an exquisite little area which beckoned us to tarry, so out came the camping stove once again. The Earl Grey and cereal bars were a welcome elevenses and we loitered long at Pla de Boet taking a 2nd mug of tea and tucking into our supplies of dried fruit and nuts. We sat and watched the white cattle grazing on the lush green meadow, the bowling green qualities of which were broken only by the lazy stream which meandered through its midst. The peaceful scene was shattered somewhat when a mother and her two children and a mad Labrador pulled up in their 4x4 gas guzzler on the dirt track some

50 metres away. Upon release from the car the dog went berserk and came leaping through our little lunch spot and tearing across the meadow scattering cattle in all directions. No amount of calls and whistles from the owner made the slightest difference. This was fun and the mad hound was intent on making the most of its liberation. After several minutes of utter mayhem it eventually came loping back to its owner, completely breathless, tongue lolling to one side from its slavering mouth. She was none too pleased and kept the balmy mutt leashed from then on as the family wandered off up the valley.

Entertainment and tea break over we resumed battle and after crossing the meadow and stream by a tiny footbridge and a brief ascent we diverted off the path to refill our water bags and bottles at the romantically named Barranc d'Arcalis, well above the area where the cattle grazed. Even so, not wanting to take a chance we used the purification tablets. The next section of the trail was a steady ascent up to the pass at the Port de Boet where we would once again cross the border back into France, the first time since our excursion to Bagneres de Luchon. The day was pleasant, ideal for walking in many ways. As we approached the pass we could hear voices of French climbers somewhere up on the ridge to the south of the col. They never came into view although they sounded no more than feet away at times. Beyond the col and upon our descent to the Etang de la Soucarrane Michael developed problems with his ankle which caused him to start limping. It slowed him up quite a bit and I was worried this may be more than just an afternoon twinge. Just when we had got going again! Fortunately this was a short day and we were close to our destination, a wild camp, at 2300m next to the picturesque lake. This would at least allow Michael to rest up.

We found an ideal flat area of grass near the lake and pitched the tent as the sun came out to greet us. It was quite early, 2pm, so after a late lunch we opted for an afternoon siesta. After a couple of hours dozing in the tent I decided to make myself a cuppa and treat Michael to some of my expert singing in the process, giving a very Sinatra like rendition of My Way as I washed out our socks at the lake's edge. For some strange reason he didn't appreciate my efforts and said I was just disturbing his sleep. Thats the trouble with the youth of today, they just don't recognise a class act when they hear it!

Tonight's menu comprised of the dehydrated delights of beef and potato hot pot (for me) and chilli con carne (Michael) followed by a dehydrated version of apple pie and custard, which, I have to say, though it was inconceivable beforehand that it would taste anything like the original, again, I was pleasantly surprised. It was actually quite good!

It clouded over in the evening and we stayed in the tent, inside our sleeping bags, reading and completing Sudoku puzzles to pass the time. Unbeknown to him the top half of Michael's sleeping bag had got wet in yesterdays awful weather and the dry lower half only covered as far as his waist. He had to use his fleece and our 2 coats to cover his top half which was never going to be enough 7500ft up in the Pyrenees. It was a cold and windy night and probably our most uncomfortable under canvas, especially for the one of us with only half a sleeping bag. Stupid boy!

# Day 35, Saturday 5<sup>th</sup> August, Etang de la Soucarrane to Refugi de Sorteny

*Day 35, Saturday 5<sup>th</sup> August, Etang de la Soucarrane to Refugi de Sorteny*

The sky had cleared overnight to leave a bright sunny morning and a covering of frost on our tent as I arose at 6.40am. Poor Michael had suffered with the cold overnight and upon his emergence from beneath the 2 waterproof jackets that had provided scant insulation for his upper body he sat hunched up coaxing every last ounce of heat from his mug of steaming Earl Grey tea. He said his leg felt ok so following a customary bowl of hot porridge each we broke camp just as a series of fisherman were arriving having ascended from the head of the dirt road some 1000 feet below in the Vallee de Soulcem. I envied them the warm, dry, and comfortable beds from which they had departed to come and partake in some weekend sport. This was our full time habitat with no home comforts to which we could return.

We crossed the outfall of the lake and headed down the fisherman's path into the valley. Once the sun rose above the Cap de la Coste Grande on the Andorran border to the east the temperature shot up. It looked like the unsettled couple of days we had just gone through had come to an end and we were back to sunshine again. Our travels were to take us to a new country today, the tiny Pyrenean principality of Andorra. Our route into this new land was via the exquisitely named Port de Rat which was little more than a narrow notch in the steep and craggy ridge that defended the border. The approach on what was a decent and well defined but narrow path was most impressive, picking its way carefully up the ever steepening ramparts that protected this particular border of the tiny principality from the outside world. We passed a group of some six or so French walkers near to the top of our ascent who were too clean-cut to have been out for more than just the day. Three days now without a shower set us apart from any day trippers. Such imposters were not true mountain travellers like us. You had to look and, more importantly, smell like a mountaineer to really be one!

Once again the attainment of the col opened up new horizons. Such daily milestones along our route were always an uplifting aspect of all our days probably because they usually heralded the end of the up and the start of the down. Today was no exception. We were to descend into the civilisation of a busy ski resort which was also popular with summer walkers and day trippers and, more importantly for us, contained the luxury of a bar/restaurant where we eagerly anticipated the welcome distraction of a hearty lunch. As we looked down from our lofty perch at the Port de Rat, some 2540m above our lowly beginnings at Hendaye, below us lay the nursery slopes of the Station d'Ordino-Arcalis with the metal pylons marking the course of the chair lift on the far side of the valley. It was clear from the guidebook that this was not Ton Joosten's favourite place. He clearly did not relish his encounters with civilisation along the HRP. We on the other hand more than welcomed the prospect of some real food at the bar/restaurant and any artificial ugliness of the surrounding resort was an irrelevance when compared to the prospect of a good feed.

We threaded our way carefully down the narrow and precarious path towards the valley floor. Upon reaching the more level ground we romped over barren slopes down the valley towards the restaurant at La Coma. It was a popular place with a full car park and many people milling around outside. Once inside we were like 2 kids at a party and filled our trays with all manner of snacks and sandwiches, cakes and crisps and fizzy drinks at the self serve counter. The restaurant was mostly empty and no doubt intended to cater more for the winter sports tourists. Upon reaching the till I was struck by the change of language, for some reason expecting Andorrans to be French speaking. Their official language was Catalan and I struggled to communicate with the lady at the counter, eventually resorting to my usual garbled mix of unintelligible Anglo-Franco babble. She scanned each item and announced the amount which made absolutely no sense at all to me. Usually, especially with numbers I am able to extract some translation from the words I hear. She could have been asking me for sex I wouldn't have had a clue. I played safe and despite a pocket full of coins and numerous small denomination notes I handed over a 20euro note. She could see I had lesser amounts but accepting the communication impasse thought better of asking for anything less and simply handed me my change. I smiled and muttered a pathetic 'muchas gracias' and scuttled off with Michael to one of the numerous empty tables. It was our most luxurious lunch since our days at the camp site at Arties a week ago and we gorged on a feast of carbohydrates the likes of which were unknown to us in the wild and remote lands of our Pyrenean wilderness.

The excesses of our lunch weighed heavy as we set off again, uphill behind the cafe/bar, along with a horde of day trippers heading up to the Estanys de Tristaina. The lakes were a popular picnic spot and there were scores of people on the path. Ascent was not easy with full packs and full stomachs and we laboured along, generally much slower than everyone else. I had noticed that the HRP route was somewhat contrived at this point and this excursion to the Estanys de Tristaina was a rather unnecessary uphill diversion from the general direction of the route which continued down the main valley from La Coma towards the small village of El Serrat. The drawback to the direct route was the fact that it was all on tarmac road, hence no doubt the diversion.

We reached the lower of the lakes, Estany del Mitg de Tristaina and, whilst I must say it was most picturesque, it was too densely populated for me. I was beginning to see Mr Joosten's point of view. We headed round the northern shore of the lake, stepping over sprawled picnickers along the way until, leaving the hollow of the lake behind on an increasingly faint path we soon ended up on rather steep ground. Our initial line led us directly towards a vertical crag and as we approached this impasse I began to wonder where on earth this mad bloody path was leading us now. My question was answered when it took a sharp and unbelievable turn downhill on to what I can best describe as vertical grass. (This is a phrase used by a good friend of mine and fellow hill-walker Pete Smith, whose life I have seriously endangered on several occasions on previous encounters with what he fondly refers to as vertical grass).

We stood atop a mountainside which fell away beneath our feet. I suspect many of our predecessors had probably turned around at this point and retraced their steps to the cafe bar since there was little evidence of previous footfall on this latest addition to our Pyrenean assault course. The 'path' plummeted down to a stream some 500 feet below on loose and treacherous ground that barely clung on to the mountainside in places. My progress was extremely slow as I meticulously selected each crucial foothold on a slope that dared us to negotiate its vertiginous ramparts. Once again I found it hard to believe that this death defying line formed a recognised long distance route through the mountains. It was inconceivable that a proper 'path' could ever be designated on this most improbable of ground. As usual Michael was far more sure footed than me faced with such vertigo inducing steepness and stepped confidently ahead, sometimes leaping four or five feet at a time to some precariously balanced slab of rock or minuscule patch of flat ground as he careered downhill at an impossible speed. How he managed such amazing gravity defying progress on such slopes was beyond me. He had the balance and surefootedness of any mountain goat but on just two legs. I had witnessed this on several occasions previously including a time on Tryfan in Snowdonia when as a young lad of around 14 he leapt back and forth between the two natural stone pillars (Adam and Eve) which adorn the summit, entertaining the crowds with his undoubted prowess and frightening the shit out of his dad.

My slow, careful and rather nervous descent culminated at a small dam across the small stream emanating from the lakes above, the Riu de Tristaina, where Michael was awaiting my arrival. He was sat at one end of the dam enjoying a drink and eyed me up and down closely as I approached.

"I may be slow but I get there in the end," I asserted.

"Yes, if you don't die of old age in the process."

"Have I ever told you the story of the young bull and the old bull," I said.

"No I don't think so," replied Michael inquisitively.

"Well there are lessons to be learned from that particular tale that could apply to you and I now."

"Oh yeh!"

"Yes, very much so," I confirmed. I stopped and teased him with a pause, prompting an impatient reponse.

"Well, …are you gonna tell me or what?"

"No, I think not. It's a bit crude and not the sort of thing to pass down from father to son".

"What, oh my god, you've got to tell me now!" He pleaded.

I laughed at his youthful snappiness.

"Ok then, but don't tell your sisters."

I began, "there was a young bull and an old bull in a field one day when the young bull spots a herd of cows in the next field to which someone had left open the gate. Barely able to contain his excitement he turns to the old bull and says, "hey look, someone's left the gate open, quick, let's run down there now and shag one of them cows!" The old bull looks at him and says, "no, let's *walk* down and shag 'em all!"

Michael looked at me thoughtfully before announcing, "sounds like a load of old bull to me."

Leaving the small dam behind and after another slightly less steep descent down a grassy ski piste we ended up back on the road which led down from La Coma. As we stepped onto the tarmac surface it was somewhat of a relief to be walking on even and relatively smooth ground for a change. We turned down the road and after some 50m or so left this modern highway for a section of the original and slightly less even road, now closed to vehicles but accessible to pedestrians, subject to a rather awkward limbo manoeuvre beneath a dangling strand of electric fence. Such contorted movements did not come easy. Whilst we were by now quite fit and certainly in my case, significantly lighter than when I started, after several hours on the go the muscles around the back and torso were stiff and not accustomed to any contortions other than those required to walk and carry our packs, or at least they were in my case. Bending and twisting sufficient that no part of you was more than 2 feet above the ground was out of the ordinary and beyond the norm of our daily uphill and downhill routine. The electric wire was too high to risk stepping over. The prospect of a 100volt shock via the groin area being ample deterrent, and in the end the only way I could negotiate this latest obstacle was by lying on my back and shuffling across the ground like some upturned crab. Michael of course managed this latest obstacle with far more grace and elegance than I and sort of stooped underneath the highest section of wire in a single movement whilst I was still getting up off the floor.

The old road hugged the north side of the valley whilst its modern equivalent disappeared over to the southern side in long sweeping zigzags. It was pleasant ambling down this long perished traffic free strip of tarmac in the afternoon sun where shrubs and brightly coloured wildflowers closed in on either side as the road surrendered its ground to the inevitable march of nature. It wasn't long before we rejoined the main road once again and were reduced to our normal single file walking, but this time to avoid the traffic. The road wasn't too busy with just the occasional passing vehicle, but this was the first time I could recall that the HRP had resorted to such a long stretch of main road since our travels in Basque country.

After some 2.5km we turned off to the left onto another road and the change to uphill from a previous steady descent immediately slowed our pace. Similar to La Coma road this new road was also a cul de sac, leading to a car park which gave access to the Parc Natural de la Vall de Sorteny. Our objective for the day was the unmanned Refugi de Sorteny situated in the high pastures of the Sorteny Valley. The remainder of the day we spent chatting as we gently ascended at first on tarmac and then on a dirt road through forest. We discussed the merits of shaving ,of all things, which after some deliberation, we deemed to be an unnecessary chore, and not suited to mountain men such as ourselves, so resolving to concede to the rough look which so suited our day to day apparel. After some half an hour of gentle ascent the dirt road ended at fenced garden area of indigenous alpine plants, such as alpine gentian and Pyrenean lily as well as the now commonly encountered purple iris. Beyond the garden we stepped through a small gate and ascended amongst native pine, oak and birch lined pastures to the sturdily built Refugi de Sorteny.

It was a fine looking building with walls of natural coloured stone and a slate roof, with 2 stone built chimney stacks and barred timber framed windows. It seemed quite a substantial building for its lowly status as an un-manned refuge.

It was mid afternoon and we discarded our packs and sat on the doorstep of the refuge drinking cool, fresh water from the spring just outside. This venue for our latest siesta was directly beneath the flight path of many southerly headed jets that introduced a steady drone to our lazy afternoon as they streamed their white vapour trails across an otherwise blue sky. A Canadian girl and Spanish bloke stopped briefly at the refuge having travelled over from Camping d'Incles, our destination for tomorrow, informing us that the campsite was closed. They had ran out of food and were headed down to the village of El Serrat looking for accommodation and soon headed off again.

The inside of the refuge was furnished with steel tables accompanied by steel benches, but it was the steel bunks which adorned the perimeter walls which most caught my eye. Steel bunks makes sense you may think. Robust, long lasting, less prone to damage and wear and tear, but the perforated sheet steel plate incorporated into each bunk bed structure, and the absence of anything resembling a mattress made me cringe at the thought of what sort of nights sleep I was going to have. If it was the bunks that caught my eye then it was the toilet that assaulted my senses most. In a corner of the refuge was a toilet cubicle from which the most deplorable stench emanated. Even though the door was closed the insidious reek still permeated into the main area of the refuge. Of course curiosity determined I must take a closer look and upon opening the door the overwhelming stinking odour that hit me was beyond human endurance. I slammed the door immediately balking at the as the putrid stench grabbed my throat.

"Oh my God, how the hell could anybody possibly bear to use that place for it's intended purpose? You can't breathe in there!" I stammered.

"It doesn't smell any worse than you do at the moment." Michael countered.

"Come on, I'm not that bloody bad! The smell in that bog is completely unbearable!"

"Yeah, that's about right."

"Well, I tell you what, how about we lock you in there for the evening and you can compare pongs? I think you'll find that even I, in all my putrid sweatiness am but a sweet rose next to that stinking hole!"

Ok, I'll take your word for it. You're a close second though," he retorted.

I decided there and then that there was absolutely no prospect whatsoever of me using this disgusting latrine and I headed off downhill into the woods for a crap. I thought to myself, I couldn't hold my breath long enough for the time it takes me to have a dump and I could not face more than one second of breathing in such a choking stench. An alfresco poo was far more appealing.

As the afternoon became evening we resorted to this our third consecutive night of dehydrated food with a minestrone soup starters and pasta carbonara main course, followed by a yoghurt we had each picked up from the cafe at lunchtime. These meals were at least functional but barely provided the basic sustenance required in view of the thousands of calories we were burning each day. They were supplemented with the supplies of dried fruit and nuts that we each carried which at least made up for the otherwise nutrient starved diet that this powdered food provided. I longed for a plate of steak and chips again and eyed up our walk tomorrow which culminated close to civilisation in the form of the small Andorran town of Soldeu. Maybe a chance to dine like kings?

We were joined that evening by 2 Spanish blokes and a French guy travelling alone, running the HRP and intending to complete the whole trip in 25days which I found completely astonishing. He carried the lightest of packs and had running shoes, vest and shorts as his only attire. His tiny pack contained the skimpiest of sleeping/bivvy bags and basic food provisions of dry pasta and half a baguette. I couldn't begin to contemplate how he had managed to sustain himself in this wild and remote Arierge region, but he had, and overall he had completed in 18 days what had so far taken us 31 days of walking and he was intending to complete the final 12 days in just 7 more days. Remarkable! With this thought and a distinct feeling of inferiority and unworthiness we retired to our metal beds for a night of physical torture, agreeing to rise at 6.30am.

# Day 36 Sunday 6<sup>th</sup> August. Refugi de Sorteny to Vall D'Incles.

*Day 36 Sunday 6<sup>th</sup> August. Refugi de Sorteny to Vall D'Incles.*

Dawn was a sweet release from a night racked with pain. Even the therma-rest made little difference to the hardness of the metal beds. I felt I'd been run over by a small steamroller when I awoke. The two Spanish guys were already up and about and the French bloke was gone when we arose at 6.30am. As usual it took us an eternity to have breakfast and pack up and we didn't leave the refuge until 7.50am.

We were headed for the Collada de Meners which was a 650m ascent up to the head of the valley. It was a pleasant warm and sunny morning and we had the valley to ourselves as we slowly ascended through meadows adorned with alpine flowers on a faint and barely discernible path. The vegetation thinned as we ascended into the upper reaches of the Sorteny Valley until we were enveloped in a world of stone. The headwall of the valley was steep and the last half hour of ascent was in the shadow of the northerly spur of El Pic de la Cabaneta.

As we approached the Collada de Meners we began to hear voices from up above and soon noticed what appeared to be runners in shorts and running vests scrambling down the ridge towards the col. It was a mountain race. At the col we encountered the curious sight of an official handing out and collecting tags as each runner checked in and then out heading off up the Pic de Serrera to the north. Our sudden appearance clearly confused the official who, like some absent minded latter day border guard approached us for our respective tags. Feeling rather sheepish he returned to seat on a nearby rock muttering away to himself. The presence of the race competitors and our funny little race official was a peculiar invasion into our mountain world especially in such a remote spot. We sat and rested a while at the col as each competitor came scrambling down the ridge towards us, before disappearing off to their next checkpoint. Some of them looked a little confused. One even asked me for directions. I sent him off in the direction the last 'runner' had gone. Such was the terrain this was not running, more suicide really. Each athlete put in a token 10 yards of jogging at the col in between the vertical scramble down and the immediate vertical climb up. Looking around at the section of the course that I could see I couldn't envisage there would have been many opportunities for actual running anywhere. Plenty of opportunities for flying if they were to misplace a hand or foothold at any stage, but running? No!

We headed down into the Vall de Ransol where we bumped into a middle aged English couple who had walked up from the road head. This was our first encounter with our fellow countrymen since we parted company with Richard some three days ago and we dearly welcomed the chance to talk to someone other than each other. We stopped a while and chatted. The couple were on a walking holiday in the area and were heading up to the Pic de Serrera, which at 2912m was one of the highest in Andorra. They too were clearly pleased to talk freely in their mother tongue having spent 2 weeks in Andorra without having met another English speaking person. After ten minutes or so we each went on our way.

Our route became somewhat confusing at this point, with less than helpful directions in the guidebook. The main path headed off downhill into the Vall de Ransol ahead of us but our route crossed to the north side of the valley heading for the Coms de Jan refuge. The non existence of any path was always disconcerting and resulted in repeated references to the map. After sometime dithering it turned out that the guidebook instruction to "follow a vague track in the grass that goes ENE" was actually more useful than first appeared, and we found a hint of a long abandoned path which contoured along the north side of the valley. After some half hour we rounded a grassy bluff and the Coms de Jan Refuge came into site some 100 feet above where we stood. The intervening path got lost somewhere amongst the jumble of loose rock and we made our own way to take a seat on a large slab of rock fronting the solid and robust but rather austere looking stone building. It was a gathering point for a number of walkers who congregated in numerous groups in and around the hut.

We made this our lunch stop before the second major ascent of the day. It was unique for us to find such a well populated spot for lunch. The hut door was open behind us and smoke rose gently in the light breeze from a small metal chimney pipe that emitted from an opening in the wall. People milled around the refuge door as the irresistible smell of home cooking wafted from within. There were no English voices amongst the crowd and despite the temptation to investigate the source of the cooking aromas we settled for the last remnants of dry toasties and a somewhat dishevelled looking final piece of everlasting saucisson. When my aching jaw had reached a stage of submission and could no longer compete with the impressively durable saucisson I resorted to the more edible contents of the bag of dried fruit and nuts that we each carried.

It was in some way reassuring to be amongst a hubbub of people again after our enforced exile in the wilds of the Haute Ariege. Although we had encountered other walkers in these remote regions of the Pyrenees it had tended to be at night in the refuges where all the random wanderings of these lonely mountain travellers briefly came together for rest and recuperation before setting of on their respective journeys again the following morning.

Our route that afternoon took us on a diagonal ascent over the southerly ridge of the Pic de la Portaneille on the French border. Upon setting off from the Coms de Jan at first it was once again difficult to identify any path but in the distance we could see the slanting line of a track which headed towards the top of the ridge crossing a ravine near the summit. This gash which cleft the ridge from top to bottom appeared a somewhat formidable obstacle. It was given a specific mention in the guidebook with the cautionary words recommending that "a little care" was required in its crossing. This set off my alarm bells and immediately elevated its status to that of a Himalayan glacial crevasse in my imagination. Given Mr Joosten's let's say occasional inclination towards the understatement, by the time we reached this ravine it had taken on mythical proportions in my mind. Hence my surprise when upon reaching it we found the passage across quite straightforward. I think its dramatic appearance from a distance meant it dominated the view and probably the thoughts of any person approaching from below and when accompanied by the warning it was difficult to be anything but apprehensive but its traverse was quite simple and barely merited a separate mention.

We topped out on what was a bare, flat topped and grassy ridge before descending steeply down grassy slopes towards the Vall de'Incles some 700m below. The path was less than clear once again and made a meandering detour in a general north east direction before rounding a broad ridge and making a traversing descent on exceptionally steep ground towards a very solid and pristine looking Cabana Sorda refuge, located near the outfall of the beautiful Estany de Cabana Sorda. I wonder what the lake was called before they built the refuge?

Like the Coms de Jan the Cabana Sorda was a honey-pot for hikers, many of whom were probably intending to spend the night within its solid coloured granite walls. We however we had a date with some home comforts of our own down in the Vall d'Incles, and upon reaching the foot of the crags across which we had descended, we turned away from the refuge and headed down through the forest to eventually emerge on the narrow tarmac road that threaded its way up the valley. Knowing that Camping D'Incles was closed we headed down the valley to another campsite, which we reached some twenty minutes later. It had showers and real toilets that didn't smell like a Mumbai open sewer.

After we'd put the tent up a visit to the showers was the absolute No 1 priority but we had a short wait because the hot water didn't come on until 5pm!? The sheer pleasure of a hot shower is an indescribable feeling when it's the first you've had in 4 days. I didn't smell too good and was convinced that parts of me, especially the feet and groin area were beginning to rot. I had heard that crotch rot was something suffered by Sir Ranulph Feines on his polar expeditions so I was in good company. The pong emanating from my nether regions resembled a cross between a festering blue stilton and a dead skunk. Standing beneath that hot spray of water was so invigorating and washed away the toils of the day. The sensation of feeling clean again was absolutely wonderful. Afterwards, whilst Michael spent an eternity in the shower, I sat in the campsite bar and polished off a couple of bottles of San Miguel served by the rather surly looking lady who seemed to run the place. It was late afternoon and the small bar, which doubled up as the site office, was empty.

We had decided to have a night on the town as a treat for five days of hard slog and dehydrated food. We headed down the valley towards Soldeu, more of a village than a town. Upon reaching the main road we encountered a bar/restaurant and not wishing to delay our evening of excess any further dived inside. There were a handful of locals at the bar and we ordered our first of many rounds of drinks. The barman/waiter spoke some English but more significantly he had the most pronounced of camp mannerisms. Each round of drinks was met with a Kenneth

Williamsesque, "was that nice for you?"

After a while and several more rounds of drinks this had us in stitches. The bar cleared of other customers and our camp waiter entertained us with his effeminately delivered array of remarks,

"What would sir like now," or,

"Would you like me to put a big one in there?"

The more we laughed, the more he played on our reactions and the more we drank. After an hour or so of soaking up more alcohol than we'd had in all of the last 5 weeks put together we ordered our meals, reverting once again to the magnetic lure of red meat. We both enjoyed what was termed a beef chop with chips and veg and a sizeable baguette, washed down by a local wine and followed by a homemade Christmas tree shaped ice cream. The meal was exquisite and with sizeable portions, most satisfying.

Intent on making a whole night of it we returned to the bar following our meal where we enjoyed a mixed array of beverages from Tia Maria coffees, some local, very potent liquors and more beer. We chased the barman off to some far distant storeroom where he managed to retrieve a bottle of Southern Comfort and we virtually emptied the whole bottle between the 3 of us. I can't remember an awful lot about the return journey to our tent except that it seemed a lot shorter than on the way there. I left Michael somewhere by the entrance to the campsite whispering sweet nothings to his girlfriend Haley on his mobile while I went and crashed out in the tent. And boy did I sleep! Fully anaesthetised against any discomfort and pain I hit the sack and didn't move until around 7.30am the next morning when the pain of a full bladder became overwhelming. Wow what a night!

## Day 37 Monday 7<sup>th</sup> August. Vall d'Incles to Hospitallet pres l'Andorra

Ughh what a morning! A Monday morning at that! There was ice on the tent when we arose, a measure of the cold night of which I had known nothing at the time insulated in the cocoon of my sleeping bag. It was a beautiful blue sky morning but I was in no fit state to appreciate it. No number of cups of tea were going to revive me today. My tongue had welded itself to the roof of my mouth and my head hurt. The thought of any type of exercise at all, let alone lumping a honking great backpack some 18km over rough mountain terrain, was not something I welcomed. My only consolation was that Michael looked worse than me!

We were tardy that morning and it was 10am before we set off up the Vall d'Incles. We had a few miles of road walking which was at least a gentle introduction for the rigours to come. It was a popular walking area and there were numerous cars parked at the road head with people setting off in various directions into the mountains. The accessibility of this valley made it a popular starting point for those heading off into the mountains. It was a warm day and we suffered on our ascent as pure alcohol oozed from our every pore. Our first objective was the unmanned refuge at Juclar where we would stop for lunch. At an altitude of 2294m it was some 500m or so above our starting point and we felt every last centimetre. The path was clear and well defined, which was a significant change for us of late. It wound and twisted its way up the steep and heavily vegetated upper valley in between the tangle of boulders, rocks, crags and waterfalls. After 2½ hours, and a profuse amount of puffing, panting and perspiration, we arrived at the refuge which we had all to ourselves.

The refuge was of a similar construction to all others we had encountered throughout Andorra with solid coloured granite stone walls and a slate roof. We sat at the stone benches on the patio area outside and picked through the final scraps of food that we cobbled together as a lunch. I let Michael have the last of the saucisson as I didn't think my digestive system could take any further onslaught. I satisfied myself with the final shattered segments and crumbs of toastie bread along with a rather smelly and curled up gnarl of cheese that had spent 6 days sweating in a cling film wrapper inside my pack. It was edible and that's about the kindest thing I can say about it.

We pressed on upwards passing the two Estanys de Juclar via a cliff top path. A concrete dam just beyond the Juclar refuge contained the lakes within this steep sided valley. The crystal clear waters revealed massive submerged boulders that disappeared into a deep deep blue of hidden depths towards the centre of the lakes. I was surprised at the nature of the path which traversed some hundred feet or more above the southern bank of the western most of the lakes before descending down a vertical face with the aid of a fixed rope. A feature apparently not worthy of a mention in the guidebook? The path crossed the valley between the two lakes through a scrapyard of glacial debris before heading up to the first of two cols, the Collada del Juclar on the France/Andorra border. The attainment of a col usually meant the next stage would be downhill but not this time. We continued upwards, following the border line to the next col the Port de l'Albe where our three day venture into Andorra ended.

By now we were both pretty much recovered from our alcohol induced incapacity having perspired away the toxins in a sweaty and laboured 3 hour ascent to the col. The Port de l'Albe was our highest point of the day and I wrongly assumed that it also signalled the end of the days ascent and that the main difficulties were now behind us. Not so! The next hour or two took us down into France past a series of very picturesque lakes but the nature of the terrain while beautiful to behold was less attractive to walk upon. Our passage past the Etang de l'Albe then a series of small un-named lakes was over very rough ground indeed, comprising rocks and boulders which contorted and twisted every footstep. What appeared a relatively straightforward route descending through a valley on the map was anything but, with a couple of awkward scrambles over difficult exposed sections high above the lakes. Such rough ground was always hard on the feet and psychologically draining as well. Progress was slow as we carefully picked every foot placement through a sea of ankle breaking propensities.

The area was quite popular with hikers and we encountered numerous other parties on our trek that day. Stopping for a rest at the east end of the Etang de Couart I released my throbbing feet from their incarceration within hot and sauna-like boots and immersed them in the cool waters of the lake. I could swear I heard them hiss as they broke the surface. The sensation was verging on the ecstatic. I sat there on a boulder wearing a satisfied grin as I dangled my feet into the cooling balm of this mountain lake. Immersed in sweet contemplation I reached for the guide book to confirm where our route took us next only to discover to my surprise that the next section entailed an unexpected ascent. Damn! I had wrongly assumed that the remainder of our day after Port de L'Albe was all downhill but from our resting point we next had to cross the outfall at the end of the lake then ascend over and around the end of the north east ridge of the Pic de l'Albe to a further col, the Couillarde de Pedoures. There was only an altitude difference of 21m between where we were now and the col but this clearly belied the amount of ascent involved. I could see at least 50m of ascent from where we were sitting. The map revealed an intervening descent and then re-ascent to the col. It sometimes didn't pay to micro-analyse the route like this and just to take it as it came, but experience had frequently demonstrated to me that the minute you stop paying attention to the map is the time you end up getting lost, and maybe having to correct your mistake with miles of backtracking and possible re-ascent.

Re-acquainting my battered feet with my trusty boots we set off in search of the Couillarde de Pedoures through what Ton Joosten described as a "chaotic landscape full of rocks." Upon rounding the shoulder of the Pic de l'Albe we entered a large bowl in the centre of which stood a tall and rusted metal tower. We couldn't figure out its intended purpose. It looked like an oil derrick or a solitary pylon. It appeared to have the remnants of hoisting gear suggesting either mining activity or possibly a cable car/ski tow but the latter option seemed unlikely since there was no evidence of any other similar structures in the vicinity. I was intrigued as to why it didn't receive a mention in the guide book. It seemed such an obvious and prominent landmark. It remained a mystery and we pressed on to reach the broad and stony col a few minutes later after a gentle ascent from the mysterious metal tower.

The remainder of the route that day was thankfully in descent although it did seem interminable at times. From the col we descended to yet another Pyrenean lake, the Etang de Pedourres (getting bored with these now). Beyond the lake stretched a long and gently descending valley through which meandered the wonderfully named Rau de Baldarques river. The path was well defined and for the first time that day we were able to bowl along at a decent pace. We were becoming very focused on the objective as our trek progressed and at the end of each day, when weary and footsore the scenery passed us by almost unnoticed. So it was that we entered the tiny border post of Hospitalet pres l'Andorre, tired and weary and oblivious to the last few miles of scenery through which we had passed.

It was 5pm and we had booked into a gîte for the night and were looking forward to a night of relaxation, good food and a comfortable bed, followed by a whole day of rest the following day. My knees were sore from the constant pounding of repeated descents with a heavy pack and they needed a reprieve from the constant punishment. After a welcome shower and a change of clothing we sat down to a really smashing meal along with another 10 or so guests, all French. I was too tired for social chit chat and my French wasn't up to it anyway, so after dinner we retired to our room where I soon crashed into a deep sleep in the satisfaction that we had just completed the hardest stage of the HRP and were about to embark upon the final section which would take us through to our final goal, the Mediterranean.

# Day 38, Tuesday 8ᵗʰ August. Rest Day at Ax les Thermes

In 2006 Hospitalet pres l'Andorre was a small border village of some 107 occupants. The name Hospitalet apparently refers to a refuge or hostel and not a small hospital as may be inferred from a direct translation. Probably it's main focal point was the railway which provides the only non coastal cross border train route between France and Spain since the closure of the Pau – Zaragoza line in March 1970. It was opened on 20ᵗʰ October 1908 and at 1428metres the station at Hospitalet is one of the highest in France. Today we were using the station to travel down to the spa town of Ax les Thermes, some 15 miles north into France and 700m lower. Our journey there was as much to pass the time as for any practical reasons although we did need to obtain some supplies for our next few days in the hills. The next 3 nights of our trek were in remote areas where we would be camping and have little opportunity to replenish dwindling food stocks.

We spent the morning around the market where I was struck by sight and smell of the profusion of shrivelled cured meats. It was like a set from a stage version of Lord of the Flies. The various hams, gammons, cured pork, saucisson and other unrecognisable and somewhat putrid looking meats dangling from meat hooks at butchers stalls produced an overwhelming but not unpleasant smell throughout the market and attracted seemingly every fly from southern France. Michael, sanitised from an upbringing that presented all his food in sealed plastic from the cooler displays of supermarket shelves was aghast. This was just that bit too close to the abattoir for comfort for him. The massive cheeses too had an air of durability. They could probably be left to fester for years without detriment to the taste or edibility. I purchased some cheese, comfortable in the knowledge that there was no prospect of it ever going beyond its 'eat by' date, even if I kept it stuffed in my pack and wrapped in my dirty socks and underwear for years. Michael purchased a particularly malodorous piece of saucisson which, for me lacked any nutritious benefits whatsoever on the grounds that it was completely inedible and was guaranteed to result in Michael being escorted by a cloud of flies all the way to the Mediterranean.

We had time to kill in Ax les Thermes which was a pleasant change and much of the afternoon we spent in quiet relaxation at the open Bassin des Ladres (Lepers' Pond) where, along with various other participants we sat bathing our battered feet in the hot sulphur spring waters. The springs were developed in the medieval period on the orders of Saint Louis to treat soldiers returning from the Crusades afflicted with leprosy. The waters, which were used by the Romans, are claimed to treat rheumatism, skin diseases, and other maladies which today included battered feet. At 77c it made a change to the icy waters of the various mountain lakes that had acted as our previous foot spas. We treated ourselves to 2 lunches that day but tempting though it was we kept the alcohol consumption to just a single pint of cold beer not wishing to suffer another hangover for tomorrows walk. Mid afternoon heralded the onset of thunderstorms so we sheltered in a nearby internet cafe before catching a bus replacement for our train which had been cancelled for some unexplained reason. A second night in the gîte was luxury indeed and following another wonderful meal and a more concerted effort at being sociable this time, we eventually went to bed around 9.30pm.

## Day 39, Wednesday 9th August.
## Hopitalet pres l'Andorre to Estany de Lanos

The day started overcast as we set off uphill through the woods above the village of Hospitalet pres l'Andorra. The recommended finish point in the guidebook was the manned Refuge des Besines which makes for a relatively easy section taking little more than 3 hours. We were intending to press on from the refuge to a small shepherds cabane near the northern shores of the Etang de Lanoux. This would have the effect of shortening the following day which included a traverse of the summit of Pic Carlit, our highest point on the whole of the HRP at 2921metres. A days rest, good food and comfy beds had left us in fine fettle and we were both eager to resume our walk that day. Ton Joosten had broken down his version of the HRP into 5 sections with this, the final section coming with a warning as being the longest of all and containing a number of "serious obstacles". Namely Pic Carlit, Pic du Canigou and the Catalonian Pyrenees.

After half an hour of ascent we caught sight of a small French family group up ahead comprising of what I presume were father, mother and daughter. We slowly caught them up on the ascent. It became clear from the few snippets of conversation that I could translate that the father was driving the two women onwards, somewhat reluctantly in their view, from what I could gather. When we caught them up it wasn't easy to pass them on the rather narrow path and there seemed no intention on their behalf of stepping aside to let us pass. Eventually the mother, who was at the rear of the group, stepped to one side and allowed us through, soon followed by the daughter. We nodded with a friendly bonjour and left them behind. The father however was not to be overtaken and strode ahead in front of us with no intention of stepping aside. After ten minutes or so we became detached from the two women who dropped back out of sight but still our French patriarch would not relent. It was as though to be overtaken was a sleight to his personal pride and he stepped up the pace. After some five weeks of hard walking with heavy packs we were fit and not to be shaken off so easily. It became a international battle of wills,

France v England. After a while I became convinced his female companions had taken advantage of their freedom in being taken off the leash and turned back and gone home but still our French leader did not relent. We were snapping at his heals for maybe twenty minutes when he finally stopped and stepped to one side. He growled a begrudged bonjour to our greeting and craned his neck searching for his tardy womenfolk. We pressed on and left him and his battered pride behind.

Out of earshot of our rival I turned to Michael and said, "he didn't want to be overtaken him did he?"

"God yeh I know. What was his bleedin' problem?"

"Don't know, but those women are gonna get it in the neck when they catch up with him!"

Our route continued to ascend and soon brought us out of the forest and onto more open hillsides as we turned east to enter the Besines valley.

As the path entered the valley it followed the line of a former railway line which made for easy walking at a gentle gradient for a while. The line had apparently been installed to service the construction of the dam which contained the Etang des Besines and many of the sleepers were still in position. It was 11am as we reached the dam where we stopped for an early lunch for Michael. After some twenty minutes or so we were passed by our French galley master and his two slaves, who clipped along at his heels like two obedient dogs. I gave them a sympathetic wave as they scurried along at an unrelenting pace. Their tyrant master chose not to glance in our direction and strode away into the distance, head held high smug in the unexpected reclamation of victory. We didn't see them again after that.

Lunch over we set off again making our way along a broad, tree root infested path on the south bank of the lovely Etang de Besines. The waters' edge contained many an idyllic camp spot and a number of hikers had recognised this and taken up residence along the banks of the lake. A curl of smoke rose gently into the tranquil late morning air marking the home of a huddle of tents near the west end of the lake. The temptation was to linger at such a peaceful and enchanting spot but our purpose did not allow such distractions. There were many places on our journey where the desire to tarry and savour the surroundings was strong but our ultimate goal always summoned us on and away from such diversions. Beyond the lake we climbed between the pines of an open wooded hillside where somewhere just above us and out of sight lay the Refuge de Besines, the end point of day 33 in the guidebook. We secretly passed below the refuge and on out of sight up the valley. We still had a couple of hours walk to reach our overnight accommodation, the unmanned Cabane de Rouzet.

Beyond the refuge we were re-united with our old companion the GR10. Not since Gavarnie on day 18 of our trek had we encountered this once familiar trail which we had taken on our first steps in to Pyrenees from the Atlantic coast at Hendaye nearly six weeks ago. The ascent beyond the refuge was of a gentle gradient in a picturesque and deserted valley through the centre of which gurgled a lazy stream. There had been numerous walkers in the lower valley and around the lake but we had this upper valley to ourselves. It was always nice to get away from the crowds. The cloud that beset the morning was now well broken and the sun broke through and brightened the day. We plodded on at a generally modest pace on mostly easy gradients and that leg of the journey soon passed in pleasant surroundings to bring us to our next high point, the Col de Coume d'Agnel. The attainment of the col brought a distinct change in the scenery. Gone were the wooded and steep sided, enclosed valleys. Beyond us to the east stretched open mountain and hillsides with not a tree to be seen. A desolate landscape of tough grass, scattered with rocks and boulders, and interspersed with the pointed peaks of Puig de la Grava and Puig Peric, but it was the steep ramparts of Puig Carlit that held our gaze. Its conical summit rose above all others in the wall of mountains that barred our easterly passage on tomorrows walk. The clear and well defined path dropped gently down from the col passing an archipelago of minor lakes towards the massive Estany de Lanos, of which we could only see the northern half.

Some half hour later we arrived at the Cabane de Rouzet which was to be our home for the night. It was 1.45pm and I caught up on lunch that Michael had consumed some 2 hours earlier.

The cabane was a very basic shelter and we were tempted to erect the tent when, upon looking inside we could see we were going to have a rough night on a hard dirt floor. An old spring bed in the corner of the hut had been covered by a series of mangy looking blankets which looked like they had recently provided the bedding for a herd of goats and were to be avoided at all costs lest the occupant cherished the onset of an infestation of flees and ticks. Needless to say the bed didn't present a viable alternative to the compacted ground.

We had the afternoon to relax in the sun accompanied by a herd of inquisitive wild ponies. They were clearly accustomed to the presence of people and approached quite close nosing for titbits. We didn't really have any spare food although the boldest amongst the herd was rewarded with a dextrose tablet which he seemed to enjoy. We soon realised that the cabane was a busy crossroads for travellers, many of whom passed by that day. It was peculiar that we hadn't seen a soul since passing the Refuge de Besines, the mountains seemingly being deserted, but here was a veritable Picadilly Circus of trekkers and fisherman. Nevertheless, it was a peaceful spot and the periodic arrival and departure of numerous travellers did not intrude upon this restful scene as they made their way on their journeys. The lush pastures around the hut, as well as attracting the dozen or so wild ponies also brought down a herd of izards, a Pyrenean cousin of the chamois. We sat drinking our beloved Earl Grey tea doing Sudoku puzzles in my little paperback puzzle book and just watching the day go by. Despite the sunshine it was quite a cool afternoon with a chill breeze springing up from the east and the frequent hot teas were a necessity if only to warm the hands. We were after all over 7000' up in the Pyrenees and the altitude was having a greater influence than the latitude that afternoon.

We had carried 2 large tins of food with us from our shopping trip to Ax les Thermes yesterday and were spoilt with a pork curry (me) and a beef cannelloni (Michael) and half a baguette each. Whilst we sat eating outside of the hut, it was too dark and dreary inside, first two French girls followed by a couple of French lads arrived and set up camp in front of the cabane. It gave the place a sort of communal feel and a basic reassurance that is provided when in the proximity of other humans in such a remote desolate place. Apart from the initial friendly greetings we each remained distinctly apart in our own isolated worlds, though their presence introduced a certain comfort just through being there. Comfort however was in short supply inside the cabane.

By 8.30pm the sun had dropped behind Puig Pedros to the west and the chill evening air chased us inside of our shelter. Despite the cushion of the therma-rest and bed-roll there was little sleep to be had that night as I turned one way then another in search of a comfortable position. I spent the night in permanent motion and dozed fitfully inside the dark stone walls of the Cabane de Rouzet.

## Day 40, Thursday 10th August, Cabane de Rouzet to Estany de la Pradella

The dawn crept beneath the bottom of the steel plate door and into the Cabane. It was 7.15am. I was relieved to be released from another night of torture. Our neighbours were still encamped outside with no sign of movement. The ponies had gathered all around the hut, no doubt in search of more dextrose tablets. The word was out! We had our usual porridge and tea breakfast and set off along the eastern shore of the Estany de Lanos towards our next major challenge, Pic Carlit, leaving the campers still to emerge from their tents. At 2921m (9580ft) Pic Carlit was the highest point we would reach on our trek. We departed from the GR10 once again and headed southwest on a path some hundred feet or more above the shores of the lake where a group of fishermen were camped. The summit of Carlit was hidden for most of the morning as we traversed above the lake on open slopes before entering an area of sparsely scattered and stunted pines. Hardly a forest! As the dam at the south end of the Estany de Lanos came into view our route took a sharp left turn uphill to follow a tumbling stream, the Ruisseau de Fourats up into the high valleys of the Carlit massif. Following the left bank of this stream the landscape transformed from pine forest to more barren and rocky slopes until we entered an open valley at a small lake the Etang de Fourats.

Ahead we were faced with an intimidating wall of rock. The remaining 1500 feet summit cone of Carlit towered above us in a final defiant barrier to our onward progress. It was hard to conceive that a pedestrian route existed between where we stood and the summit, such was the angle of the slope. As we pushed on past the tiny Forats lake the path entered a massive area of incredibly steep scree through which the route zigzagged ever upwards. We ascended cautiously as the thread of a path became more and more precarious the higher it climbed. The slope was treacherous as we sent rocks cascading down behind us with almost every step. We had to stay close together so as not to shower each other in the deluge of rock that crashed down the mountain in our wake. Once again we had ventured onto a section of the map where the 'path' was defined by the dreaded dotted line, in other words not suitable for any beast that was not equipped with a set of wings. Such was the gradient that it became difficult to look down. There were fewer and fewer places where it was possible to stand safely and view the route behind us. We just had to keep moving and facing in towards the mountain. Our highest summit was not going to relinquish its crest without a fight. I was just glad we were ascending this section and not descending!

We eventually emerged at a narrow col just below the summit having tried our very best to reduce the overall height of the mountain by sending as much as possible crashing down into the valley below. It was a relatively easy stroll to the summit for the remaining 60 feet where we joined a number of other summiteers. Carlit was the highest mountain in the eastern Pyrenees and attracted a large contingent of aspiring ascendees. It was cool on the summit and after a brief photo shoot we headed off down what was deceivingly referred to as the 'tourist route'.

Now to any ordinary person the term 'tourist route' would convey an image of a gentle afternoon stroll in shorts and t-shirt up what must of course be the simplest and easiest of paths, well within the capability of anyone who is merely able to stand on their own two feet. This misnomer is seemingly applied liberally to many popular mountains and the two most obvious examples in the UK, the so called tourist routes up both Snowdon and Ben Nevis are serious undertakings and not to be underestimated. The same could be said of Carlit. The 'tourist route' up from the road head at Lac des Bouillouses was a long, hard and for the final section, a giddy vertiginous ascent requiring the frequent use of hands in a vertigo inducing scramble up and across the east face of the mountain. As usual Michaels mountain goat instincts came to the fore and he raced ahead of his pondering father who I have to say was taken aback that this 'easy' way down Carlit seemed just as hard as the hard way up on the other side of the mountain. As usual I was slow on such ground and took endless care over every hand and foot placement. My reward for such laborious progress was survival and I relished it's sweet taste as I stepped down from the last of the scrambling section on to less vertical ground. Away to the east we could see our final major obstacle of the trek. Pic de Canigou, still some four days walk off.

We continued down a steep ridge still having to resort to use of the hands on occasion, passing more and more people heading for the summit. It was a popular mountain alright and there were many families and relatively young children amongst the would be climbers that day. After descending some 2000 feet we stopped for lunch by a small lake, the Etang de Vallell that was clearly much favoured by all those heading for the summit with hordes of people dotted around its rocky shore. Delving into the contents of our packs the smelly cheese put in an appearance along with the disintegrated remains of our toastie breads that never seemed to survive the rigors of our backpacks. Accompanied by the indestructible sauscisson, which I had decided was best treated as chewing gum as it had the consistency of an elastic band and no matter how much mastication it was subject to would not break down to a point whereby it was actually swallowable, this made up our lunch.

Heading on down away from the mountain we passed literally hundreds of people that day heading up Carlit. It was a marked change to the previous solitude we had come to expect through the Ariege region. We were returning once again to civilisation. The end of the road at Lac des Bouillouses provided the ideal place from which to ascend Carlit and this fine sunny day attracted many would be mountaineers from far and wide. It was like Snowdon on an August Bank holiday. The land to the east fell away with wooded hills and valleys stretching into the distance, dropping away towards the Cerdagne. This heralded a distinct milestone on our journey. We were within touching distance of the end. During this last few weeks we had become walking automatons. Walking, eating, sleeping, walking eating sleeping had become our life. Such was the immensity of the trek it felt like we were on a treadmill at times with mountain after mountain appearing at every col and every summit. It was like the unrelenting hordes of an invading army or the battling the nine headed Hydra, whence upon severing one head another two would grow in its place. The psychological aspect of the challenge was sometimes overwhelming , but now there was light at the end of our long tunnel. On occasions it had sometimes been difficult to see beyond the objective and enjoy the journey, but here at long last our goal seemed within reach and we were fit and strong with no recurrence of the injuries that had plagued us only a few weeks back.

The descent to Bouillouses was a long one but we were helped by the presence of good, well used and well defined paths. A number of people stopped us along the way, clearly unaccustomed to ascending serious mountains, clad in their Nike trainers, enquiring how far to the top. My estimate of "trois heures et demi" and "six heures pour retour a ici" was met with astonishment.

"Non!"

"Mais oui," I ascerted, "six heures pour aller et retour."

We left them deliberating, probably as much at my pigeon French as much as at the prospect that it would take them six hours to get to the top and back to where they were standing, which in turn was still an hours walk from Bouillouses.

We trundled on down through beautiful scenery, dotted with glacial lakes that sat amongst an arid and stony landscape. For the most part we passed all other walkers who were clearly out for more leisurely strolls with the exception of a party of young French trekkers who steamed past us like they were in a race. They were by far the fastest walkers we had encountered on the whole trip and were very soon lost amongst the trees ahead of us as we entered the more densely wooded sections of the lower reaches of the Carlit Massif. Our incentive to push on was the prospect of a cold beer at Bouillouses.

We descended to the western end of the large dam that held back the waters of the Lac des Bouillouses and joined the throngs at a busy hotel terrace. Threading our way through the crowd to an empty table we carefully removed our packs and took our seats amongst the other, less smelly and more smartly attired clientele of the Hotel de Bones Hores. I ordered a 'grande bierre' and Michael a coke. My beer arrived in a glass of bucket proportions and I swear I heard it sizzle as it touched my lips. That initial infusion of ice cold lager to a hot and dehydrated mouth is one of life's great pleasures. I savoured the moment as the carbon dioxide fizzed around my teeth and the cold bitter liquid hissed its sweet way down my throat. I closed my eyes savouring the moment as I emitted a huge 'aaaaaarrrrhhh' as I lay back in my chair, raising the cold , wet glass up to the afternoon sun.

"Oh my god that is absolutely wonderful," I announced.

"Better than sex?" Michael enquired.

"Infinitely," I declared. "Far less effort, and it doesn't pass comment on your performance when you've finished!"

It would have been so easy to spend the rest of the afternoon, feet up on that terrace just boozing! The temptation was strong but we needed to press on to find ourselves a campsite amongst the lakes and forest to the east. I found the beer had gone straight to my legs when we eventually stood up and how me and my pack managed to extract ourselves from the midst of that busy terrace without inflicting mortal injury upon numerous customers I do not know. We headed off across the dam and after a short walk down the tarmac road away from all the hubbub we struck off on a narrow path into the forest. It was late afternoon and we were tired and in search of a suitable bit of flat ground with a convenient fresh water supply on hand where we could stop for the night. The walk through the woods past numerous small and picturesque lakes was exquisite but it was lost on us. We were very tired and hungry and just wanted to pitch the tent and rest. We passed a few other people along the way including a group of people gathered at what would have been an ideal camping spot next to the Estany Negre. The path ascended from this lake, still in dense woodland where we encountered two mounted police officers, who took the opportunity to point out that there was no camping allowed in the area before 8pm. I was not in the mood for stupid rules and after smiling politely and thanking them in my very best French we continued up the path and they trotted off in the direction from which we had just come.

"If they think I'm gonna hang around until 8 o'clock before pitching the tent and cooking dinner they can kiss my bleedin'arse!"

"Not a very nice thought," Michael pointed out.

"There's another lake coming up in a few minutes and I'm not walking any further than that. I haven't come all this way to be bossed around by some jumped up little jobsworth French squirt in a uniform with an inflated opinion of his own fuckin' importance," I announced angrily.

"Oh no, we're goin' to jail." Michael said nervously.

"8 o'clock, what a ridiculous bloody rule. It's obviously only there to be broken. Jesus we're in the middle of bleedin' nowhere, what effin difference does it make when you pitch the tent?"

"I'm too young to go to jail."

"For god sake have some backbone will ya. We're gonna pitch the tent at the next available spot 'cos I couldn't walk an inch further, I'm knackered. If they come back we'll just act soft!"
Yeh, well that's easy for you!"

"Watch it shorty or you'll be sleepin' outside with all the crawlies and the BEARS!"

"What, as opposed to sleepin inside with all the fartin', snorin', smelly feet and the enormous old grizzly?"

Some ten minutes after our meeting with the 'forest police' the Etang de Pradella came into sight through the trees as did our obvious campsite, a clearing in the forest with a couple of large logs in its midst and a mere fifty yards from the lake.

"Home sweet home," I declared.

"Look it's even got a couple of chairs and a view back through the trees, across the lake to watch the sun set behind Pic Carlit. What could be more perfect?"

"A 5 star hotel, jacuzzi, sauna, big soft feather bed and one of them blond Swedish masseuses you were goin' on about the other week!" Michael declared.

"Some folk are never bloody happy!"

I dropped my pack to the ground and slumped down onto one of the massive logs and just sat there waiting for the aches and pains to melt away and for the tent to pitch itself.

"Phew, that was a long, hard day."

It was 6.30pm and we'd been on the go for some ten hours. The bivvy site was ideal except that it was right next to the path in full view of all, including our two over zealous mounties. Being so late in the day I didn't expect we would see many people out and about now and I was too damn tired to be bothered about officialdom so we just said 'to hell with it' and put up the tent. Dinner was of the dehydrated variety once again, but most welcome nevertheless. Our two friends did not return thankfully and soon after eating we both crashed out, comforted by the thought that we had that day overcome one of the last few remaining major obstacles in Carlit and were at last within reach of our goal.

## Day 41, Friday 11th August. Estany de Pradella to the Valee d'Eyne

This morning there was an extraordinary role reversal, unprecedented throughout previous nights under canvas. Michael was first up and actually made me a cup of tea. This was a rare treat indeed and I didn't say too much, other than to thank him, lest I put him off the prospect of future similar indulgences. I enjoyed my gentle awakening to another glorious sunny day, sat at the entrance to the tent, sipping Earl Grey, still half encased in my sleeping bag, watching the morning sun light up the distant slopes of Carlit across a misty, flat-calm Etang de Pradeille. It was a most civilised start to a comparatively easy day that would see us finish in ascent into the Catalonian mountains for a third consecutive night away from civilisation.

We packed up the tent before the police arrived to tell us we couldn't camp after 3am or something equally daft and setting off soon picked up a wide forest track that we were to follow for quite some miles. Whilst the use of what amounted to a major highway for us made for fast progress and minimal fussing around with the map we were encased within the claustrophobic confines of a mature pine forest. Hemmed in by a 60 foot wall of pine needles with just the occasional glimpse of the outside world where a fire break or adjoining path would provide just a hint of a view. We cracked on at a strong pace for what seemed like an eternity, passing under a chair lift and beneath a couple of ski pistes. The presence of winter sports paraphernalia seemed out of place. It didn't feel like we were still in a mountain region. However, although we were essentially walking along a valley we were still at an altitude of some 1800m. We stepped out along that forest track forcing the pace for some 4 miles or so but it felt like 40. After about an hour and a half we finally emerged onto a tarmac road, the D618. From the map we could see we were quite close to a number of villages and towns although any sight of them was obscured by a surrounding wall of forest.

We turned left along the flat road and after a short while made a 90 degree right turn on a narrow track with forest on our left and the open ground, long since cleared of trees on our right. This reassuringly distinct track stopped after a couple of hundred metres and we were deposited on a vague and infrequently used hint of a path that headed off into the forest. This narrow thread of flattened earth meandered into the trees and dispersed in a web of minor little trails each as unconvincing as the next. The guide books reference to "just follow the most obvious track" convinced me we were lost again since it would be too great a stretch of any imagination to describe any of these vague trails as 'obvious'. They were clearly the last fleeting evidence of some previous lost soul who was probably still wandering aimlessly somewhere through this perpetual forest. I took a bearing and we headed down the section of lightly compressed earth that came closest to heading in the direction we required. After 30 seconds it had turned through 90 degrees and plunged deeper into the dense woodland. We blundered on, picking up bits of trails here and there until, as if by magic, we were once again deposited onto another road, which according to Mr Joosten was the D10c, where the Haute Route meets the GR10 once more.

After another brief shortcut downhill through the forest we returned to this road and soon descended into the small village of Bolquere. This was our first opportunity to restock our food supplies since leaving Hospitalet 3 days ago and we were relishing the prospect of fresh food. It was 11am and we were ready for an early lunch.

A single general store in the centre of the village seemed to stock a wide variety of food including some rather irresistible looking chickens that were revolving on a rotisserie near the shop entrance. There was simply no way we could have left that shop without one of these succulent looking French fowl. The pair of us were drooling at the prospect of feasting on something so incredibly wholesome after weeks of pasta and dehydrated mush. We duly purchased a large chicken, along with various other foodstuffs for our journey and retraced our tracks outside to a small picnic bench next to the small stream just on the outskirts of the village. The subsequent scene was something akin to a stone-age feast. It was a throwback to the hunters returning to the cave with a brontosaurus for dinner. After the initial, almost civilised, apportioning of the chicken there followed a 10 minute feeding frenzy akin to that of the shark fests of the southern oceans as seal pups first venture into the water only to be ripped apart by these lurking great white predators. I doubt that this sleepy little village had ever in its history witnessed such a scene of utter carnage. The chicken carcass was devoid of all flesh upon culmination of our feast.

It must have been a peculiar sight to have witnessed. We barely raised our heads and didn't speak throughout the whole period of consumption. I could just envisage a David Attenborough commentary of the whole scene.

*"Here in a remote corner of the Eastern Pyrenees we find two primitive males of the homo-carnivorous-scousicus species feasting on their unfortunate prey. Such is their concentration on the food before them they are blissfully unaware of the presence of our camera crew only a few feet away. Thanks to the expert photography of our skilled team we are able to witness the fundamental savagery of these wonderful beasts, especially the large silverback. Look as he jealously guards his kill whilst ripping apart the remains of his meal with those powerful incisors in a display of unparalleled primeval barbarity. Such scenes belie the otherwise gentle nature of these most resourceful and intelligent of beasts."*

After probably our most satisfying of lunch breaks in nearly 2 months, followed by a brief siesta we ambled back through the sleepy village and on down a narrow country lane which rolled gently downhill in the hot afternoon sun towards the Col de La Perche, a tiny hamlet at the highest point on the main N116 road. This would have been our finishing point had we not opted to travel onto Salardu, missing out the High Pyrenees. This was the Cerdagne region on the border of France and Spain. A geological anomaly that made up the largest open space in the Pyrenees, 26 kilometres long and some six kilometres wide and all above 1000metres. It harboured a number of oddities within its relatively small area, including a series of peculiarly named villages such as Ger, Alp, Das, Age, Err and Hix and the even more economically named Ur. It seemed to me that someone in a hurry had cobbled together a seemingly random assortment of letters that had drawn them from a hat to form a haphazard collection of truly bizarre placenames.

Through the middle of the Cerdagne ran the renowned PetitTrain Jaune, the Little Yellow Train, whose tracks passed through the highest SNCF railway station in France at 1593 metres. The line, 63km in length, was opened in 1910 linking Villefrance-de-Conflent and Mont-Louis. It was extended to Latour de Carol in 1927 to link up with the Trans Pyrenean railway that we had used some days previous at Hospitalet. As we ambled down the narrow lane towards Col de la Perche we came by the station just before reaching the main N116 road. Stopping at a convenient bus shelter outside of the deserted station, we stepped into its shade and out of the hot afternoon sun for a drink of the still cool water we had collected that morning from the Estany de Pradella. This was our lowest altitude since leaving Alos de Isil some 10 days previously and the corresponding increase in temperature was noticeable. We were both feeling a little soporific after our lunchtime over indulgence and we loitered in the shade of the bus shelter for quite some time savouring the respite from the burning sun. The stop allowed us to access our water bottles as opposed to the hydration bags where the water was always warmed through close contact with our bodies and from the heat of the sun. The drinks bottles on the other hand were cool and refreshing and the sensation of cold water running down our throats cut straight through our thirst.

Another strange quirk of this Cerdagne region was the Spanish enclave of Llivia, measuring some 6km by 3km which was cut off from the neighbouring Spanish territory by some 2 km and completely surrounded by France. This bizarre situation arose from the poorly drafted Treaty of the Pyrenees in 1659, which split Cerdagne between France and Spain. Under the terms of the treaty Spain was required to cede only villages to France. Since Llivia was considered a city and not a village due to its status as the ancient capital of Cerdanya it remained under Spanish rule. In 1939, at the end of the Spanish Civil War, there was some discussion of Llívia remaining a free territory of the defeated Republican government, but this was never carried out.

With some reluctance we emerged from the protective canopy of our lonely bus shelter and ventured back out into the afternoon sun. Passing under the railway line we crossed the main road of the N116 and headed off up the gently rising D33 road towards the small village of Eyne. It was an inconspicuous little place and I'm almost sure we passed through unnoticed. We were soon off-road again amongst the familiar territory of a woodland path heading up the Vallee d'Eyne and into the Catalonian Pyrenees. It was late afternoon by now and many parties of walkers were heading down the path after their day in the hills. It was at this stage that I became distinctly aware of the pong that was emanating from every pore in my skin. As we ascended steadily and my heart and lungs worked harder to supply the blood and oxygen to my muscles I began to sweat more. This in turn seemed to re-active the old stale sweat that had become engrained in my clothing and especially the shoulder straps of my backpack. Each time we passed another group of hikers descending the path towards us I grew more and more conscious of this unearthly whiff that filled my nostrils constantly. I was convinced that anybody within a few metres would be overcome by such a decrepit odour. I even took to passing people on the opposite side of what was a quite wide path in order not to offend them too much.

I stopped for a second and turned to Michael, "whose turn is it to do the washing tonight? I've got a few items that could do with cleaning." I announced.

Michael looked at me, knowing full well that I was not serious and replied curtly, "if you think I'm going anywhere near touching any items of clothing that have been even remotely attached to your body then you're clearly even more mad than I thought you were!"

"What do you mean?" I questioned, as innocently as I could.

"Do you own bleedin' washing," that's what I mean.

"Oh well I'm glad we've got that cleared up then. We wouldn't want you getting your little hands dirty would we?" I smiled.

We emerged from the cover of trees and continued to ascend a straight valley scanning the opposite bank of the river for a suitable campsite away from the path. We eventually found a spot of flat ground at the end of a grassy ridge as the the last few stragglers wandered down the valley towards Eyne. One of the first priorities, for me anyway, was to bathe away three days of cumulative stench. Checking there were no more day-trippers descending past our camp I stripped off and ventured into a pool of ice cold water in the fast flowing stream. I crouched down and struggled to catch my breath as I splashed water over my body, struggling to work up any sort of lather with the remaining sliver of soap. As I was concentrating on keeping my feet and not stooping so low that my genitals were immersed in the icy waters I was unaware that Michael was stood on the bank merrily taking photos, of me. Little rat!

We had purchased pork steaks at Bolquere for our dinner that evening and decided that the best means of cooking them would be on an open fire, so as I washed various items of clothing in the river Michael set about collecting firewood. From our vantage point high up in the Eyne valley we gazed back west towards Carlit and other distant pinnacles of our earlier travels. Two portions of meat in the course of one day was an unprecedented treat for us as we sat on conveniently placed boulders outside of the tent transfixed by the dying embers of our campfire. A peace descended upon our lofty home nestled high above the last vestiges of human habitation some thousand feet of more below. We had the Vallee d'Eyne to ourselves and sat chatting and drinking endless mugs of tea followed by a nightcap of hot chocolate as another days sun set in the western sky behind grey folds of endless mountains beyond the twinkling lights of the Cerdagne far below.

## Day 42, Saturday 12ᵗʰ August. Vallee d'Eyne to Refuge d'Ull de Ter

Saturday morning dawned cool and breezy with thick cloud masking the summit of Carlit and heading our way. We were up at 6.45am and away soon after continuing up the Valle d'Eyne onto the border ridge at the Col d'Eyne or Col de Nuria, depending upon which side of the border you came from. It was a long ascent and for once I was trailing in Michaels wake. He was very fast that day and I couldn't sustain the pace of his younger legs. We passed a large herd of izards which scattered ahead of us just before the col. The final steep climb led us through a large bank of snow which had failed to succumb to the summers thaw. It was cold at this altitude and in a stiffening breeze we each donned our fleeces and jackets to try and hold onto some body heat.

The col was a flat, barren rocky landscape where the only vegetation that could survive the harsh conditions were the hardy lichens and mosses that clung to the rocks. The cold wind swept across the col from the north west belying the warning by Joosten of the hot and arrid conditions we could expect to face as we neared the Mediterranean. This was the coldest we had felt on the whole walk! Our route was to take us along the border ridge over a series of high peaks, Pic d'Eina (2786m), Pic de Noufonts (2861m), Pic de la Fosse du Geant ( 2801m) and the Pic de la Vaca (2826m) all of which sounds somewhat ambitious in a single days walk but with modest ascents and decent paths the peaks came and went without any difficulty. After the second and highest of the summits we dropped down to the Coll de Noufonts were we joined once again by our old companion the GR11. Not since a brief encounter at the Pla de Boet on day 34 had our paths crossed and it was reassuring to have the red and white paint flashes of a well defined path to guide us once more. The GR11 had ascended from the curious settlement of Nuria some 2000 feet beneath us in the valley.

The most notable feature of Nuria is that its only means of access other than by the web of paths and mule tracks that approached from both France and Spain, is an electric railway. These days this is mostly used to carry tourists and skiers up to the village that is dominated by the enormous prison like structure of the sanctuary.

The railway built in 1931 climbs up the Nuria Valley from Ribes de Freser via Queralbs to Nuria and ascends some 1062m (3484feet) in its 12.5km. There are no roads beyond Querelbs and the railway is the only form of transport into Nuria as it ascends alongside the old mule track. 7km of the line is a rack railway which is necessary in order to provide the traction needed to overcome gradients of upto 15%.

As we ascended from the Col de Noufonts towards the Pic de la Fosse du Geant we noticed a group of 3 hikers ascending the GR11 path, maybe a hundred feet below us on the ridge. One of the most striking aspects of this group was that we could smell their perfume/deodorant/after shave from such a distance. It wafted up the mountain towards us. We speculated for some moments as to whether these people had maybe bathed in the stuff but concluded that this was what normal people smell like and we had become unaccustomed to such aromas in our narrow world of sweat and body odour. A more sinister aspect of our environment though was the weather closing in behind us. Although it was still clear as we reached the summit of Pic de la Fosse du Geant we could see all around us the valleys filling with mist and dark cloud approaching from the west. As always in the Pyrenees this really spooked me. One encounter with near death in the form of a thunderstorm was already one too many and I eyed these dark clouds as harbingers of the storm to follow.

We quickened our pace and after a few more ups and downs arrived at the Col de Nou Creus or Col des Neuf Croix which as its name suggests is marked by a series of 9 metal crosses.

I have since tried to discover the significance of the nine crosses but have been unable to obtain any information. I am left to wonder whether they mark the passing of nine petrified souls in some terrible tempest that beset these mountains in some previous era. Who knows?

We stopped at the col for lunch until the crump of far off thunder invaded our little world and reminded us we should not tarry. We left the nine crosses behind, now heading for our final summit of the day, the Pic de la Vaca, with hastened stride. The mist rose higher in the valleys below and dark clouds finally caught us and enveloped the ridge ahead. This was still early in the day. Not the normal time for the once customary thunderstorms. The thunder remained someway distant as we ascended to our final peak and then beyond, stepping into Spain, on a compass bearing towards the Col de Tirapitz which would lead us down from the border ridge. After some initial confusion we found the col in swirling mist and beat a hasty retreat down into the valley of the Torrent de las Barracas. All the time the gloom deepened and whilst distant rumblings of thunder remained distant they held us in a grip of fear. Even though we were off the high ridge this was open terrain with no opportunities for shelter. We had no option but to press on to the Refuge Ull de Ter, still some 5km distant and over yet another col.

We hadn't seen anybody since leaving the Col de Nou Creus. The mountains had become abandoned only to fools such as us who persisted with their forlorn and wretched objectives. All the sensible people had long since abandoned the cause and were sitting in a comfy bar drinking sangria, laughing at the suckers still out and fleeing the teeth of the storm. We scurried over the low Col de la Marrana and descended in to the Circo de Ull de Ter where surprisingly some other fools were gathered, including two particularly stupid fools who were descending the Puig Gra de Fajol towards the col. These two individualshad decided upon a short-cut down which was leading them onto a vertical cliff. They were probably some 500 feet above us and I whistled and shouted to gain their attention. They were descending on steeper and steeper ground and heading directly towards a series of what appeared impossibly vertical crags. They heard my whistle and I beckoned to my right, (their left) to try and encourage them to abandon the folly of their impossible descent route. They hesitated for a few moments and then continued on their original course just as a sinister rumble of thunder echoed around the valley walls.

"Stuff this, I'm not hanging around to watch these two idiots get stuck on a cliff face in a thunderstorm", I declared, and without further ado we set off ever faster on the last mile to the Refuge. I don't know what happened to those guys. I can't envisage that it would have been possible for them to descend the way they were going and I just hope they had the sense to turn back before they got into really serious trouble. We arrived at the Refuge d'Ull de Ter at a very early 2pm just as the first drops of rain were beginning to fall.

The refuge was empty when we arrived and we sat in the deserted lounge area relieved to have escaped the impending storm, which actually never arrived. It was wet and miserable with rain all afternoon but any rumblings of thunder were always distant, at least a couple of valleys away. The early afternoon passed slowly, punctuated by the occasional arrival of another group of guests including a party of 3 Spanish girls, probably in their early thirties, who livened the place up with their laughter. They invited us to play a Spanish version of Ludo/Frustration which in my case lived up to its name. I could not roll a six to save my life and on the few occasions when I did manage to get out of the starting blocks I was immediately pounced upon by one of my opponents much to their obvious delight. I came fourth out of four, as any decent Englishman would do in such a situation.

We spent much of the afternoon in their company awaiting the formal opening of the dormitories. They fortunately spoke good English and proceeded to teach Michael and I Spanish, with limited success I must add. Amid much laughter at our pathetic attempts at some of the more guttural pronunciations the rest of the afternoon passed quickly as we stumbled through our impromptu Spanish lessons. It was quite cool in the refuge and I was pleased to eventually be able to get a hot shower, which was coin operated and on a very short timer. I emerged from the small shower cubicle after half a shower and still partially soaped, in my (clean) undies and with my towel over my shoulder to be greeted by the one of the Spanish girls stood outside patiently waiting her turn in the shower. She was draped loosely in a skimpy towel, which barely covered the front of her body and tantalizingly left her exquisitely sexy bottom on full view. She skipped past me with a smile and a giggle and after returning my eyeballs to their sockets and collecting my chin from the floor, I and resisted the urge to skip in after and regaining a modicum of composure I ambled off to the men's dorm, partially stunned, even mildly embarrassed but secretly delighted at my unexpected encounter.

We joined them all later at dinner, all fully clothed, where they described their last 2 days in the Catalan Pyrenees during which they had got lost on 2 occasions and ended up climbing the wrong mountain and descending to the wrong valley, resulting in them having to make massive detours to get back on track. It appeared that the concept of using a compass was quite alien to them and I wondered how on earth they had survived this long. What they lacked in mountain skills they made up for in social skills and it was probably amongst our most socially enjoyable evenings of the entire trip.

We retired to the dorm around 10pm after a pleasant evening of social chat. The sleeping arrangements were on alpine bunks of about six beds in a row. This is ok generally so long as the person next to you is not a snorer or restless sleeper. Tonight was not my lucky night. After lights out it soon became apparent that the guy next to me wanted to practice starfish impressions all bloody night and I would continually encounter an arm or leg flung over onto my section of bed. After an hour or two of this I was getting really hacked off and retrieved my backpack from the bottom of the bed and placed it between us which wasn't easy in the dark. The pack didn't smell too good and it's presence had the effect of forcing my unwelcome bed partner to face the opposite way and focus his attentions on the guy in the next bed. I dozed off with the aroma of stale sweat in my nostrils from the backpack but safe in the knowledge that I had a barrier between me and the sea creature in next bed.

## Day 43, Sunday 13<sup>th</sup> August 2006, Refuge d'Ull de Ter to Refuge de Mariailles

I'd had another crap nights sleep, what with trying to avoid the effin' octopus in the next bed and then spending the remainder of the night trying to suppress the urge to fart, sleep had been hard to come by. We joined the 3 Spanish girls for breakfast. They were walking to Nuria on this their final day in the mountains and for the first time actually set off early (7.50am) following some tardy starts. We set off (8.15am) into a bright sunny morning and descended from the refuge towards the tarmac road, crossing a rotten and flimsy looking bridge across a small ravine. Michael asked to go first as he was convinced the bridge would not survive my crossing. It did, although I couldn't envisage it being around much longer in all truth. We reached the road and immediately turned up hill towards the Vallter 2000 ski resort. Upon arrival at a large car park we skirted around a scruffy looking building in search of our path. It was by no means clear at first. The ascent continued behind the empty building, on quite steep and rough scree. Our fitness was at its peak by now and we quickly devoured this 300m ascent to arrive at the entrance to a large plateau, the Porteille de Mourens.

I was somewhat concerned at the forecast, which according to our 3 Spanish friends, was for rain, cold winds and possible thunderstorms in the afternoon. It was ok for the moment with largely blue skies predominating but we could see dark clouds far over to the south and west so we didn't hang around. The Porteille de Mourens gave access to the first of a number of plateaux that we were to encounter that day, the Pla de Coma Armada. It would have been a tricky proposition finding the way across this featureless wilderness except for the fact that the path had been marked by a series of large flat stones that had been set into the ground. The walking was relatively easy on almost level ground and skirted to the north of Pic de Coma Armada and Puig de la Llosa on the border ridge. We were now back in France again.

On approach we didn't appreciate the significance of the next col on the ridge until upon our arrival we eyed the most delightful of sights in the distance, The Mediterranean. It's sudden appearance in a distant haze of blue to the east was both unexpected and inspirational. We were still over seven days walk away and I hadn't really expected to be able to see the Med until the section of Pyrenees Orientales during the last 3 days of the walk after Amelie les Bains, but there it was! We were looking down upon the Badia de Roses on the Spanish Costa Brava. It was a most uplifting sight and generated a buzz of conversation between us, which was in itself quite unusual.

We continued east across another plateau, the Pla de Campmagre, leaving the border ridge behind for the final time that day and skirted the next peak, the Roc Colom, at 2507m the last border summit above the 2500m height, another indication of our progress. Arriving at another col, our onward route was by no means clear and the guidebook was once again somewhat misleading. "Walk NE on a vague path," actually led us to the edge of a steep precipice above the valley of Les Conques. The path disappeared completely after about 100m distance from the col we had left and a short period of reappraisal was required. Referral to the map indicated that we were supposed to be following beneath a ridge to our right that ran in a ENE direction. Our error was easily corrected but reliance on the guide book alone was once again shown to be a flawed tactic. We easily corrected our mistake and picked up a faint path that brought us to the next col Porteille de Rotja. From there the path became more distinct and we sped along with the white pinnacles of les Esquirdes de Rotja ridge on our right. Frequent notches and gaps in the white rock allowed for repeated glimpses of the Mediterranean on the horizon.

After an hour or so the path contoured away from the ridge and became lost in a rocky wilderness leaving us to improvise our own route up to the next col, the Collades des Roques Blanche where we joined a wide dirt road that had ascended some 2500 feet from the French Pir Valley to the south east and continued over to Vernet de Bains and Villefranche de Conflent, the starting point for the Little Yellow Train. The next stage took us along one of these dirt roads, in a north easterly direction, ascending steadily to our final plateau of the day, the Pla de Guillem. We left the road here and set off across a featureless wilderness with no path, heading away from the ridge that had guided us for many miles that day. The cloud that had chased us all day was now covering parts of the ridge we had walked on that morning and we hurried away from its relentless pursuit passing a wild and remote Cabane du Pla Guilhem high up at the edge of the plateau. We scurried on down the ridge to the north of the cabane on an improving path to pick up the same dirt road we had earlier left behind at the plateau at the Collade de la Roquette. After two short-cuts that avoided a couple of prolonged and drawn out hairpin bends we picked up the dirt road for the final time that day and it accompanied us all the way to the Refuge de Marrielles. It was 2.45pm and we had once again escaped the rain which had consumed the mountains in our wake.

The refuge was only half full if that, according to the eccentric but likeable warden.

"Ah, Monsiour Taylor. My tailor is rich." This was taught to me in my first English lesson!" announced the mildly potty warden upon our arrival.

"You are English and of course you will like a cup of tea now, yes?"

"Oui s'il vous plait monsieur."

"Ah, vous parlez Francais?

"No, not really," I responded quickly before things became too complicated.

Dinner was an interesting concoction of rabbit stew, veg and rice. A large pot containing the stew was placed in the centre of the table from which all the guests helped themselves. The trouble with rabbit stew is that rabbits are so scrawny there is never much meat involved. However, Michael was adventurous with the ladle and managed to scoop a large block of meat onto his dish. It was only as the meal progressed and he removed the gravy and bits of meat and onions etc that he finally realised he was looking at a rabbits head, teeth and all, that was looking back up at him!

"Oh my god, it's a bleedin' rabbits head," he announced. "Shit what have I been eating?"

The warden, who was sat opposite, roared with laughter and informed Michael that it was regarded as a delicacy and that he should consider himself privileged.

I could see Michael wasn't convinced and he moved the remains of the head to the side of his plate and continued with his meal, examining every mouthful in minute detail thereafter.

We met an American guy from New York, Tim, who was travelling around southern France with his mother in law. He was an interesting chap and we were engaged in conversation for quite some time after dinner. When we had finished eating, we all wandered outside into what had become a rather grey and dismal evening, with oppressive grey clouds shrouding the surrounding mountain tops. Then, quite suddenly, in a spectacular and unexpected show of impressive grandeur, the sun dipped beneath the clouds beyond Carlit to the west and lit up the sky in a spectacular fiery sunset that for several minutes turned the whole world orange.

## Day 44, Monday 14ᵗʰ August. Refuge de Marrielles to Refuge de Cortalets

Today we were to face our final major test on the HRP, Pic de Canigou. At 2784metres (9134ft) it is well down the league table in seventh place in order of altitude so far as Pyrenean summits on the HRP are concerned, behind Pic Carlit (2921m), Tusse de Montarque (2889m), Pic de Noufonts (2861m), Pic de la Fosse du Geant (2801m), Pic d'Eina (2786m) and Pic de Nou Creus (2799m), four of which we went over yesterday. However, it is regarded as an iconic peak in the eyes of the local Catalans. Its relative isolation at the end of the Pyrenean chain, steep flanks and close proximity to the coast give it a dramatic appearance when viewed from the plains of southern France around Perpignan, such that it was considered to be the highest mountain in the Pyrenees until the eighteenth century. This mountain has symbolical significance for Catalan Nationalist groups. On its summit there is a cross that is often decorated with the Catalan flag. Every year on the 23d June, the night before St Johns Day (*nit de Sant Joan*), there is a ceremony called *Flama del Canigó* (Canigou Flame), where a fire is lit at the mountaintop. People keep a vigil during the night and take torches lit on that fire in a spectacular torch relay to light bonfires somewhere else. Some estimates conclude that about 30,000 bonfires are lit in this way all over Catalonia on that night.

This mountain held its own symbolism for us. It was the last big challenge on our trek. Beyond Canigou the peaks diminished to around half of this altitude on their final defiant march to the Mediteranean. We were up at 6.55am and away by 7.55am. The guidebook recommended a finish at the refuge at Mines de Batere but we had cut this short and intended to finish at the Refuge des Cortalets. The route initially followed the GR10 path and we were accompanied by numerous other walkers along the way. After about an hour of steady ascent we struck away from the GR10 uphill on a less well defined path marked with yellow paint flashes, soon passing a basic stone cabane, Cabane Arago. As we moved higher the terrain assumed a more barren appearance of rock and scree. The path ascended in long sweeping zig-zags on steeper and steeper ground before a final incredibly steep ladder of rock led to the summit. This was probably the most serious bit of scrambling/climbing on the whole route. The last 50 feet were almost vertical and required careful placements of hands and feet and a clear head. Looking back I would not have fancied the same route very much in descent, that's for sure!

The summit brought us into the full icy blast of a cold north wind. We were the only fools on the top in shorts and T shirts. All the sensible people had long trousers and windproof jackets. After a brief photo shoot we scurried off in search of warmth and immediately encountered a constant procession of people ascending on what was deemed the tourist route up from Cortalets. The path was narrow in places and we frequently needed to stand aside to allow others to pass or on occasion others would stand aside and allow us to pass. This convenient arrangement of mutual courtesy worked well until we got caught behind a family who were descending particularly slowly and were not prepared to stand aside to let us or anybody else past. When I realised the extent of their rudeness I actually became embarrassed when not a single thank you, merci or gracias passed their lips as they marched on downhill almost brushing people aside in the full and unyielding expectation that it was everybody elses duty to stand aside and let them through. It was a family of four, father and mother with a teenage son and daughter of northern European origin from their occasional conversation. I cringed as people remarked at their rudeness and made sure I thanked all of those who had stepped aside to let us pass in case they thought we were all together as one party.

After some ten minutes or so I asked in both English and French if we could pass. After a few attempts the daughter, who was back marker of the four, stepped to one side and let us through. Similarly the son did the same a few minutes later. The parents however had no intention of giving way and presented a formidable wall of north European resistance at any attempts to pass. I persisted in requesting that they let us pass but they refused to acknowledge our request despite actually turning to look behind on a couple of occasions. I was becoming really pissed off with this ignorant duo who seemed to regard any concession of ground as a sign of weakness to be avoided at all costs. I bided my time. Michael and I were fit, strong and particularly agile by now and the opportunity to skip past these two dinosaurs was going to present itself.

Patience eventually paid off after some twenty minutes of being stuck in the middle of our slow moving convoy. A large party of some dozen or more hikers were ascending towards us and I could see we were all going to meet on a particularly narrow section of path with very steep ground below. I turned to Michael as the two muppets ahead of me came to their first and only stop and announced sharply, "follow me!"

I scooted up some ten feet above the path on a narrow balcony, almost running, much to the astonishment of the people ascending towards us and apparently much to the annoyance of the bloke we passed who shouted some untranslatable angry insult after us. As we jumped backed down to the path ahead of the traffic jam I couldn't resist a loud whoop of "Yeeeeeehaaaa!

I turned to see a red faced look of anger as our path blocker shook his fist in the air in frustration as we danced on down the path unimpeded. I must confess I was completely baffled at their behaviour could not comprehend why anybody would be so unco-operative in such a situation. I was almost tempted to do a moonie as a final parting gift but resisted the temptation in case I lost my balance and fell down the mountain. Imagine the ignominy of being found by the French Mountain Rescue Team with your trousers around your ankles. Mmmm, no, not a good idea!

We zipped on down the mountain into a thick grey mist arriving at Cortalets at 12.05pm, just in time for lunch, which we ate outside at a picnic bench. We had taken 4hrs 10mins for what was designated a 5hr 30min day. This would have been completely beyond us some weeks earlier. Six weeks of humping massive packs up and down mountains had brought about a level of fitness unprecedented in my whole lifetime. I could see I was probably some 2-3stone lighter. Gone was the belly bulge that had hung over my belt at Hendaye. I barely had the hips to hold my shorts up anymore and there was hardly any belt left to tighten on the waist strap of my backpack. On the downside I no longer had the insulation that protected me from the cold and after our lunch we had to retire to the inside of the refuge that was actually quite busy with midday diners by now. We ordered a procession of hot drinks and changed out of our damp clothes in the toilets but had difficulty keeping warm despite donning our fleeces and attaching the leggings to our shorts. It was by no means warm inside that refuge.

We could probably have quite easily walked on to Mines de Batere and I regretted cutting the day short. It left us with a whole afternoon with nothing to do and as per the procedure in the majority of hostels we were not allowed into the dorms until at least 4.30pm. At 4.30 on the dot we were shown our room. I scurried off to the shower to try and warm up. It was coin operated again and after my allocated 3 minutes I stood there covered in soap which I had to rinse off with cold water, completely defeating the bleedin' object of getting warm altogether. I didn't like this place. There were rules everywhere, in French, Catalan and English. In the bedrooms, the corridors the bathroom, the bar, everywhere!

Don't eat your own food in the refuge.

Don't take drinks outside of the bar.

Don't wear your boots.

Don't smoke.

Don't have lights on after 10pm.

Don't talk after 10.30pm.

Don't talk before 6.00am.

Don't, don't don't!!

The assistant who directed us to our room even gave us a demonstration on how to fold our blankets before leaving. This was all far too regimented for me. I felt like screaming. I couldn't abide such a strictly run regime after our weeks of freedom in the hills. It was like a bloody boot camp. The discipline of the place robbed it of any atmosphere or character for me and I wanted to be a million miles away. I actually felt like a criminal for leaving my rubbish (biscuit wrappers etc) in the only waste bin I could find in the whole building, located in the toilets that had inscribed above it, Paper Towels Only!

The evening meal was a more relaxed affair thankfully and we met up with Tim and his French mother in law, Michelle again. They had walked the GR10 route which skirts around the flanks of Canigou. For some reason there was a large amount of wine on our table and Michael and I ended up with at least a litre and a half between us. Unbeknown to me he had somehow procured a larger glass than mine and each time we poured the wine he ended up with proportionately more. It wasn't until near the end of the evening that I realised when it was too late. For someone who six weeks ago didn't like red wine he had certainly acquired a taste for it now!

## Day 45, Tuesday 15ᵗʰ August, Refuge des Cortalets to Mines de Batere

*Day 45, Tuesday 15ᵗʰ August, Refuge des Cortalets to Mines de Batere*

All blankets folded in the regulation manner, I flicked a corner of the top one in an act of petty defiance before we departed Cortalets at 8.30am on what promised to be a relatively easy day. Most of todays walk was in descent with a modest climb of some 250m over the Col de la Cirere towards the end of the day. We ambled off on a wide dirt road that descended steadily through pine forest. Yesterdays mist had cleared and there were fine views of the French coast towards Perpignan. The gradient was easy on the legs and I didn't realise that when after some 4km we came to turn off the dirt road onto the Balcon du Canigou we had already descended some 400m. The Balcon was a delightful path that descended in a gentle traverse across the east face of Canigou and we savoured our morning stroll on what was probably our easiest walking day yet. (Tomorrow would be easier again). After half an hour or so we stopped by a small cascade that crossed the path and we broke out the pans and gas stove for a brew-up. Our trek so far had demanded a certain amount of haste, with mostly tough and challenging daily schedules and chasing storms. This was a pleasant change being able to take our time and to take in the surroundings at a more relaxed pace.

Tim and Michelle passed us as we sat enjoying our tea and snack bars though we soon caught and passed them once we had resumed walking. We slowly descended and soon entered a dense natural woodland whereupon the familiar sound of ominous distant thunder could be heard. Unlike our day on the Catalan Pyrenees two days ago when the storm remained some way off this grew closer with every minute. We quickened our pace heading for what we took to be some sort of shelter, the Maison Forestiere de l'Estanyol, where we hoped we could escape the storm. The path began to zig-zag downhill just as the heavy rain arrived and in a few minutes a building appeared ahead through the trees. We dived inside the solid stone built house just as the peals of thunder were getting closer. A moment later a young French couple arrived followed by Tim and partner some ten or 15 minutes after that. By this time the storm was directly overhead and a deluge of rain battered on the roof. It was a spectacular storm with repeated lightning flashes with barely seconds between them. One particularly close strike made the hut shake and the windows rattle and somewhere close by there was the resounding crack of timber and the crash of a falling tree.

I was sure as hell glad I wasn't outside in it. This was an untimely start for a thunderstorm, late morning and it had caught us unawares. It was quite cool in the hut so we collected some bits of firewood that were piled in an adjacent outhouse and got a fire going. The storm continued unabated outside and after about an hour amidst a succession of deafening thunderclaps the door to the hut was suddenly flung open in dramatic fashion and there in the doorway stood a tall and lean old man. Another lightning bolt silhouetted his substantial frame in the doorway at which the young French girl let out a startled yelp. His entrance could not have been more dramatic had it been stage managed. It was like a scene from an old Dracula movie. He stepped inside, removing his sodden and dripping hat and unbuttoning a tweed jacket revealed a full grey beard, beneath a weathered and wizened old face. With a cloak and a pointy hat he would have passed for Gandalf.

"Les horages, les horages, toujours le quinzieme d'Aôut!" he declared as he closed the door to the raging storm. He went and stood by the fire and steam rose all around his damp clothing confirming his appearance as some mystical wizard. Tim and Michelle began talking to our new resident and discovered that he was a shepherd who tended his flocks high on the slopes of Canigou. Apparently another shepherd, a close friend of his had been killed by lightning on this very day some years previously. Hence his curses upon arrival about 15th August.

We sat out the storm until the peals of thunder were far distant and emerged from the hut around 2pm. It was still raining, but not the torrential downpour of earlier. I wanted to press on to our destination at Batere over the other side of the Col de la Cirere. We set off uphill through the trees on a drenched and slippy path. I was nervous. The thunderstorm was not as far away as I thought, maybe just the other side of Canigou. The canopy of trees held some protection from the rain and a degree of psychological protection from the lightning but I faltered at every distant rumble, tempted to turn back to the shelter of le Maison. As we pushed on ascending more and more, the trees thinned out until we emerged from beneath our protective canopy traversing across open hillside. As we reached the col I felt naked and vulnerable to the threat that loomed ahead in the black clouds to the south. A crack of lightning ripped out of the sky to strike the far summit of La Souque, a satellite peak of Canigou some 3-4 miles distant.

"Come on son lets shift. I don't want to be around here when that storm is upon us. There's no bloody shelter here."

"It's miles away dad, we'll be ok."

"Yeh, that's what I thought at Arlet and next minute it was right on top of us. Come on we've only got just over a kilometre distance, all in descent, we can be at the refuge in less than fifteen minutes!"

"I don't think there's anything to worry about, it's even stopped raining!"

"Michael, just listen to yer old dad and shift yer bleedin' arse will yer! That storms headin' our way or I'm a monkey's uncle."

"Monkeys uncle? What does that make me then?"

"Barbequed chimp if you don't get a bloody move on, NOW JUST SHIFT!"

The sky continued to darken as we came upon the first of the mine workings above Batere, including a small concrete shelter that contained a dead sheep. If it wasn't for the sheep I'd have been tempted to remain in the hut even though, with no door or window it was open to the elements and would provide limited shelter. I felt we were losing the race against the weather as black clouds streamed across the valley in our direction. Leaving the hut we pressed on downhill at an alarming pace arriving at a tarmac road a few minutes later, just as the proverbial dam burst and we were overwhelmed in a deluge of rain. The thunder and lightning remained across the other side of the valley but the rain bounced high off the old and worn out tarmac surface. There wasn't time to stop and don the waterproof leggings. At least this time we were wearing our jackets. We scooted down the road and soon after a hairpin bend arrived at the refuge with no time to spare. A lightning bolt smashed into the hillside above us as we drew alongside the old converted mine building. I was momentarily deafened by the explosion as we dived into the doorway of the refuge.

"Jesus, I'm getting tired of these close scrapes. We were standing where that bloody lightning struck only five minutes ago."

The refuge was quite luxurious so far as refuges go. We had our own bedroom with 2 single beds and real bed linen! The storm raged outside and the tarmac road became a river as torrents of muddy water rushed downhill. Such drama outside was of little consequence as we took full advantage of the basic comforts inside. After an unlimited amount of time in a wonderful hot shower where I just let the soothing water ease my aching limbs, we went down into the basement of the building where we had a large common room to ourselves. On the back wall a large fireplace begged to be put to good use and we duly obliged. Soon the roaring log fire made our latest encounter with the elements a distant memory as cascades of water washed down the windows outside.

It was a few of hours before Tim and Michelle arrived. They had sat out the second wave of the storm at Estanyol and not set off until 4.30pm. We all sat down to a most satisfying dinner together, comprising sausage, pasta and vegetable casserole, accompanied of course by the obligatory red wine. A relaxing end to yet another eventful day.

## Day 46, Wednesday 16th August. Mines de Batere to Amelie le Bains

We awoke to bright, clear, blue sky day. The storm had washed the air and drenched the land. We had corn flakes for breakfast for the first time in months so I had 2 bowls. Today our walk was mostly downhill to the French border town of Amelie Le Bains. Setting off from the refuge at Batere in the company of Tim and Michelle we ambled down the road in the morning sunshine and after about a kilometre struck off on a dirt road that ascended gently around the southern slopes of the Puig de l'Estelle. We parted company with Tim and Michelle who left us at the start of the dirt road to follow the GR10 down to Arles sur Tech.

After some half an hour's walking we arrived at the crest of the ridge at the ruins of an old watchtower, the Tour de Batere where we switched to the north side of the ridge with panoramic views out over a sea of white mist that filled the coastal plain.

Our route, mostly on the gentle gradient of dirt roads took us past numerous abandoned iron ore workings of Formantere that had apparently been operational until the mid 1980's but were now just tumble down and rusted relics being reclaimed by the relentless march of time and nature. After a couple of hours of gentle descent on various dirt roads a short section of tarmac and the occasional isolated farmhouse heralded the first signs of civilisation. The final mile into the town was a confusion of disjointed minor paths and ancient tracks that wound their way down through wooded hillsides and ancient olive groves above the town.

The guidebook was open to some very broad interpretation at times and omitted a number of crucial landmarks and junctions which frequently had us scratching our heads but we somehow muddled our way through and emerged through a small housing estate into the busy little town of Amelie. It was lunchtime, just, and we landed at a deserted little cafe bar across the road from the River Tech adjacent what looked like a boules court. These occasional encounters with civilisation and especially food were always met with a celebratory beanfeast and we proceeded to eat and drink everything in sight, starting with an enormous baguette each crammed full of cheese and tomato. We were like two kids in a sweetshop with a years worth of pocket money to spend.

Following our hearty lunch we wandered into the centre of Amelie which at a mere 240m above sea-level was our lowest altitude since leaving Hendaye some six weeks ago. Peculiarly as we stood in the main square contemplating which of the street bars we would select first a large chunk of masonry about the size of a half brick, disintegrated as it crashed to the ground from a cornice high above all of the hustle and bustle.

"Did you see that?" I asked.

"What?"

"A piece of that building just fell off and nobody seemed to notice except me!"

"Oh yeh," remarked Michael completely disinterested.

Following a second lunch and more drinks we booked into the somewhat dated but rather quaint Hotel Joan d'Arc where I enjoyed my second shower in less than 24hours. Well it was more of a drip than a shower really and attaining a state of all over wetness, all at the same time, prior to the onset of evaporation was a major achievement.

We were planning a rest day in Amelie with the opportunity to do some washing and get a haircut even! Our cropped heads had taken on the appearance of a less than tidy Wurzel Gummidge in the six weeks since they were last attended and upon finding the town barbers shop we were duly able to make ourselves understood by reference to some well known French footballers. Michael asked for a Fabian Barthez while I was struggling to remember the national team captain.

"You know Michael, the one with a Z at the beginning of his first and second name. The tall guy, brilliant ball control? Come on you know!"

"Two Z's, mmm…I know, Zsa Zsa Gabor," he announced triumphantly.

"Zsa Zsa Gabor?" I looked at him wondering whether he was serious for a second, when a wry smirk settled on his face.

"Zinadine Zidane," the barber announced and gave me exactly the same haircut he had just given Michael.

Our next excursion was to the launderette where we bumped into a strange guy that had stayed at the Mines de Batere refuge with us the night before. He was actually walking the HRP. He was unshaven and particularly unkempt looking but the most striking aspect of his character was the smell. He was drying his walking socks in one of the tumble dryers, which in itself is not particularly unusual you may think. The problem was that he had not washed them first (they had got wet the day before when he was caught out in the thunderstorm) and the resultant and most obnoxious, nauseating smell, that hit us like a cricket bat in the face, was absolutely overwhelming. Unsurprisingly there was nobody else in the launderette. Fortunately our trip to the launderette was just recce visit to suss out the place so we would know what coins and how much we needed for a wash etc. etc. The bloke was French and intent on engaging us in conversation. We were after all, fellow compatriots of the HRP! We on the other hand were intent on survival through the conventional means of breathing oxygen and backed our way out of the door as quickly but politely as possible, gagging for air.

"Oh my God that absolutely stunk. Don't you ever complain about me being smelly ever again, or I'll make you share a tent with him and his socks," I asserted.

"That was bad," acknowledged Michael. "No wonder he's on his own!"

I returned to the launderette later that afternoon while Michael had a nap at the hotel. There was still a rancid aroma of our friends socks, despite the fact that he must have long since departed, and I had to go and find a bench in the town whilst waiting for the washing to finish because the pong was unbearable. That evening we bumped into Tim and Michelle again at a restaurant where we were having dinner. It was somewhat of a surprise as they had earlier that day headed off to Arles sur Tech, some 4km up the valley. Apparently they had been unable to find accommodation. We chatted for an hour or so. Tim gave us an insight into one aspect of life in his home town, New York with regard to the status of dogs there and how in down town New York those citizens with large dogs are considered wealthy as they must also possess large apartments in order to accommodate them! He eloquently described a whole industry that had sprung up around pampered pooches, with whole blocks dedicated to the well being of dogs with vets, dog psychiatrists, grooming parlours, poodle manicure specialists and canine dieticians. His tales had us in stitches. Only in New York!

We were tired after our exertions of the previous week and were back at our hotel for 8.30pm.

# Day 47, Thursday 17<sup>th</sup> August, Rest day Amelie les Bains

Breakfast was taken at leisure in the terrace garden overlooking the trickling waters of the River Mondonoy, a tributary of the Tech. I could quite happily have sat there all morning with my coffee, French bread and assorted preserves but the kitchen staff were only employed until ten and we were in danger of being tidied away with the condiments.

This was our first rest day in the last nine, since Hospitalet pres l'Andorra, but such had been the easy nature of the last 2 days since leaving Cortalets we were hardly in need of such a break really. We were both physically strong and fit and whereas the rest days during the first few weeks of our trek provided an opportunity for rest and recovery, that was usually essential and always appreciated, today was a somewhat unnecessary diversion from the task in hand. However, our pre-planning meant we had committed to stay put since we had booked our accommodation for the next few nights as far as Col d'Ouillat.

As usual I was a restless soul and lamented the decision to lay up in Amelie for the day. My irrepressible urge was to press on to Banyuls at the earliest opportunity. We had enjoyed a full afternoons rest yesterday and were fully recovered from our exertions. This was bad planning!

We wandered somewhat aimlessly around the town which quietly went about its daily business oblivious to our presence. I was mildly amused to see that the Spar chain had a presence in remote corner of southern France as we picked up our lunch there for tomorrows walk. The day passed slowly in sleepy Amelie as we whiled away the hours at pavement bars snacking on pizzas and French beer. Our evening meal was taken at the Green Pepper Restaurant, curiously emblazoned with its English title in this staunchly Catalan town. Our usual preferred option of steak was excellent but I'm afraid the portions were more suited to patrons with the appetite of a budgie. The pavement bars and restaurants all closed up just after 10pm and the town square fronting our hotel emptied of people, heralding our return to the hotel room.

The room on the first floor was hot and stuffy and we threw open the window to try and create some airflow. This was unfortunately more successful in sustaining the flow of noise as various parties of drunken youths clattered noisily through the town until around 3am when some semblance of peace finally descended. However, as it was market day on Fridays the silence was short lived when at 4am equally noisy market traders began assembling their stalls. Oh give me a flapping tent on a windy mountain top any day!!

## Day 48 Friday 18th July Amelie le Bains to Las Illas

We arose at 6.45am to a deserted hotel. At least it was deserted by staff anyway. My discussions the previous evening with the manageress requesting a 7am breakfast had clearly fallen on deaf ears. At 7.25am a member of kitchen staff finally arrived and after a frugal repast we eventually got away at 8.10am. We had recce'd the exit from the town the previous afternoon and soon left Amelie behind, heading up a steep and narrow tarmac lane that reduced to a stony path after some 100metres or so. We ascended on quite steep paths mostly in the shade of a dense canopy of deciduous trees that afforded occasional breaks and brief views back to the town. It was a hot and dry day and we were grateful for the shade of the trees, though the lack of view made the walk tedious and rather boring. After some 2 hours or steady ascent and several million trees later we arrived at a rather sinister and intimidating farmhouse high up on the ridge, Can Felix. It was surrounded by barbed wire and innumerable keep out signs. Ton Joosten in his route description referred to the section with the words, "don't go through the gate which gives access to the farm (don't even think about it) but follow the marks on the right side of the building and the fence." This made me wonder just what he knew of the place or was he, like us, just intimidated by the profusion of barbed wire and keep out signs? Can Felix was a foreboding place with no sign of life within its grounds. We skirted the perimeter of the property expecting a pack of Dobermans to come rushing through the grounds and snarling at our heels. Shortly after passing this mysterious property we joined the GR10 path again but noticed that all of the red and white paint flashes had been painted over with black paint, which meant the path became difficult to pick up in places still within dense forest. It was a mystery why the path markers had been obliterated and my suspicions led me to believe that it had something to do with Can Felix. However I was to discover later that the GR10 had been re-routed away from its original course and now took a line further south. I concluded that Can Felix was actually a nudist colony whose occupants did not appreciate any fully dressed intruders.

We picked our way carefully on well disguised and seemingly little used paths, ever upwards, frequently losing our way and having to retrace our steps. As we got higher the trees thinned and allowed for a better perspective of our surrounding terrain. After a final steep scramble we reached the Roc de Frausa, (Roc de France) just after twelve noon from where could see both the French and Spanish Mediterranean coasts from its lofty summit. Somewhere in this section of the Pyrenees was the where Laurie Lee had returned to Spain to fight in the civil war in his book "As I Walked Out One Midsummer Morning". His trek across the mountains up from the small French town of Ceret was in December. It was hard to envisage him struggling through snow drifts and blizzards as winter approached. The seasons clearly held some starkly contrasting conditions in the Pyrenees Occidentales between August and December.

We pressed along the border ridge through open glades on pathless terrain until a sharp descent into dense woodland blotted out our views once again. Arriving at a dirt road our route led us down through the forest into Spain and into the grounds of a remote hermitage, Ermita de las Salinas. It was lunchtime and we sat at a picnic table in the grounds of the Salinas sanctuary harassed by wasps which were probably attracted by the fizzy drinks we purchased from a small cafe within the building. A few adventurous tourists had made their way up into these quiet hills by vehicle along the rough and dusty dirt roads that criss-crossed the area and were milling around the grounds. They gave us curious looks. We were not one of them!

After filling our water bottles at a hidden spring in the woods behind the hermitage we sought out a meandering path which snaked its way from the back of the Ermitas de las Salinas and soon lost itself, and us, amongst the trees. I knew from the map there was a dirt road somewhere above us, probably no more than a few hundred yards away, so rather than play cat and mouse with our elusive path we struck off uphill and sure enough soon arrived at the dirt road, where we turned south east gently downhill. We spent the next hour on this dirt road which stayed just on the Spanish side of the border before arriving at an imperceptible pass, the Coll de Lly, where, stepping through a small metal gate we stepped back into France for the final time on our trek. Our route from here to Banyuls, whilst following the border in a number of places on the final day, remained otherwise entirely in France. We followed what appeared to be a long abandoned way down through the forest towards our destination that day, the small village of Las Illas. Once again our path had a look of abandonment. As we descended, the soft soil of the path had become eroded and formed an awkward gully in which it was impossible to walk. There were fallen branches from the pine trees that lined the lost path which forced numerous mini diversions into the trees. After about ten or fifteen minutes of this we emerged on a wide forest track where there were signs of much recent logging activity with large swathes of forest felled opening up the views across endless forested hillsides.

The village of Las Illas, though quiet, had a modern look about it as we ambled down the single road that ran through it's centre in search of the gite we had booked for the night. The gite was empty but we went and found the owner, a Madame Martinez a few doors away. This accommodation was positively luxurious compared to what we had been used to and for the moment at least we had it to ourselves. The property was a medium sized detached bungalow with two bedrooms containing bunks and a most homely and comfortable dining kitchen with real armchairs. After a brief guided tour by our host we were left to our own devices. After a few clothes washing chores and a shower each we sat and relaxed, nibbling on some Madeira cake that Michael had bought in the Spar at Amelie. We made ourselves at home, lounging in the sumptuous comfort of softly sprung armchairs, supping numerous mugs of Earl Grey, revelling in our comparative luxury.

We didn't have the place to ourselves for much longer. Around 5pm Madame Martinez was opening the front door to two further visitors, whose Englishness was immediately apparent from their staccato French as they conversed with the owner at the front door. Matt and Hazel had like us started from Hendaye, but, unlike us they had walked every inch of the way on a combination of HRP, GR10 and GR11. We had numerous tales to trade with them and spent a pleasant evening in their company, which included a visit to the village restaurant, dels Trabucayres for dinner.

## Day 49 Saturday 19<sup>th</sup> August, Las Illas to Col d'Ouillat

Departing our 5 star accommodation at 8.15am with Matt and Hazel we ascended out of Las Illas on a deserted and pothole ridden tarmac road which soon became the now familiar dusty dirt road. After some twenty minutes or so we left the final remnants of civilisation behind as we headed off over densely forested hills on an wide and undulating track towards Le Perthus, a bustling border town just off the main A17 motorway between France and Spain. We were a mile outside of Las Illas at the imperceptible Col de Figure, marked by a junction of roads, but otherwise easily missed, when Hazel announced the need for a toilet stop. Out of courtesy Michael and I pushed on as Hazel headed for the trees, leaving Matt resting on his trekking poles at the side of the track. The interlude allowed us to move a good distance ahead and we were soon out of sight. We had grown accustomed to our own father/son fellowship on our walk and it felt good to once again be out on our own. Whilst we had enjoyed the company of our new friends our weeks of solitude had somehow isolated us and we appreciated simply being able to make our own decisions, without the need for compromise. We could stop when we liked, have lunch when we liked and at our own pace. The imposition that was enforced by walking in the company of others was almost an intrusion to our world, so we stepped out and forced the pace, leaving our two companions trailing probably a good distance behind.

The dirt road we were on entered an ancient beech forest where the trees towered above us like massive monoliths well over a hundred feet tall, each striving for their share of sunlight. The air beneath the lofty green canopy was pleasantly cool, and a damp, woody and musty aroma filled the air. We pressed on with regular glances behind to see if our pursuers were in sight but they did not appear. Leaving the soothing shade of the forest we emerged into more open country with scattered hillside farms and the distant barking of dogs. The dirt road made for fast progress with little need to consult the map and we soon put the miles behind us. The sun was hot at this lower altitude and we seldom had our drinks tubes away from our mouths. Entering an area of pine forest once again we rounded a ridge and began a marked descent towards Le Perthus. At a point where the HRP left the dirt road and struck off through the trees on a faint and narrow path avoiding a long sweeping zig-zag in the track we stopped, for the first time since parting from Matt and Hazel, and sat awaiting the arrival of our abandoned companions. Some fifteen or twenty minutes later we heard their voices long before they appeared around a bend in the track some 100m metres back. They were pleased to see us and us them. We walked together in single file on the narrow shortcut path through the forest before emerging once again on our dirt road.

We descended towards the Col de Panissas, the scene of many previous battles between the French and Spanish. The col was dominated by the imposing Fort de Bellegarde which stood high on a hill overlooking the pass. Built by the French in 1679 to defend the frontier it had been the scene of numerous battles including having been laid siege to by the Spanish in 1793 but then retaken by the French the following year. It's more recent history had witnessed a more sinister use by the Gestapo during WW2 as a prison for PoW's and enemy agents. There were various ruins alongside the dirt road as we approached the fort, which I suspect were of Roman origin. I later learned that the track we were on was the course of an old Roman road, the Via Augusta, that stretched 2725km from Cadiz to Rome, passing through the Col de Panissas.

The Col de Panissas had been the main route through the Pyrenees in ancient times and its strategic position had meant it was a much sought after and fought over position on the Franco/Spanish frontier. The famous Battle of the Cold de Panissars dates back to 1285 between Phillip III of France and Peter III of Aragon. It was a severe defeat for the French, who were already retiring over the Pyrenees when the Aragonese fell on them. It was the last battle of the Aragonese Crusade, a papally-sanctioned war on behalf of Charles of Valois to secure the Aragonese throne from the excommunicate king Peter, who had conquered Sicily against papal interests. The battle followed on the heels of the naval victory at Les Formigues on 4th September.

It was a fascinating place, so much so that Matt and Hazel decided to explore the fort in more detail and we parted company once again after our brief reintroduction and Michael and I headed down into Le Perthus for lunch. We were all headed for Col d'Ouillat this evening so would meet up again later. Descending from the fort we passed by hillsides covered in ancient stunted cork oaks, each with their tell tale girdle of missing bark from previous harvests. I suspected this was an industry destined for terminal decline in view of the synthetic alternatives now available.

Le Perthus was an assault on the senses. We stepped onto a bustling main street of supermarkets, restaurants and shops displaying all manner of useless tourist tat, and all manner of tourists. It was 11.30am and we reluctantly landed on the garden terrace of an otherwise deserted restaurant, where we ordered lunch. Our arrival seemed to be the trigger that heralded an invasion of customers who had all seemingly been waiting for someone else to make the first move. We enjoyed a round of sandwiches each followed by an ice cream and then gratefully fled the mayhem that was Le Perthus.

Our route for the next few miles was a steady 650m ascent on a secondary road into the mountains east of the town. Fortunately the road itself was relatively quiet with just the occasional passing car. It was a hot afternoon in which we spent most of time in the full heat of the Mediterranean sun. Occasionally the gradient of the uphill slope to our right (the south) would be steep enough to cast a shadow across the road allowing a brief respite from the searing heat. I took the opportunity on each of these occasions to remove my hat and so allow a degree of cooling to my frazzled head. There were a number of welcome fountains and a couple of accessible streams at the side of the road which brought impromptu showers and some sweet relief from the relentless heat. After some 3 miles and nearly a thousand feet of uphill slog it was with some relief also that we eventually stepped off the road and onto a rough stony path to enter an area of woodland and a further short reprieve from the suns heat. We arrived at the tiny hillside hamlet of St Martin de l'Albere and got ourselves lost yet again amongst a confusion of paths and tracks that proliferated around the settlement. We doubled back through the hamlet, much to the amusement of some youngsters who were playing outside of one of the cottages. They clearly didn't see many strangers passing their front door and to see the same two twice in ten minutes was probably quite unusual, although if they were all following Mr Joosten's advice I would have thought the sight of strangers wandering up and down in front of their house would be a regular occurrence. Being kind, his directions through St Martin de l'Albere were rather vague, with comments such as, "work your way up to the hamlet," "pass the church," each of which could be construed to refer to a number of alternative routes. My conclusion was that Mr Joosten had actually included such ambiguities as an initiative test for a readership who he will have acknowledged possessed a certain degree of tenacity and determination anyway having undertaken the challenge of the HRP in the first place, and to have actually got so far despite his sometimes ambiguous directions.

After a couple of false trails we got back on track and continued uphill towards Ouillat. As we ascended the trees thinned out and we were left under the baking heat of an unforgiving sun. Another aspect of the conditions above St Martin de l'Albere which made the going just that bit more unbearable were the flies. Clouds of flies gathered around our heads and settled on our faces constantly. These were the sort of persistent little bastards who wouldn't be deterred by a flailing hand or a sharp blow of air from pursed lips. They were in our ears, up our noses, on our lips and eyes and generally in our faces both literally and metaphorically. Their persistence was exasperating. I removed my hat to use as a swatter and must have resembled some delirious maniac in my efforts to repel these winged pests. No amount of swatting would prevail. They were like Zulus, for every one that was killed another ten would come and take its place. At one stage I stopped and in a unbridled fit of pique flailed my arms and hat wildly in the air screaming in a mad outburst of temper, "why don't you all just fuck off and leave me alone, arrgggh!."

Just at that moment we were passed by two athletic looking, sickeningly cool and bronzed young men wearing only speedos and flip flops and carrying small day sacks who came tearing up the hill at a break neck pace. They clearly had no desire to engage a mad Englishman in the midst of an epileptic fit and barely acknowledged our presence, soon leaving us behind. Two minutes later we in turn passed them as they struggled with their route directions at a path junction. At a signpost for gite d'etape we took a 90 degree left turn, traversing across the hillside, leaving the open ground for the shade of a mature beech forest where the problem with the flies diminished. Ten minutes later we emerged from the trees at the of the Col de l'Ouillat gite. I couldn't believe it, the place had a bar! We released the burdens of our crushing packs and I enjoyed a very large beer (1 litre I would guess) whilst Michael stuck to his coke, as we took a seat on the elevated terrace and gazed back west to the distant horizons of Roc de Frausa and Canigou. It was 2.45pm and we had the remainder of the afternoon to relax. What bliss! Matt and Hazel rolled into camp at

3.45 just as we were finishing our drinks. We arranged to meet them at dinner and headed off to our room.

There were two buildings separate from the bar and dining room that formed the accommodation blocks and we made for the first of these two blocks to find our room for the express purpose of a little siesta. It was more of a large box than a room really. Once it contained two people and two packs in addition to the existing two beds there was no room left as such. The 'box' was probably about 7 feet square containing two small single beds, between which there was a narrow gap, just barely space to put our backpacks.

"For my next trick I am going to do an impression of a sardine!" Michael announced.

"Bit compact innit", I said back.

Such was the limited space we had to co-ordinate any standing manoeuvres so that there was only one of us on our feet at a time. In the event that we both needed to stand at the same time then one of us had to leave the room. After a spell of clothes washing and exhausted from our afternoon ascent in the hot sun we both crashed out for a welcome rest.

Dinner was at 7.30pm where we sat together with Matt and Hazel chatting over the numerous trials and tribulations we had each endured along the way. It was hard to believe we were here at the eve of the final days trek to Banyuls. Michael and I agreed an early start and ordered a 6.30 breakfast which was to be delivered to our rooms along with the additional luxury of a packed lunch. This really was civilised! We sat and watched the sun set behind Canigou and tripped off to bed around 9.30pm.

# Day 50, 20*th* August, Col de l'Ouillat to Banyuls sur Mer.

A pot of coffee and some biscuits were on a tray outside of our room when we arose at 6.30am. I couldn't believe this was the final day. I carried my gear downstairs to pack my stuff and put on my walking boots outside in order to try and keep the noise down in a building where every movement echoed and creaked around the walls and floors. Michael joined me a few moments later and sat at the bottom of the flight of stairs tending his feet. I hadn't realised just how badly his heels were blistered. They were both completely red raw. I cringed at the sight. An area of both heels about the size of a 50p was devoid of flesh and red and angry.

"Jesus, how the hell have you managed to walk with heels like that?"

"I didn't realise they were quite that bad."

"You're going to have a job getting your boots on aren't you?"

"Mmmm... probably."

I was astonished at his fortitude. He hadn't mentioned his heels for weeks and they had obviously been causing him some severe pain. That moment was a defining one for me in my understanding of a son that never really spoke an awful lot not even to complain of his own suffering. How he had managed to continue walking without breathing a word about his shredded heels was unbelievable. He had some guts I must say, but in many ways such silence epitomized Michael. He had demonstrated a strength of character beyond his tender years to have tolerated such pain and discomfort without complaint and I was proud of him and the resilience he had shown.

We dressed his heels with the compeed dressings that we had in our first aid packs and rooting through the depths of his tardis like pack actually found a brand new pair of socks that Michael had carried all the way from Hendaye, without even knowing. The shredded socks that had worn to destruction were consigned to the nearest bin. They were more hole than sock anyway. (An epilogue to this tale is that upon return to the UK we actually found a further pair of unworn socks in the depths of Michaels pack.)

"No wonder your bloody heels are like that, look at the state of these socks, didn't you think to change them you bleedin' berk!" I nagged.

When we set off at 7.45am, there was no sign of Matt and Hazel. The first mile or so was in steady ascent through a mature pine forest towards the curiously named Roc de Trois Termes, which was to be outdone later that day at the Pic de Quatre Terms. We stepped out from the forest onto a narrow tarmac road that headed up towards the TV masts perched atop the nearby Pic Neulos, which would be our highest point of the day. In contrast to yesterdays heat there was a strong, cold northerly wind which whipped across the east ridge of Neulons, chilling our bones. For the first time in over a week we resorted to donning our fleeces although we did stick with our shorts. The road ended at the TV masts and we descended steeply down the back of Neulos on rocky ground through dense scrubby trees and bushes to emerge on a broad grassy ridge where the GR10 path that we were following became less distinct until we arrived at a rather basic stone refuge, Refuge de la Tagnarede, from which the overnight occupants were still emerging. (It was only just turned 9am)

Beyond the refuge the path entered a forest where we completely lost our way and had to proceed on a compass bearing over rough ground, through brambles and general forest undergrowth to eventually emerge at a col which we believd must Col del Faig, although I wasn't entirely confident of where we were? A myriad of minor paths fanned out in all directions so we took the one that most coincided with the direction we needed to be going according to the compass. After a succession of minor cols and rises in the border ridge we ascended to the summit of the Pic de Quatre Termes from where we had our first sighting of Banyuls a distance away in the Mediterranean haze. It was an uplifting sight. We were on the doorstep of completing our trek and it felt good.

Descending from the summit we made our way down grassy slopes to a small spring where we stopped for lunch. The water there was little more than a slight trickle and couldn't be separated from the gritty soil through which it oozed to make it drinkable so we had to be content with the tepid contents of our drinks bags. After lunch our route led us over several more bumps and dips to the summit of Pic Sailfort at 981m from where our route to the sea, still some 5-6 miles away, was entirely in descent. Michael was suffering badly with his blistered feet and his progress was slow as we descended the steep and rocky east ridge of Pic Sailfort. I could see that each step was accompanied by a labour of agony as his face contorted against the pain and I had to grit my teeth just watching him struggle. He still never said a word. At the Col de Baillaury we reached a stony dirt road that contoured to the south of and beneath the Balcon de Madeloc. According to the guide book the HRP avoided this obvious route and opted instead to ascend around the northern slopes of a minor subsidiary peak of the Balcon de Madeloc to arrive at the next col, the Col de Formigau. However, we had not contemplated the prospect of any more 'up' sections and such a proposition, however minor in nature, was beyond the will of our exhausted spirits and worn out feet. We opted for the slightly longer, but generally more level dirt road which rejoined the HRP a mile further on.

Our dirt road arrived at the Col de Gascons on a high ridge overlooking the olive grove and vineyard slopes that tumbled down to the Mediterranean, still some 3 miles and over one thousand feet below. This point marked our release from the high mountains to a more gentle and Mediterranean like climate and environment where the hand of man was the dominant factor in shaping the land. We momentarily joined a narrow tarmac road from which a couple of steep shortcuts removed the prolonged and drawn out hairpin bends. To our pleasant surprise a water font at the side of the path, the Font de Chasseurs, provided a welcome relief from our labours as we stopped to enjoy a cooling drink and took the one and only opportunity all day to refill our dwindling water supply.

Upon resumption the steep sections of path made for a new agony for Michael as he wrestled with his blistered heels and our progress became interminably slow. The path wound its way ever downwards through vineyards and olive groves on ancient paths and tracks until we finally stepped onto the back streets of Banyuls. Similar to the start of our journey it seemed peculiar to be marching through the side streets of this seaside town with backpacks and we stood out from the crowd although I dare say it was probably a common sight for the locals. In a few minutes we emerged in to the bustle of a busy promenade and crossed to a wide shingle beach that was adorned with sun-bathers more suitably attired for their environment than we were.

We hadn't really planned what we would do upon arrival at Banyuls but it was only fitting that we should finish at the sea on our coast to coast adventure. It's difficult to describe my mixture of emotions as we crunched through the shingle towards the waters edge but I swear to god I just floated down that beach, oblivious to the hundreds of eyes that followed our every step. I wanted to whoop with delight but settled for a punch of the air and a big hug from my son as we stood in the lapping waters of the Mediterranean. Here we were at an objective that for so long seemed so distant and unattainable but now was here! Through all the toil and disappointments we had prevailed and overcome the obstacles along the way. We had succeeded. I was overcome with a deep satisfaction and emotion and promptly stripped off and went for a swim in the sea in my underpants as Michael sat on the beach and tended his bloodied feet.

As I lay floating on my back in the soothing waters of the Med I contemplated our achievement. I wanted to capture that moment forever and bottle it. What a bloody walk!

The culmination of 7 weeks of absolutely draining and all-consuming effort; Struggling with injuries and all the weather could throw at us; The heat, the cold and the wet; Close encounters with terrifying thunderstorms and the awesome power of nature. Probably 4 Everests worth of ascent and descent and some 400 miles of often pathless terrain; Lost tents, claustrophobic mountain refuges, vertical paths, dodgy (and good) directions, useless maps and, it could be argued, an equally useless map reader. Running out of water, dehydration, exhaustion, insatiable thirst; 50 days worth of physical and psychological adversity that ended here on a western Mediterranean shingle beach. I had a raft of emotions too complex to convey; a deep contentment in our achievement, a profound pride in my indomitable son, and a real sadness that our adventure had finished, but a relief as well that it was all over.

Tomorrow we would awake to a new day and not face the considerable demands of the HRP, our companion and adversary for the last two months of the summer, and we would head back to our ordinary lives. But tomorrow was another day. This was here and now and I was more than happy to bask in the self satisfaction and reflect upon what had been a very different and demanding way of life for a whole summer.

So far as adventures go I dare say it would pale into insignificance in the realms of time. It was no first ascent, polar expedition or venture into the unknown depths of the Amazon rainforest. But for simple souls like Michael and I this was our Everest. An achievement of a lifetime. A tale of adventure to tell the grandchildren in years to come.

# Epilogue

It was inevitable that I would return to the Pyrenees. The section of the walk we had missed out between Heas and Salardu nagged at me like a persistent toothache for the next 2 years until in the Summer of 2008 I returned with my youngest daughter Rachel and my brother-in-law Charlie, along with our trusty Sherpa, Keith. By this time Michael had settled down into a full-time job, bought a home with his wife-to-be, Hayley, and they'd had a daughter together so he was somewhat pre-occupied and unable to accompany us on this occasion.

We completed the intervening section in 10 days, with the assistance of ice axe and crampons over the high sections between Refuge de la Soula and Refuge du Portillon. It was a thrilling and most enjoyable trip with many more tales to tell but not in this journal.

It was satisfying to have completed the 'missing link', however, for me the challenge still remains, to complete the whole trek in a single trip from coast to coast. Any takers?